T0364256

WHAT KIND OF ARCHITECT ARE YOU?

Udo Greinacher

ORO Editions
Publishers of Architecture, Art, and Design
Gordon Goff: Publisher

www.oroeditions.com
info@oroeditions.com

Published by ORO Editions

Copyright © 2021 Udo Greinacher

All rights reserved. No part of this book may be reproduced, stored in a retrieval system, or transmitted in any form or by any means, including electronic, mechanical, photocopying or microfilming, recording, or otherwise (except that copying permitted by Sections 107 and 108 of the U.S. Copyright Law and except by reviewers for the public press) without written permission from the publisher.

You must not circulate this book in any other binding or cover and you must impose this same condition on any acquirer.

Author: Udo Greinacher
Project Manager: Alejandro Guzman-Avila
Managing Editor: Jake Anderson

10 9 8 7 6 5 4 3 2 1 First Edition

ISBN: 978-1-951541-56-9

Color Separations and Printing: ORO Group Ltd.
Printed in China.

ORO Editions makes a continuous effort to minimize the overall carbon footprint of its publications. As part of this goal, ORO Editions, in association with Global ReLeaf, arranges to plant trees to replace those used in the manufacturing of the paper produced for its books. Global ReLeaf is an international campaign run by American Forests, one of the world's oldest nonprofit conservation organizations. Global ReLeaf is American Forests' education and action program that helps individuals, organizations, agencies, and corporations improve the local and global environment by planting and caring for trees.

CONTENTS

Architecture is commonplace. We inhabit it and use it; it is constantly present; it serves as foreground and background and usually has a story to tell. Numerous volumes are devoted to its typology, history, construction, and design. But apart from its most illustrious makers, we know almost nothing about the people who conceived it: the architects. *What Kind of Architect Are You?*, the question most architects encounter when they reveal their profession, is difficult to answer. Is the underlying expectation that we specialize in a type — office buildings, for example, or parking garages? Or that we limit ourselves to a specific market share — commercial, residential, or communal? Maybe it is our role in the design process that is of interest — procurement, design, detailing, construction supervision, and post-occupancy evaluation? Aspects of all of the above define all of us, and not at all. Clearly, a short and succinct answer does not suffice.

PREFACE

What Kind of Architect Are You? showcases a panoply of architectural practices to a reading audience that shares an interest in the profession. Topics range from the theoretical to design-build, from installations that challenge our preconceptions to the set of TV shows on home remodeling, from instructing future architects in the US to expanding the reach of the profession worldwide. Inspired by *Working*, Studs Terkel's journey into the everyday history of working life in America, the collection of interviews records the extraordinary dreams of ordinary architects. The oral history is driven by a search for inspiration, recognition, and meaning to the work beyond a paycheck, as well as musings about education, clients, and the future of the profession. Almost all of the contributors are employed by architectural firms; many are principals, some are sole proprietors, some are partners. Almost everyone teaches, at least occasionally, or part-time. A few have left the profession for the arts, landscape, or TV production. Some have joined architecture from other disciplines. All are consumed by what they are doing.

The collection offers a glimpse into a vast array of professional possibilities and points out meaningful alternatives to the prevailing myth of the "starchitect." It provides those in search of an architect with insights into how we work and helps them to formulate expectations. It challenges practitioners to think introspectively and examine how they fit into the architectural spectrum. And finally, the collection documents the cross-section of cultural and architectural practice across America.

The reader may find that the "voice" varies throughout the collection. That variation is consistent with the variety of architects included — in fact, it underscores the myriad responses to *What Kind of Architect Are You?*

4

My father was an important civil engineer. He built natatoriums and ski jumps, and as a kid I was on the construction site a lot. It was fascinating. As a civil engineer, he developed new concrete support connections, he did a lot of math and that was too technical for me. That was not what I wanted to do. So when I was 18 I decided to study architecture and I graduated at age 23. I studied in the GDR, at the Art Academy Weissensee. At that time Marzahn, a socialist housing community, was built and I realized that I did not want to do that kind of work. That's why I majored in preservation. I have always been very interested in history. My thesis project was the conversion of a monastery into a concert hall and a restaurant for the socialist society. The west wing of the complex was missing, and I designed a modern interpretation of it. That was my debut in the realm of preservation. As a preservation architect I was lucky – I did not plan it that way - but it was much easier for me to work in the west than for many of my colleagues. Historic preservation is more compatible with western customs and designs than socialist architecture.

Martina Abri is no stranger to crossing boundaries. As a conservator and architect she constantly navigates between old and new, history and practice.

It became clear to me that preservation requires background knowledge and that's when I got into research. Shortly after graduation I was fortunate to restore two buildings by **Karl Friedrich Schinkel**, the *Friedrichswerdersche Kirche* and the *Alte Museum*. So as a very young architect I started learning everything about Schinkel. It was important to me, not that it was required of my job, but I needed to look behind the ideas of the building to discover Schinkel's thought processes. I was curious how he developed his designs. In my mind this is a necessary part of any restoration concept. That's how I got into Schinkel research.

In January 1985 I emigrated to West Berlin, and, because of my expertise I was soon able to pursue a university career. I became an assistant to Professor Hans Junecke at the Technical University of Berlin, where I worked on two volumes on Schinkel's life's work: *Karl Friedrich Schinkel: The Prussian Province of Saxony*, and a volume on Schinkel's work within Germany but outside of Prussia. Schinkel was responsible for all public buildings in Prussia. Professor Junecke had collected a lot of material before the war, all originals. They consisted of archival copies and photos of buildings destroyed in WWII. By the time I met him he was 86 years old and needed an assistant to help him. Many applied for the position. Originally, he did not like that I came from practice and he asked me to read an entry written by Schinkel himself. I could read Schinkel's handwriting because I had studied it. That was my way in.

What I love about Schinkel is that on one hand, the man was trapped in the structures of a tightly regulated Prussian administration. On the other hand, his Italian diaries reveal a sensitive person. In his early sketchbook — he was eight years old, a normal boy — he drew his teacher shitting behind the bushes. He is not so stringent, so straightforward, but can be very sensitive when it matters.

You have several choices when working in preservation. Either you ignore the monument altogether, emphasize it through your design, or you provide the background for it. You try to find a dialogue between old and new, between main complex and addition. I believe that establishing such a dialog is the ultimate goal, as did Schinkel. Then, in the province of Saxony, he wanted to demolish a Gothic cloister vault because he considered his design proposal to be more important than a Gothic cloister. Learning about it, I thought that maybe he had never been there ... but no. He saw the cloister and wrote that he could not imagine a better building than his proposal in its stead. This contradiction was fascinating to me.

Nevertheless, Schinkel managed to bring together large configurations of architectural space. It is mind-boggling to see what architectures he managed to create, their quality and innovation, while he had to cope diplomatically with the Crown Prince. To do all this he ruthlessly exploited his own body; he slept only 4 - 5 hours a day, got up early, and went to the library. He lived in the *Building Academy*, and his apartment and his office were in the building so he could use the huge library at night. I am fascinated by his many talents; he was really interested in urban design and its architectural spaces. He also designed dioramas from Petersburg and Palermo and produced stage sets and incredible many paintings. He was an all-round genius.

Professor Junecke and I edited the 22nd volume, *Schinkel in the Province of Saxony*, which finally appeared in 2014. It took us over 17 years, but the volume contains more than 780 pages. The professor had died during the process, at the age of 93, and on his death bed left me all the material he had collected on Schinkel. That's a huge burden for me: we had written only one volume, and now I have to write a second volume alone. But I will retire at some point, and I look forward to writing it.

On the other hand, I really love being a practicing architect. I cannot sit in a chair and write all day. That's why I decided to practice as a building conservator. And due to the preservation work that I undertook in East Berlin, I had a very, very good start in the West. For example, the DDR restoration of the Friedrichswerder Church, Schinkel's first brick-built building since the Middle Ages in Berlin, had used very bad bricks. As the chief architect I advised against the use of new standard bricks which were burned too hot and were thus too hard. The bricks were used nevertheless. After the reunification it turned out that the hard-fired bricks could not absorb enough moisture and thus destroyed the historic soft bricks surrounding them. That meant every brick used during the GDR time had to be replaced again. Administrators in the Federal Office for Building and Regional Planning found my stance courageous and they asked me to supervise the reconstruction again.

In addition to the *Friedrichswerder Church* there is another original Schinkel building in Berlin: *Schloss Tegel*, built for Wilhelm von Humboldt. In 1988 the owner hired me to restore the castle and I am still working on it today. Some of these projects extend for a lifetime. That's how I founded my architectural office with Christian Raabe in 1994. Together we have restored many important buildings in Berlin. A partner is necessary when you are teaching at the university.

In 1993 I became a professor of historic preservation at the University of Applied Sciences, Potsdam. I teach theory, history and methods of historic preservation, heritage conservation design, and building survey. I pick a new topic each semester — I supervise both bachelor and master's theses — and the topics must fascinate me as well. You can only excite others when you are enthusiastic yourself. That's important for the students and me as well. There is no room for monotony, you have to be fascinated again and again.

In the preservation program we educate people in historic stone, wood and metal construction. I often work with my students outside the academy at historic buildings. For example, I restored the roof of a large Coptic Orthodox Church in Lichtenberg, and now the community needs help restoring the interior. My colleagues and I offered the project as a master's thesis, and with help from the city conservator the church received support for scaffolding. We recently received additional funds from the State Office of Monuments to implement the concept of the student thesis. The link between the university and practice is very important, and I am one of the facilitators at the school. I am the only architecture faculty who teaches both the preservationists and the construction supervisors. Two years ago, I received an award from the BDA for the best Master's thesis in preservation, and two and a half years ago, the research work of one of my students received the Berlin-Brandenburg Science Award. That made me proud.

Of all the architects who share my interest in the dialogue between new and old I find **Peter Zumthor** the most interesting. His *Kolumba* museum in Cologne is wonderfully consequential in its design. I also introduce my students to his more recent buildings such as the *Brother Klaus' Field Chapel*. I consider him to be a very sensitive architect, a role model. **David Chipperfield** is good, too, but sometimes his work has too many inconsistencies. While I admire his attitude in the *Neues Museum Berlin*, I find his treatment of the large staircase too harsh and without a goal. Originally the Erechtheion terminated the ascent and was worth climbing these stairs, but the Erechtheion is no longer there. Now I can only glimpse a statue of Friedrich Wilhelm IV on horseback through the windows, but that was never the intention. Originally the stairs had a transparent railing. Instead of separating the handrail with a strip of glass, he pulled the railing all the way up, which emphasizes the presence of the stairs. If only he had put a statue on top to make one climb to Olympus?

My own architectural design work is contemporary. I do not decorate houses with capitals, with pilasters, or with half-columns, unlike many of my colleagues who follow that fashion. That does not work for me. In my preservation work I deal with original portals from 1732. I would never come up with the idea of dressing up a new building. I have a huge problem with this yearning for an imaginary world that never existed, with a newly emerging postmodernism.

We experienced the same thing in Uzbekistan. We restored a tomb from 1372, and the locals could not appreciate the tiles where the glaze was chipped. They cut out the original tiles from the 14th century and replaced them with contemporary tiles which do not have the quality of the historic ones. People just have to learn to appreciate the original substance and accept that a reconstruction never approaches the quality of the original.

We restored one corner of Schinkel's *Bauakademie* in Berlin, and of course now I am asked: why did you rebuild that corner when you are against the reconstruction of historic buildings? We did it to reconstruct Schinkel's progress; my office partner did his dissertation on this corner, so it was research for us. We wanted to see how the Bauakademie came about two years after the Friedrichswerder church, to understand Schinkel's development as an architect. The Ministry of Foreign Affairs of the GDR which had replaced the Bauakademie was demolished after reunification, and we found 2,400 artifacts on the site. We photographed and cataloged all of them. Because the found bricks were dirty, we could determine exactly where they had been placed within the wall. Although the building academy is very well documented, some things just cannot be shown in a photo. Because we found all those amazing blackened bricks we were able to make the reconstruction as true to the original as possible.

For me it has never been an issue to be a woman in the architectural profession. I finished at 23 and managed my first construction; all the workers listened to what I said. What is still an issue, though, is that I'm the only faculty member from East Germany in my department. Even though preservation qualifications have been the same in East and West Germany, several of my colleagues still think that their western education and training was superior to mine, due to the many possibilities they had. There are often tensions. For example, the whole college attacked me when former students and I tried to prevent the demolition of the old Fachhochschule — a GDR building — and attempted to reinterpret the structure within its historical context.

For me, the stratification of a city is incredibly important. We cannot pretend the GDR did not exist. But today at the old market, there is now Barberini, there is Kulka with the castle, an interpretation of a memorial architecture, there are the original *Nikolai church* of Schinkel, Knobelsdorff's original town hall, and the GDR construction of the University of Applied Sciences. Now there is a desire to tear it down and replace it with a dollhouse that used to be there before World War II, complete with all these decorative elements. They want to turn Potsdam's city center into a dollhouse. Nobody cares about the people who lived in the GDR for 40 years, who were born in the GDR. We cannot erase their lives completely; I have problems with that.

My colleagues were annoyed and asked why they had to listen to the East crap again. But the students — that's the good thing here — a lot of students wanted to work on the topic. They realize that their parents come from the East, which does not exist anymore. A lot of people argued against the demolition. It was, of course, a democratic process. Immediately after the reunification, it was decided to rebuild the city center. But after twenty years one could reconsider, be open to investigate anew, reinterpret the findings. The University building was not listed as a historic structure, although it dates back to the 60s, 70s, and structurally parallels a house built by **Mies van der Rohe** in the USA. The GDR architect who built it said he did not even know Mies. We had limited access to Western publications; only the main West German architectural magazine was available in the State Library, but that's about it. Tearing it down is a tragedy — the wrong policy — in my eyes.

I have seen little of the world and I really want to travel. But of course, I have to finish writing the volume on Schinkel. I can draw very well, too, but miss out on that lately. There is so much going on right now and to do justice to everything some things must be done superficially. It hurts because I do not want to. Of course, I will continue my office as long as possible, since the work I started at the Sophienkirche will most likely continue well into 2022. But I have good employees these days, so I can leave them to it occasionally for a couple of weeks and travel.

What we call architecture now is a small fraction of what it could be and really what it should be. We have focused intensely on structure, aesthetics, and technology. Most recently, we may have given some relevance to our profession in the environment where we failed entirely to show the greater social and economic reasons for our profession. And when we don't show that relevance, we are, in fact, irrelevant to a great number of the issues in the world. People don't think of calling an architect when they have a problem. They don't think of calling an architect when there's an economic problem. They don't think of calling an architect when they're facing a public health problem. They don't call us. We don't get those jobs. We get jobs for very small, very limited reasons. Our profession is nowhere near what it could be or should be, and nowhere near contributing what it could.

Bryan Bell: If This Is Architecture, I Don't Want To Be An Architect!

We actually have to go out and find the need for design and then demonstrate how design can address that challenge. If we do that, and if we demonstrate how we can address all these other issues, then people will start to call us. I'll give you a quick example. I taught at the Rural Studio in central Alabama, which is not the cultural design mecca of this country, but when they have a challenge, they call up the Rural Studio and asked us to come and sit at the table with them to discuss what we could do to help. There's not even any design on the table at that point. There's no built solution on the table. This is just step one of the conversation because they've seen the proof that design is potentially the start of a solution. And if that can happen in rural Alabama in ten years, that can happen across the whole country and in the world in not that long a time. That's what I mean by being an activist. We're at a phase right now where we have to prove what we can do. The public is not calling us. Our work is decreasing, not increasing. We need to push hard to make sure it goes the other way. The burden is on us.

The most interesting jobs that are out there never come to us because people don't understand what we do. The *Butaro Hospital* by **MASS** in Rwanda is an amazing example. The client was Dr. Paul Farmer. He is a Harvard Fellow, I would say one of the smartest guys in the world, and has helped very many people throughout the world. Through Partners in Health, he was building hospitals in Rwanda where the old military bases used to be; what could be better than that? I'll tell you what can be better than that: hire an architect. He was building these hospitals without an architect. Michael Murphy, a Harvard student, walked up to him and asked whether he could serve as the architect for the next hospital. Paul Farmer was building hospitals where people with contagious diseases would come and spread those diseases. Michael Murphy, a student who had never done a hospital before but had a creative mind that Paul Farmer didn't have, realized the problem came from simple things: air exchange, quarantine areas. Michael Murphy's hospital was going to reduce communicable diseases more than any of the other hospitals Paul Farmer constructed. Today, Paul Farmer is an incredible design advocate.

I talk about expanding the roles we play. Let me just address why that's important. Right now, we play this very limited role in the middle of a project. The project is formulated by others before we become involved. The budget is finalized before we become involved. The site is often selected before we become involved. The program is written to a large degree before we become involved. Therefore our ability to creatively solve the problem is incredibly limited at that point because we weren't involved. And I think we are the group with much of the creativity of the culture. That's our luck. But it's also a responsibility. And if we're not using that creativity earlier to help craft better solutions, we just come in late in the game and shape a form to some criteria others have laid out without the iterative brainstorming collaborative process we can bring. Our creativity is incredibly limited. And we also have to play a role post-form, because post-form is where we can share the credit for the good our buildings do. Right now, we do the punch list, hand over the keys, we get our picture, and we're gone. And then somebody else moves in the building, goes on to save lives, to provide daycare, to cure tuberculosis. So we walk away and say, "Great I got my photo for the magazine, it looks beautiful, I don't care what happens after this." We're not given credit for what happens in our buildings, and we're not held accountable for the positive or negative results. Both of those are big problems. If we're irresponsible and insensitive and don't take the users into account, we ought to be called out for that. We have a big reputation for being like that, unfortunately, and we've got to take some responsibility for that reputation. At the same time, I really believe that if we are part of these solutions, we ought to be up there with everybody else getting credit. When I can show examples of buildings that spurred downtown renewal in Durham, North Carolina, or buildings that taught people trades and reduced tuberculosis in Rwanda, or buildings that created jobs in Marion, Alabama — that's when the public is going to start calling us. The buildings are a key player in that, and people that design those buildings ought to be given credit. So this link — what happens in a building after us — is one of these steps we need to make, so the public understands our contribution.

Who pays for these public benefits of design? When we demonstrate public value, the public will pay for it. We have to demonstrate public value clearly, and then public dollars follow. That doesn't mean we tell the government to give us a big pool of public interest design money and we'll do what we want with it. For example, I get a lot of my fees from the department of agriculture. They don't really see themselves as paying architects and designers. They need certain things done to support agriculture, including housing for farmworkers, and if I demonstrate a value for achieving those goals, I get money from the Department of Agriculture. There's all this public funding to solve public challenges. Designers need to insert themselves, insert their value into those sectors, and the funding comes.

I never do volunteer work. Never. I mean I can't; it's my job. This isn't something else, this is my job. So I always have to clearly demonstrate what the value is and then somebody pays for it. This is not like I'm making up a value and think somebody will pay for me. I have to go to the client and say: look, this value, if you pick the wrong site, or if you have the wrong program, it's going to cost you. You really need me upfront. In the case of the Durham Performing Arts Center, the architect became the developer because nobody would do that project. And he was from Durham and knew how much was needed. The project was incredibly successful. The first year, they had targeted to have 100 shows. They had 200 shows. Even a project like the High Line in New York, I think the initial economic impact was 9 billion dollars for buildings around it, having just revised it, to 90 billion dollars. This was a vision from the designers on how to utilize an unused piece of material in the city. Those two guys who came up with it can go anywhere else in the country and say: look, hire us on your economic development budget and we'll find some liabilities in your city and make them into assets, and here's our track record. There are a lot of projects like that. The Beltway in Atlanta was made up by a thesis student at Georgia Tech who sent a letter to the city council, instructing them to do this. City council is indeed doing it, a multi-billion dollar project made up by an architecture student. Nobody called Ryan Gravel up and said, "Ryan, we need you to come up with a proposal to solve our public transportation problem." He had the creative vision to see something. He saw these abandoned railway lines and thought: we've got these and we also need to make a beltway.

Now, do you think Ryan can get paid from those billions of dollars? Yes, of course. A small fraction pays Ryan out of the multi-billion dollar benefit to the city. So that was a value he created. And that's what I'm talking about the creative contribution we can make, not if we just sit around and wait for somebody to call us up. Some people think that entering a competition is like getting a call. I never enter a competition. I don't like the odds. And somebody's already defined it. I feel redundant since there will be maybe hundreds of applicants. I have a great ego, but somebody else is going to solve that problem pretty well. I'll go find something nobody else is doing, which is easy to do, and there is no competition.

My own education — graduate from both Princeton and Yale — is supposed to be a good one. I was always handed a program on a piece of paper. I was never taught to formulate a program or even go find a need for design. I was given a piece of paper for a hypothetical client and told to design for the hypothetical client. I never had the opportunity of having a real person sit in front of me and not only try to understand the challenge in built form but find poetry where it might not be obvious. So, I learned to design for hypothetical clients. But that isn't the way design works. There's a real client sitting there, and that real client actually has real qualities and challenges and issues, and unfortunately, this becomes an immediate conflict with the hypothetical client. That's why architects typically think of the client as "the enemy." He is the enemy of the way I was taught to design.

When I left architecture school, I got a job with **Steven Holl**. After six months, I was saying to myself: if this is architecture, I don't want to be an architect. As much as I admire him and love a lot of what he does, Steven Holl's philosophy is to ignore the client. In one magazine article, he said, "I agreed to do this house because the client promised not to interfere in the design." Another example of this approach was when we got a grant from the Graham Foundation for the Fine Arts. It was a project for Phoenix, Arizona, called *Edge of the City*. Nobody in our office had ever been to Phoenix. And I just couldn't believe that we were that smart, that we could make up something for Phoenix, without ever bothering to visit or even talk to anybody in Phoenix. The project went into the Museum of Modern Arts, so you'd think this was a good design. But did it do anything for anybody in Phoenix? No. Anybody at all? Well, it was good for our resumes. I do think there's something wrong with that philosophy.

I'd also worked for **Samuel Mockbee**, and Sambo showed me not to ignore the client, but that design poetry can come from the client. It's not just in the materials and in the light, but no matter who that person is or how "poor" they are, there's always something wonderfully poetic about them, you just need to believe that and look for it. Our challenge is to dig, and look, and listen, and find what is heroic and poetic and magnificent about that person and also about that place, regardless of the budget. The budget is never an excuse.

I think there's something we teach students that is linked to that hypothetical approach to design, and I think that's a problem. Somehow, we need to teach students more about what Sambo showed me. It's not just about helping "poor" people, but it's about respect and giving dignity to the lives of all those we serve through their designs.

My first mentor in architecture was **Bill Abbe** in high school. He said, "Don't just look at the sidewalk, look up at the buildings." So I say, "Be pro-active and look for the public need for design." I believe I can walk a quarter-mile in any direction from this building, and I can find a design project, I can find a job. I tell students to keep their eyes open for design opportunities, not just for beautiful forms, or precedents but also for the need for design. In 36 hours, they have to find a need for design, they have to program it, they have to get the materials, and ideally, they should talk to somebody using it — 36 hours. The students always complete it. The project can be very simple, like one time at the University of Oklahoma. There was a sidewalk, and there was a button you had to push to cross it and get the walk signal. For some reason, it was about three and a half feet away, and there was inevitably a mud puddle in that gap. Everybody had to do it, even design students. It was that easy to find a need for design. Do you like stepping in the mud? Aren't you a designer? Why didn't you solve this problem yourself? That's sort of pedestrian, literally. But it's not something you have to train people. You just say: do it. They can all do it.

With the job situation now, they have to go out there and look for these needs and find these challenges themselves. It's like flipping on a switch. Everyone I assign this to does it very creatively. We have this gift and the ability to see solutions that aren't there, to envision a physical form, even a step in a mud puddle. People think the mud puddle's there but somebody's saying, "Well I can change this, I can change the physical environment, I can envision what should be there." So it's not about the budget. It's about flipping that switch on and saying, "Go look, go find a need for what you can do." You could spend three hours doing it, you can spend just one afternoon. It doesn't have to be a whole semester. But it can also be an approach to a career as it's been for me.

I approach design as a collaboration, making a collection of the best ideas. The design process becomes inclusive, such as how to identify when other people have a good idea. Sometimes you do, sometimes others do. No one person has all the good ideas. That's sort of a fallacy that we believe in, "I'm the best designer, and I just got to keep trying to prove that to everybody." First of all, the client doesn't care who designed it, they just care about how great the solution is. In school I explain this by saying, "I'm grading you guys as a team, so if your partner has a good idea, you want that good idea as part of your project because if it's going to get a good grade and it's going to get published, that's success. So just recognize out of your self-interest that sometimes you want somebody else's idea, and sometimes they'll take yours. We're going to all present our ideas, and then other people are going to say who has the good ideas. And there can be no negative statements made, and nobody can defend, and you can't pick your own idea." By the end of a design-build project, everyone's got something in there, but it's not one thing that anyone person thought of by themselves. At Yale, they do a design-build project that's 40 years old, but they do a competition of four teams, and each team does a scheme, and one of them is picked. Well, what do you think the other 75 percent fell about that? It's like: I win, you lose. That doesn't create a team or shared ownership. The result is students really don't want to build somebody else's design. They didn't contribute anything to that. Now they are supposed to just build your design? That's a really bad idea. They should take those four proposals and say, "Let's put the best ideas from all of these, and let's go further." There is a fear in this process that the results are unknown. But isn't the goal always to go beyond what we know, to something better than anyone person could have conceived of at the beginning?

When I went to teach at the Rural Studio, I said to Sambo, "How do you do this? Auburn students aren't that good. I mean, they're good, but these buildings are all exceptional. So how do you get this great work all the time?" He said, "We beat the bushes until the good ideas come up, and then we grab them." It's that simple. It's sort of like: just throw out ideas, don't just fall in love with your own idea and then defend it — which is what we are taught in school. Just keep throwing out ideas, and as a group, when the good ones come up, we all say, "Hey, that's a good one, and this is a good one." And you put the good ideas together and you get these great projects like they do down there, not because the students are better, but you keep the good ideas and lose the bad ideas. At the end of the day, when they learn to collaborate, it's a real feeling. I mean, I love the last moment of the design-build projects when people say, "That's not one person's design, but we can all find something in there." In the Design Corps summer studio, they don't even get grades, so they're only there because they are self-motivated. So if I don't get them feeling ownership and like this is their project, if I did it the "Yale way," 75 percent of my students would just show up at 11 am and leave at 2 pm. But to have a successful project, they need to be there from 8 am to 8 pm. They have to be motivated, and they're motivated if this is their project. To achieve a great designer, I think you need to lovingly seek and embrace the unknown.

I think that serving the wealthiest two percent, which is what we consider "architecture" now, will always be there. People will hire **Eisenman** to do schools and **Steven Holl** to do houses. There's a whole culture to support that approach. I don't imagine that will ever change. But I'm talking about the other 98 percent that I feel is the other part of architecture, which is an amazing source of undeveloped potential and unimagined solutions. The greatest skill set I have is my architectural education and ability. That's who I am, that's what I like to do, and that's what this is about. I just want to use those in meaningful ways.

My mother was a fashion designer. I grew up in a house where she would throw a couple of yards of fabric across the dining table, sketch on it with white chalk,cut out drape, and have a dress made in the course of two days, beautiful clothing. I'm still fascinated by fashion because of its cycles and the relation of those cycles to architecture and construction issues. The way a garment is put together, and the way you can perceive quality in garment construction, and the way you can perceive quality in architectural construction, the nature of detailing and how flashy detailing is or is almost invisible appeals to me in terms of the things I'm interested in my own work.

Fashion has been as much influenced by the trickle-up as the trickle-down. You know, not everything comes from Dior or Prada, or whatever designer you might be interested in. It also comes from the street, right? The development of blue jeans as popular clothing, or baggy clothing, or grunge, you can see that fashion designers, noted fashion designers "mine" the everyday. I do think there's a relationship between fashion and architecture, and some of it has to do with sort of the stylization of every day things, like blue jeans, like the t-shirt, of course perhaps being the best example ever. I think it's very true that we are influenced by those things that spring up without the apparent hand of the architect.

Deborah Berke can get by on little sleep, no problem.

I am arguing for an architecture that flirts a little bit more with invisibility or is this combination of the moments of bold and the moments of subtle, or the moment of exquisite and the moments of banal, rather than the full force on statement which is closely knit to a kind of marketing strategy. It is so clear who the building is by that there is no mystery or intrigue or possibility for multiple readings of it.

My interest in the everyday has very much evolved into the dance with the bold, and the dance with the invisible at the same time because to me, that's what makes a good building, where you might look at it and go: hot damn. Or you might look at it and go: hmm, did somebody design that? And I would like that to be true in my work right down to the baseboard. You know that every piece of it flirts with a kind of boldness and anonymity at the same time.

What drives me? I love making things. I always have loved making things. I like making buildings where people make things, and that's part of the inspiration for the studio I'm teaching now. If you make buildings for other people making things, your work is backgrounded to their activity, but perhaps foregrounded in parts of their daily experience, and I love that too.

So I like making buildings for people making things or teaching things. They could be making music, they don't have to be making widgets. But making spaces for making and creating really stirs my soul.

I would describe my relationship with all my buildings as with former lovers. The affection remains, but they are in the past, and I'm looking forward. I would split our work up into two categories: ground-up stuff and unusual adaptive reuse. I hate the expression "adaptive reuse;" it sounds so ugly and belittling as a set of words, but reusing old buildings for new purposes is, of course, very exciting. So of the new buildings, I would say a favorite was the bank that we did in Columbus, Indiana (on the cover of the monograph with the big floating glass box). It is a 6,000 square foot tiny little building, sitting next to three big box stores. I loved making that building. I loved designing a building that was not a sign in the **Venturi** sense but was a sign nevertheless at a really diminutive scale, shouting its presence, but in the daytime was quite modest when you approached it. That was a hugely satisfying project, and I love that building.

In terms of our adaptive reuse work, we do a lot of this stuff, but two I remain sort of in love with. Years and years ago, we took an old Rolls Royce repair garage in what is now the NY Meatpacking district, but what was then essentially ... nothing. There was plenty of meat, but there was no district. And turned it from this derelict repair garage into fashion and photography studios called Industrious Super Studio like the one in Milan. We used the ramp that they had driven cars up to the second level as part of the circulation expression, so these incredibly leggy women and interesting things came up on dollies, up this ramp, and it was a very visible procession into where the photographs were being taken. I loved that; I still love that building, and it's still functioning as a photography studio. And the 21C Hotel in Louisville, which you know we took these old warehouses and turned them into an incredibly chic hotel and art museum. Those were party wall buildings that nobody could have conceived of as possible as a hotel. And I love that project, and I'm still happy every time I go there. Sometimes I go to projects and think, "Ugh, why did we do that" or "damn, I should have fought harder against that value engineering." But I go to 21C, and I think, "Oh, I really like this place, I still like this place."

Being a woman in architecture is no longer really an issue for me. But in terms of the profession, the fact that 50 percent of the students in many programs are women, but the number of women-led firms like mine, or senior partners at more corporate firms, or even women doing things on the periphery of traditional forms of practice or new practices or new ways of thinking about making, or being an architect or going into related fields, the fact that women are still so poorly represented at numbers that haven't improved really since I got out of school — that's scary to me. We're doing something wrong to be losing all of that creative thinking and intelligence and education. People venture that it might have to do with balancing family and the work hours expected of an architect. I just think that's too easy and simplistic an answer. I think it's more complicated than that.

I think there are maybe levels of certain discouragement as you make your way up the ladder, you know, you're often the only woman in the room; it's hard to build a voice of confidence in some of these environments. But I think women are kept out of the upper echelon and all the related professions, engineering, landscape ... through a series of dozens and dozens of tiny reasons, not one big reason. I don't know what the method would be to address it, but I do feel for the health of the profession going forward. We have to figure out what to do. We have to make it possible for more women to thrive in all the related design professions.

When we were working for a well-known American fashion designer many years ago, there was a very strict and dictatorial woman running his operations, and she was known to be just unreasonably demanding about her staff. We were designing their stores around the world, and it was eight o'clock in the evening, and we were still in a meeting, and I said: I have a young child, I need to see her before she goes to bed and I'm going home, but I promise you that everything that you ask for will be on your desk in the morning. And she kind of looked at me and she bristled, and everybody in the room, all of her underlings shared the same surprised reaction knowing you're either about to get your head cut off or be fired. And I left, and I went home, and I read my daughter a story, and I put her to bed, and I drank a cup of coffee, and I stayed up for many, many hours, and some folks in my office also stayed up because we needed to get the stuff out. She had it the next morning, and she never questioned me about it again.

I have a supporting, loving family, and I have always had a lot of energy. I have always been one of those who can get by on very little sleep and shape my work around my other requirements. So I don't think it's about being arrogant, and especially today, I think it's more true than it was back then, that if you make your priorities clear but also deliver quality work. You can have both. Or at least that's been my experience. That's something I would recommend. That having meaningful relationships, being a good parent if you elect to have children, and having a life beyond architecture is essential to being a good architect. Actually, being a culturally literate person and a person whose life is filled with experiences of all kinds makes you a better architect. So you make an effort to make time for all those things in your life, listening to live music, going to see art, traveling, eating well, drinking well, all of those things make you a better architect. So you make time for those things, but instead of letting it compromise your work, it enhances your work.

Architecture's role in the world is its ability to not only generate objects but also processes for how to develop the built environment. Architecture is not something that just happens on the back end of a process, but it factors the process itself. We're in danger of forgetting what it means to be an architect. There are so many topical diversions right now for architects, everything from the issues around sustainability, or what it is to be green or issues around social justice. All of those are valid topics to be concerned with, and design certainly has the ability to be part of possible solutions. At the same time, I fear that a lot of it is becoming the substitute for a commitment to the disciplinary knowledge that's been handed down to us, a commitment to understand the language of architecture and develop it further. We settle on easy conceptual gestures and mostly built diagrams too quickly, similar to a writer who can only do the outline but can't actually write. And the same is true for architects; I fear that all of these things become substitutes for actually being able to execute a beautifully resolute project. We can't forget, ultimately, what an architect must do.

Marlon Blackwell doesn't get 32 moves on a project; he might get three.

I became an architect for fear of becoming an alcoholic [laughter]. I wanted to be a cartoonist, and I read someplace that most cartoonists have alcohol problems. I was a very naive, young kid, and I wanted to draw, so architecture became that other default. I built some models, I took some courses, I could draw. I knew nothing, I had never even read a book on architecture, I'd heard of someone named **Frank Lloyd Wright**, and then I went to school based on that, hoping that I could somehow contribute to the world in a positive way.

A southerner, I came from a very modest background. If I were to go to college, I was going to have to pretty much pay myself. So I became a bible salesman during summers at my time at Auburn University. And I would spend the summer in one county in the rural South. I experienced a culture that people read about, but few actually experience. It's a deep immersion relative to understanding the people, and the food, and the customs, and that sort of thing. At the same time, I was selling bibles in the Bible Belt, where everybody has a bible. One of the great things I learned was the principle of selling and that this applies to whatever you're doing. As an architect, I'm really in the business of selling ideas. And the process by which I go about doing that, convincing somebody to do something that he had no idea he would do, and then to invest a lot of money to do it, I think it was an important skill to learn — all while selling bibles.

After Auburn, I worked for 10 years in practice, first five in southern Louisiana, in Lafayette, which is the Cajun part. It was a great immersion in a subculture of music and food. And then, I went to Boston, which was a much more stimulating, erudite setting. I found myself in a setting of like-minded people, ambitious, hungry, and wanting to set the world on fire. It's very stimulating, it was just dynamite to be there.

In the late '80s, Boston was a great place to live, but I found the work very unsatisfying. It was absolutely saturated with talent. The work in Boston was competent, but not critical in any particular way. It was just boring. The challenges of just getting something built, from a bureaucratic standpoint, were so great. I had to find another path, and that path was going to take me elsewhere. And it might be in that "black hole" between New York and LA.

That's why I didn't stay. I went to graduate school, with a pretty clear intention to come out of that with opportunities to teach and practice. I went to the Syracuse program in Florence, Italy. I'll never regret that because I was immersed in an amazing cultural context with really good teachers like **Thomas Schumacher**, and **Giorgio Ciucci**, and **Mark Shapiro**, and **Werner Seligmann**. I stayed a lot in Italy, but of course, I went all over Europe to see all the great modern works that I could see while I was there. It was one intensive year, and then came back to teach at Syracuse. The recession was on, there wasn't a lot of work, and I had already done a house on the side in Boston, and had been in Architectural Record Home, so there were a few things going my way, thus the opportunity to teach at Syracuse made sense.

The winters in Syracuse were criminal; I had never been so cold in all my life. I loved the school, I loved the students, but I looked around, and nobody was practicing. My people are Southern, and I felt connected with that culture. And they were folks like **Sambo Mockbee**, **Fay Jones**, and others who were living examples of some really good work in places you'd least expect to find it. I decided to go to North Carolina because there was a guy named **Frank Harmon** who had been in **Richard Meier**'s office, and had moved back to the South and was doing some really stimulating work there. I loved that collision of the kind of modernist language with the Southern traditions, and how one negotiates that.

NC State wasn't looking for someone, but I took an opportunity in Arkansas, which I thought was the South. But there are two Arkansas: the Ozarks, and the Delta (southeastern Arkansas). And the Ozarks are not the South, they're not the West, they're not the Midwest; they're the Ozarks, just like being in Appalachia. It's a very interesting place, and I just fell in love with the school. There is a great legacy there, and it had a new dean, Dan Bennett. Edward Durrell Stone is from Fayetteville. Bill Clinton had taught at the law school there. And then there were Walmart, Tyson Chicken, all these self-made billionaires who, interestingly, were all in northwest Arkansas. And a great landscape to go with it. So there was something going on there that I thought, "Well, I want to try this here." That's why I chose Arkansas. I think it's a wonderful roux of culture, of nature, of geography, all of that. The Ozarks region is not burdened by the yoke of history that New England is. The other day, my wife and I came to the conclusion that there wouldn't be a single building we've done here that could be approved in Cambridge, MA.

Our work falls outside of an accepted norm or a context because our buildings are so specific to where they are. It's not like a high modern or a low vernacular; it's that mixing, that hybridizing, and looking at both what's given to us, but recognizing what's emerging, too, in the margins or in the built environment where we could look at a trailer home and find as much value as there is in a barn or a dogtrot house. In other words, we see the building as its own type of vernacular. So we have all of that variety there and, if we're observant and attentive, we can make a lot out of it

I like Arkansas since it's been traditionally poor; what's imbued in the people there is self-reliance and a kind of independence. Still, even though it's awash much more in money and wealth today, there is no crazy money there. I can work for nonprofits, I can work for the storied families of Arkansas, and the positions are pretty similar about resources and how they are used towards design. Most folks that I work with in Arkansas don't know what they want, but they know what they don't want, and they don't want what everybody else has. And that's a great place to start versus New England, where the client tells you that he wants it to look like a New England saltbox or colonial. Whatever it is that clients want to ascribe to you to maintain the kind of perception of being in New England, it's less of an issue here in Arkansas.

Practicing with my wife, Ati, can be a challenge. Very argumentative at times. I'm 10 years older, and we come from different backgrounds. She comes from a classical modern background at the University of Miami, **Plater-Zyberk**, and that whole background, but we're both firm believers in proportion and scale and those sorts of things, and it's basically trying to find where each can contribute. I tend to be the more conceptual engine in the office and the kind of director of how we want things resolved, scale the hand, scale the building, scale the city, or the site. She has a very good eye and tends to be particularly good on the interiors with color and finishes and how to put an interior pallet together. Ati's an accomplished interior designer and an architect. It's been a work in progress because I started without her, and then she came on board, and at times it's been difficult, because she has a very strong will, and I have a strong will also.

We're not able to compartmentalize so easily, and it's tough on the kids sometimes because of architecture, architecture, architecture. There are times when I say that we should just be working separately and then other times I can't imagine it. We're interdependent. I think that it's a project, it's like marriage, we keep working on it. If we stop working on it, it falls apart. So in the business, we keep working on it. And I think it keeps work invigorating because my wife is the one person who can look and say, "What is this shit concept thing you're doing?" She will just get back in my face and say, "you need to rethink this." And we don't always agree, but often, I think she's absolutely right, and it makes me dive a little deeper.

Finally getting that first big project is traumatic. Before, I sat at the table and drew every detail by hand, sections to the ceiling, all hand-drawn, every last thing. Then I realize that I'm going to have to cede that to someone else. I found it very traumatizing to develop trust, especially for somebody who is more implicit than explicit. I'm not the kind of person that wants to stand over somebody and tell them exactly what to do. I want them to understand the framework, and then we work together. That just takes time. It was painful, that first time, realizing that I had to trust others and that I had to be more collaborative. So, yeah, the firm is sort of a benevolent dictatorship still. I mean, my name is on the door, I feel responsible for that, but increasingly, it's been more collaborative, and that's a very good thing.

Working with other firms was hard as well because I felt I was being taken advantage of. And the emotional investment wasn't the same. I finally came to a conclusion, "I will try to avoid those projects if I can." Sometimes it makes sense, like on the new architecture school, the *Steven L. Anderson Design Center*, where the quality of the firm we teamed with is such that it's actually productive. But when I first started out, others would take most of the fee, and then I would have to cover for their poorly done drawings and their bureaucratic business model. It became very clear that for others, it wasn't about the project; it was more about some kind of profit model that they had set up. I took a very dim view of that, and as a result, I keep a distance from those firms.

In practice, there are lots of things that happen serendipitously, when we're in the middle of construction, still trying to figure out what the design is going to be, that somehow work their way out because we've prolonged as much as we can. We were designing *St. Nicholas*, a church for the Orthodox Christian community, and they had to have a dome, and we had no dome. We were under construction, and there was no money, and every day it was "What are we going to do?" In the end, the contractor came up with a brilliant idea of getting a couple of cases of beer and trading them for a satellite dish. We skim-coated the satellite dish in stucco, in plaster, and then we put the Pantocrator on that, and we lit it up, and it was beautiful. But I didn't know what we were going to do until that contractor's suggestion made things work.

My initial philosophy of publishing was influenced by the late **Chris Risher**, who was from Mississippi and taught at Harvard a lot, and he yet was a guy who had never wanted to publish anything. He did beautiful work, wrote beautifully, and spoke like Faulkner, a very powerful presence. But he would not allow his work to be published. He didn't want to become a prisoner of the media in any way. So, for five years, I didn't publish anything and just worked. I stayed in one place, and I worked. It was great to quit running, quit moving from place to place, quit searching for the perfect setting, and actually say I'm going to stay here, and I'm going to carve something for myself here. After five years, I had to apply for tenure, even though I didn't believe in tenure at the time. The dean said he understood that, but if I didn't go up for it, he was going to fire me.

So I submitted a couple of projects, the small *Honey House* for a beekeeper in North Carolina, and the seven-story *Keenan Tower House* that we were working on to Architecture Magazine. They loved it and wanted to make it part of a whole issue on the primitive hut. We got it professionally photographed, we did everything right, met a writer out on-site in North Carolina, and I was excited. But when it came out, the writing had very little to do with the images they picked. In fact, the images they picked were almost unrelated. It was just odd. We had the least amount of coverage compared to the other projects, which happened to be all from the East Coast or Europe.

I let my emotions get carried away, and I called the editor in New York to complain. I brought up how the article missed the mark in covering my work. I challenged his skimpy coverage of my work compared to the works of more prestigious East Coast and European firms. In fact, I told him I was feeling a little zip code challenged. This editor essentially told me that our images were not good enough. I was insincerely assured that it had nothing to do with our project or where our practice was located, however, when I asked why he didn't give us a chance to fly back out and reshoot, he expressed his concern that we would not have the resources to do that. It was unbelievable to have to hear this as a small practitioner from the South. After defending my photographer's talent and a few expletives later, I just hung up.

Once I got over my anger, I called up Robert Ivy, the editor of Architectural Record, who had written the monograph on **Fay Jones**. I had met him briefly years before, and I knew he was from Mississippi. So I called him, said that I would be in New York, and asked if he would have some time to meet with me so I could show a few projects to him. And his secretary said that he could spare a few minutes. What he didn't know was that I was coming to New York only to show him my work. Once I got to his office, I explained to him about the Honey House, and that I would like to see it republished in an appropriate manner, which is something competing magazines don't do. And then I showed him a barn house we did, and then I showed him our Keenan TowerHouse. And I got about two images into the TowerHouse, and he ran and got all his editors, who were in the middle of eating lunch, and asked me to begin again. So I started over, and I got to this TowerHouse again, and he stopped, and he stood up and said, "This looks like **John Hejduk** grew up and built something." I had to be reassured that this was a compliment- he said it was and then said, "Okay, everybody leave!"

He shooed all of his editors out, sat down next to me and recounted how he'd been thinking about an issue for a long time about people like myself, outside the centers of fashion, that get up every day and work and try to do great work.

What I didn't know was that they decided to put the TowerHouse on the February 2001 cover. I was teaching a guest studio at MIT at the time, and there it was, on the cover. To me, that was a victory because that was a game-changer. We suddenly had the national presence, the credibility, that brought the attention back to the middle of the country, or to the margins, and began to equalize a little bit what a lot of small firms like mine struggle against. And it was a fantastic issue; I think it won a national award that year for that particular issue. It was a victory that set our trajectory higher for the practice, and really helped me understand that what I was doing had some merit and that we could move forward. It was a victory in perseverance, and the willingness to take risks. And if I hadn't insisted on it, if I'd let the other editor be the measure, well, that could have had a devastating effect on how we moved forward.

I decided when I was very young, too young to know any better, to become an architect. It turned out I had the aptitude to do it, but I think that's common for a lot of people. Second thoughts? Occasionally, but rarely. There was a period during my undergraduate education when I got really into printmaking. I enjoyed doing this but I kept doing architecture. It wasn't that I was unhappy with architecture, but I almost had my architecture degree at this point, so it was probably a little late to jump ship. If I had taken printmaking a bit earlier it might have pulled me away. My bigger concern these days is more about how I make sure that I keep loving the work because if I somehow were to become disillusioned with architecture at this point it would be a real problem. It would be like getting a divorce after 30 years. I would have to learn to live again, and I am not really interested in doing that.

Marshall Brown is fairly militant about how he works, but never asks a student to do anything he would not do himself.

The challenge is that of any person who's in the middle stages of a career, the growing pains of navigating your own practice and taking on more responsibilities. The ongoing challenge to figure out who you want to work with, who you don't want to work with, what you want to work on, what you don't want to work on, how you spend your time, what you value, and what you don't value. I am in my early 40s now, so I think more responsibilities come my way, but more challenges come as well, so I have to be careful. I have found in the last couple of years that I'm able to be more careful about what I decide to take on, based on the experience I already have had. I think about that more because I recognize there is a risk of major disasters, especially when projects become bigger, more complicated, or long-term. In the past few years, I've been lucky to have certain kinds of opportunities come my way, but some of these opportunities represent extreme divergences in terms of what I would want to be doing for maybe the next 10 or 20 years. When you're younger you get to try things on more. When you're in school try this on for a year, this on for a semester. But I think that the stakes get higher as you advance in your career. People say they put you in one box or another. So you do this product that means your this kind of architect, you do that kind of project, you are that type of architect. It's hard to go back down the path to take the other route because you have been framed or defined in a certain way. What kind of architect am I? What kind do you need? That's my standard answer these days. We live in a world of specializations and so I get this standard answer when I meet people on the street or cocktail parties or wherever. They say do you have a specialty? I ask what do you need. Then the conversation gets interesting. It took me awhile to find a good answer to that question, one that actually satisfied me.

I get a lot of inspiration from just working in my studio but that time has become rare as I have become more advanced in my professional career. The time I spend actually doing creative work becomes increasingly limited because I deal with the management of getting the work or disseminating the work. What inspires me right now is material engagement with my hands; I am drawing by hand again, doing a lot of collage work, and making models. In terms of outside influences, I am inspired by the same things that always have inspired me: film, books, living in Chicago. Chicago is an open-air museum; architecture is everywhere, it's all-around. I teach in a campus by **Mies van der Rohe** for better for worse, there is **Frank Lloyd Wright**, I got to spend a night at Taliesin a few weeks ago — not in Chicago but close enough — so there's lots that's inspiring. I guess now I've been there for eight years I can call myself a Chicago architect. To be part of that tradition is inspiring or at least it sets a high aspirational bar. I was in Italy for five weeks this summer and saw Castel Vecchio for the first time; one cannot help but be inspired by cathedrals, Venice and all that.

This past year I've been very busy. I have a lot of prestige projects such as exhibitions in Chicago and outside. There's a kind of feedback between all those spaces in the work that I do, either in my own studio or teaching and research work within the University. Right now, I'm doing a master plan on the south side of Chicago for a client — a real project for real money with a real contract — that definitely was inspired by a previous commission that was closer to research but it was paid, and that work was inspired by a series of studios that I ran at Illinois Institute of Technology (IIT) over the course of 3 to 4 years. I start teaching students about different things based on what I do in my studio and my practice. I am not interested in having my students doing work for me, or doing the work I should be doing. At the same time, I am not interested in promoting my students' work as that of my office, but my thoughts can't help to be infected by the engagement with all these spaces. I just finished a big research project at IIT about the driverless city and am already getting calls from private entities that will probably become some sort of consulting. I do unpaid research in my studio about representations, I do a lot of collage work which starts out without a client, without a place to go. Sometimes that work winds up in a gallery and maybe somebody is buying it, or I find a medium to publish it.

There is a productive relationship between all of my spaces; they are clearly divided, clearly separated, but they cross over, mostly through my mind. The ideas move back and forth. Some of these collages I am actually using in the master planning project that I'm working on right now, even though that was not my original plan. I have another example for a commission of a pavilion that I built this spring for the Arts Club of Chicago which started in this collage research and then moved into this commissioned project. I try to look for productive overlaps.

I don't know that I'm incredibly prolific and I see people out there who produce a lot more work. Compared to most architects I know, I'm fairly militant about how I work and that's what allows me to be productive, if not incredibly prolific. I like to get up and go to my studio five days a week, ideally, be in there at nine and be out of there at four or six — either side of rushhour. It's really very basic, very simple. Then subtract the time that I am teaching from that. Even on the days when I am teaching, I get Tuesdays and Thursdays to be in my office. I try to be there for the whole day. I block out that time and get in there, get to work, and get out. That works for me. I know when my productive thinking time is, I know when my productive making time is, what my biological and psychological rhythms are. I know that after 2 o'clock I don't really have any good ideas. After 5 o'clock the productivity drops off, after 10 o'clock I should not even bother because I am just making a mess. That actually puts me in a space where I know if I show up in that time and make it intense, things will happen. I don't worry so much about what is happening. Rather, I trust my training, I trust my experience, and I just make sure that I keep moving.

I'm a designer who believes that indecision is worse than the wrong decision. When I start projects I usually get into an idea pretty quickly and for me, it's less about let's try out 100 ideas — the thing that we see when we pick a Dutch architect where there are an image and a monograph with the 200 different versions of the scheme that we tried — all radically different. I think that's fine and interesting and fun, but it is not the way I work at all. My process is much more evolutionary. Once I've done some research and looked at some precedents, I come to a proposition fairly quickly, and then I try to develop along that path, as opposed to exploring 20 different paths in hopes that I get the right one. I like to play the long game. I am less interested in 100 different versions of the same product; I want to do a hundred different projects. It's just a matter of preference. I am always very concerned about opportunity cost and while I am sitting around deliberating or writing about whether I am doing the right thing, the possibility of doing other things is passing me by. I am more afraid of that.

I would not say that the future is an obsession for me. I think the idea of the future is programmatic to architecture. The things we make, the things we propose do not yet exist. They are always off into some future, especially once things go up in scale. Lots of architects say that. Even fairly conservative architects like **Andrés Duany** say that. He says, "If you know you can't think 30 years into the future you're in the wrong business." Because that's the job. That's one of the few things I would agree with him on. For me, it has become interesting to play with that as an idea and to look at techniques of futurity, scenario planning, future studies, all the stuff that is occasionally talked about in the field of architecture but hasn't been really integrated. It's not really taught much in most programs, especially not as a core part of the program, at least not explicitly. In order to get people to engage us in realizing projects or doing the things we do as architects we basically have to figure out ways to get them to imagine this alternative future. Here is a place where we might do something, imagine this place to be radically different than it is now. Can you imagine that? Some of the techniques for doing this are really interesting and engage all different kinds of creativity like fiction writing. I teach Burnham's plan of Chicago to my students and I say to them upfront: this is a work of fiction. That's how we should look at it. It is not a technical document, it's a fiction about the future of the city, it's a dream. When my students are getting desk crits or in critiques I ask one question: what is the dream? I can't judge any of what they are showing me unless I understand what the dream was. The future is about dreaming, of proposing alternative realities which are yet to come, and could be realized by myself or by others.

I believe the future of architecture to be multiplicitous. There's not only one. The future is diverse and full of discrepancies, so there is not only one. If I would propose one it would show that I have learned nothing or that I don't know what I am talking about. It's going to be multiplicitous, diverse, and conflicted. Architecture has many futures. They are already emerging in global capitals, in the Canadian oil fields, in border cities, in the west side of Chicago. There seems to be something about architecture which is part of us as human beings; as long as we are around I am pretty confident that architecture has a strong future.

The crisis of architectural education is perpetual. When has it ever not been in crisis? Going around to see other schools I see wonderful work happening. For me, the question is not change or stasis, that's not really the battle. Even since I was a student some things have changed. I started school in 1991 and that was when digital technologies came into widespread use. In the 90s people had desktop computers that actually could draw things, we had plotters, we could do things in three dimensions, and suddenly computers became a tool that could be effective. This has changed some things, maybe not everything we hoped and not in ways we expected. Still, change has no value in itself. What I find myself thinking about is the question of fundamentals. What are the current emerging and necessary fundamentals for moving forward? There seems to be less of a willingness to actually teach what one might have called fundamentals 30 or 40 years ago.

Maybe I am nostalgic, but when I was a student there seemed to be a certain amount of agreement about what fundamentals would be taught in the early years of an architectural education, let's say years one through three. Now it seems to be the Wild West: no one really knows. No one knows how the studio should be set up, no one knows if we should draw or not draw, if we should make models, do everything digitally, care about plans, care about sections, or care about any of these kinds of disciplinary techniques that we had for four hundred years. Or should we just throw them out? If we throw them out, what are the fundamentals that will replace them? Or how do we modify them? It's probably too conservative a discussion to keep most of my colleagues interested, but it fascinates me. I think it's a very radical project in the literal sense. What are the fundamentals? They wouldn't necessarily be the same for every school. But I think each school has to have a consciousness of its fundamentals. And that is a different question than the question I hear being asked a lot. Schools ask themselves what they are, and what their mission is.

Good schools are diverse intellectually and creatively, but at some point within the pedagogy, there has to be some consideration of the actual concrete fundamental techniques and sets of knowledge that we might teach today, which could be generally useful to a large number of our students. Then maybe that is a super conservative question, maybe it is more interesting to let everybody loose in a room and see what they do, which is somewhat close to what people are proposing. But then it is not a collective project anymore, and for me, that's not what architecture school should be. Architecture has always been fundamentally invested in a notion of collectivity, in terms of the spaces we make, or the way we work. Even though I work mostly alone in my studio I am still always thinking about collective engagement, about engaging a larger constituency.

I have seen it working in some places, some very advanced schools. I was able to sit on studio reviews — it was in the second year of the landscape architecture program at Harvard — and it was Professor **Pierre Bélanger** — this amazing display of pedagogical force I had never seen before. Basically, the faculty got together and developed a very collaborative semester. The idea was that the studio would be interrupted by a series of workshops that were integrated with the semester-long project. The students all worked in teams — shocking, architecture students working in teams in their second year of the program — and the faculty worked together. The faculty or people from outside with a certain expertise or certain skills would run two to threeday workshops where the students learned these skills. The whole semester seemed to me to be built around not just content but also skills. So old-fashioned, imagine teaching actual skills, and all the faculty agreeing on what skills they were to teach and what skills were important. They were focusing on the students developing some mastery of their skills. The work I saw at the end was an incredible display of force, to the point where they actually staged the final review as an exhibition. The scope of the whole operation was incredible. Regardless of whether or not you agreed with the design proposals, you could not dispute the talent of those students. It was undeniable. They weren't sitting there drawing by hand, it was all digital, CNC milled, animations, all sorts of stuff. They were asking the questions of what are the new fundamentals in our field, which were radically different from what you would have seen people doing 10 years ago. Whether they were right or wrong, I feel like they were confronting the issue in a very disciplined way.

In my studio, I'm asking myself the same question. How do I want to work every day? What gives me pleasure and what do I find useful? No defaults! Whether I turn on the computer or whether I sit at my drafting board or whether I'm cutting and pasting, I'm going to spend a fair amount of time being very conscious about those things. I also never ask my students to do something that I would not do myself. This has become the new ethic in my practice.

I come from a family of architects. As a young girl in India, I was precocious, very much a tomboy, and I would always accompany my dad to his construction sites. I particularly liked the projects where he would renovate. He would walk into projects looking at his iterations and I would walk into projects thinking about spaces: gosh, if only walls could talk. What are the stories they would tell? I loved that. I loved that there was something extraordinary about what we did within the built environment that shaped us, that changed our attitudes to all of life in general. That was my first introduction to design.

If **Shashi Caan** had to choose a role model, it would be Coco Chanel.

My father wanted us — my two sisters and I — to go to universities, study sciences and become doctors. He was very certain that we shouldn't be in the creative arts, that if we wanted professions, it should be something serious. I did not want to do that. I wanted to go to art college. It meant offending him, upsetting his ideas of what was the better education to have. I got accepted into art college but didn't know what to expect. I didn't necessarily think I was an artist but I didn't know what I was. So my undergraduate education was, in hindsight, an extraordinary journey of self-discovery. I was privileged because I really didn't need to come out of that study with qualifications for a profession. I essentially spent four years exploring. I did sculpture, painting, blowing glass, making stained glass windows, making furniture, tapestries, printed textiles, woven textiles, interiors. I did everything and loved it all but particularly enjoyed the three-dimensional spatial aspects of the disciplines. And then after graduating with a BFA, I knew I had a strong interest in interiors but needed more specific knowledge for that. I went on to study industrial design at the masters level, worked in an architecture practice, went back to school for architecture, got a second master's degree, and went back into the workforce specializing in interiors because that was still the one area that was of passion to me. It's been a long journey of exploring different aspects of design at different scales, at different levels.

After graduating from architecture school, there were two firms I wanted to work for. One was SOM. I always wanted to work for very big firms. I enjoy lots of people. And the other firm I wanted to work for was Gensler. And at the time, the reason I wanted to work for Gensler was because **Margo Grant** headed that practice. And I was very intrigued that of all the New York firms, it was the only one lead by a woman, and I wondered what that would be like. I didn't get to work directly with Margo Grant but worked at Gensler when she was still there. She was extraordinary and I admired her. I don't think it makes a big difference, though, working in a firm with a female principal.

My entire work experience has been in three major New York firms. Starting my own practice was not something that was rationalized. It was something that came about after the Trade Center fell because of the bombings. I had designed a lot of space in the Trade Center. I had designed some fifteen floors of space. That was the largest footprint of a building in America at the time. Each floor plate was an acre in size. And we lost 600 individuals of that client and I was pained by that and equally pained by the loss of the space because I knew every single closet. I knew every single space on those floors that we had designed. SOM was in the neighborhood two blocks away. I didn't really want to be in the neighborhood after that. It was traumatic. So it was more mental and emotional than it was physical or rational.

I loved my job at SOM. It was such an amazing opportunity, such a great position, and I had such a good time working in large teams, exploring lofty ideas, and doing things with the rigor that is a SOM ethos. But after 9/11, there was a period of soul searching that I think the whole nation went into. And I don't really know quite how it came about. I just know that by April of the following year, I left SOM. I took a month to figure out what I was going to do and decided to start my own practice. The practice needed to be called The Collective. A lot of the ideas and issues that we were exploring at the time were about collaboration, life balance, working in practices in ways to be most creative while managing all other aspects of life. I had done a lot of thinking about how to improve the quality of life for all the designers while at SOM.

I called it The Collective because I believe that it is the ultimate of collaborations. Our tagline is "Minds Multiplied" so two people come together and have the capacity of four. But that's not enough. It's really important that in the collaboration, we are relaxed, we are at peace, we are dignified and respectful. This requires a different set of conditions. And so The Collective is structured to be modeled after the film industry where individuals come together to work on one project at a time. I suppose I've never been one for planning life. I've never thought five years ahead. Many people do that and I've never done that. But I felt that we needed — we meaning society and culture, my generation — at this moment in time, we all need to be doing things a bit differently, thinking more profoundly about what we're doing and why we're doing it and how we might improve it. So The Collective was an idea that was about that improvement and it came to be born in 2002.

I have three male partners. And we had the choice of setting it up as a woman-owned practice and we didn't do it like that. I don't think it matters. But it is still very much a man led world in the 21st century, hugely problematic in our education institutions. In our education, sixty percent of enrollment is by women. So there's a big shift, and I don't think that in terms of experience at senior levels, we are preparing for that well enough. I don't think gender matters if you're good at what you do.

Just starting the office has been extraordinary. We are now ten years in practice. The administration is still challenging, and we haven't mastered it yet. We expanded into the UK so now we have a separate studio there, which is very gratifying, but was not planned per se. It's fantastic to be working across the Atlantic, which I think is the way of the future. I do think that when we do things from the heart driven by passion, it has its own path, and the path finds us or keeps us on the right track. I've made more time to focus on aspects of the projects that are more important. I love the conceptualization of our work. I love in particular working closely with the client, understanding his needs, his aspirations, less so the functional which are easier to deal with, but much more the dreams, the desires. And I love working to take that client to the edge of his comfort zone, but not beyond because it is important that he feels really comfortable where he is, but also progressive. That's a gauge that is unique to every single client. And so I'm very proud of the work we do. We're not trend-focused nor do we have an ideology that espouses a particular kind of work, but we're very timely, topical, focused on issues, and focused on research. In that sense, our work has supported the people we've designed for. To me, that is the ultimate success in a project.

With every project we experiment with color, but it's always a very rational, careful insertion of color. It has nothing at all to do with my Indian background; I, of course always wear black. Still, color is one of the fundamental tools in architecture, but we don't know enough about it. In architecture, we probably understand more about light than we do about color. But we certainly place form making on a higher pedestal than we do color and light. And I think that's backward. I think that without light, we don't have life, we have nothing. The moment we switch that light switch or the sun comes up, we have space, and shade and shadow begin to define the scale and shape of those volumes, and color gives us an awful lot of information. I consider color to be one of those very essential design criteria that we as a discipline must really understand.

I've learned in a more theoretical exploration of color that in any volumetric space, it's important to have at least three tonalities — a light, a medium, and a dark — and different proportions. Do you remember the eighties when we were doing a lot of beige interiors? They're deathly. You walk in and you're not really sure what's going on. Well, that was one kind of stylistic quality that we pursued that ultimately wasn't satisfying. Neither was the all-white interior or all concrete. Ultimately, it's not satisfying, anything singular is not satisfying. The human brain needs change, it needs contrast, and it understands more when there is a careful balance. And that balance includes texture, color, light and dark. Experimenting with and exploring light and color in architecture is essential.

How do we draw a client out of his or her comfort zone? I can cite several examples. We're working with the Scottish government where there is a very large approval system in place. The system is entirely based on function and in the last three or four years during the downturn of the economy, all of the requirements have become tougher and tighter. In Scotland the project is driven by function but still involves having conversations, having drinks with a client or tea with or lunch, or anything that's not so formalized, where it's possible to listen to them from a different place, and still understand or get behind why they are doing what they are doing, what they would like to see accomplished other than we need to save space to be more efficient, and somehow make people feel happier, which are the usual common criteria. We just finished designing a headquarter space for a brewery, for a distillery, a very different kind of client. It is owned by folks in Thailand but they're in Scotland and that's an interesting international mix. They know what they do best — build breweries — but they are very much in Scotland. Blending these distinct perceptions and perspectives necessitates talking to everyone, talking a lot. This is one of the mantras that I use in the office: you can't communicate enough. As human beings, all we really have is the ability to communicate, and if we can understand each other, truly listen, and do it with respect and dignity and friendship, good happens.

I've had a foot in both worlds, academia and practice, all of my life. I went straight from undergraduate school and worked for nine months in London, and went to New York to do my master's. Right after graduating with a master's, I started to teach. I graduated from Pratt and started to teach at Pratt. So I've never known another world. I've always known that there's a possibility of playing in this wonderful place we call school. Whether you teach or you're a student — in fact, if you're a teacher, you need to learn more to be able to do it — you're studying and you're exploring, researching and you're learning. The Academy was always very important for me to challenge some of the conventional pedagogies and processes that exist. It's not good enough to continually propagate what we already know. I challenge ideas of representation, of how to incorporate sensory knowledge within our applied works. Theory is great but only if it actually enhances our quality of life. If it doesn't then what's the point? But "practice" was always very important to me because it's not enough to have a theoretical understanding. It's equally important to test it in the practice. So I've always done both.

Later a third component became very important. About ten years after doing both I became involved in developing volunteer work, pro bono work within an extended community. Cultivating a sense of excellence and an awareness among the general public is an equally important component. So the three, that triangle or sort of three-way relationship is really essential.

In our practice, we are very much an academic studio. We do a lot of research. We do research for every single project and we research clients. And we have sixteen-foot ceiling heights — it's a small space but — in our main space, and two sides of it are full of books, bookshelves. Books are our primary resource along with materials because we think that's very important.

We support this madness that we all have been really driven to explore life. We all have our egos but I don't think we are an ego-driven office. Our sight for our work isn't in the next five, ten, twenty years. We don't care whether we're published or not, that's really not what it's about. In fact, we don't enter competitions because the success of the project is less about what peers think of it. For us, it is a testament of what clients come back and continue to want to work with us. And we go to the projects that we've built and we see the pride that the client takes in maintaining what we've done. When they don't change it in a hurry, we know we were successful. We love exploring and we love thinking and we have great conversations in the office. And there are times one of the partners will say okay, we should really be a little more serious about billing. But on the other hand, we can deliberate, discuss, debate, talk an issue through, and bring everyone along. We love that.

We have sort of like the United Nations in our small team where people are from different cultures. So we have fun with that. We push each other's buttons about the stereotypes that we all play with. To me, ultimately, that's what life is all about because if you can't make time to have a conversation with a colleague, then what is it that we are rushing to get done to do. And most people will say, "Well, I want to go have time for family." And to me, this is an extension of that.

I got started many different times; I'm still trying. In other words, it's an evolutionary process. I started in ceramics out of college, thought I'd be a potter, but then immediately recognized the limitations. I started in galleries in Texas after I got out of college, and then I started showing nationally at different competitions. But what I see in myself has been a forced mutation — even after a big museum show at the Hirshhorn Museum. There was a point where I just abandoned that so I could force myself to look at other perspectives and points of engagement. I don't say inspiration, sometimes these points of engagements have not been inspirational. I am compelled into action by sometimes very tragic or difficult realities. I guess that I'm always starting, I'm always starting again.

For **MEL CHIN**, making objects is also about making possibilities, making choices — that is one of the last freedoms we have.

Since my work is predicated in concept, the first thing that must drive work is how poetic is its construction. Does it have a certain sensibility that matches some kind of critical epiphany that must happen? Then I go forward. Sometimes it's works of art, sometimes it's personal and so-called studio practice, sometimes it's a political perspective that's being ignored, and sometimes it's a search for a solution for something that's totally unjust, untenable. The larger works, of course, require funding and I seek funding, and the smaller works I endure, and then there are other works that I could say are intended to be gifts, in a way, not gifts to society, but gifts to myself.

I have a retrospective coming up at the New Orleans Museum of Art, and the whole premise of the show is not just one kind of beginning, but maybe different ones. I think the curator's perspective is about how all these types of evolutions occur. Rather than trying to force one material or conceptual framework over it, she realized that there's a continual evolutionary framework. Some projects have been totally collaborative in nature; they're collaborations that were intended to suppress my dominance, so to speak. I can be the initiator, but so what? A lot of concepts can be that way. I like the reality therapy of execution, and it demands collaboration and giving up my ego, to a great degree, to make those things happen. Sometimes I do have fabricators who come in. And my chief fabricator has worked for me for 30 years, but with each new project, it's almost like we sit down and think about how do we build this or how do we execute this. And if it's a social project, then how is this delivered and how must it change. The studio is based on our economy, too. When we're flush, we hire and we have commissions. Business moves in and out, just like any other profession.

The way it happened, my father came over through New York as a legal alien, trying to avoid the subjugation of China by Japan during '39, '38. He joined the American military and became a citizen through that. He went back to China and was able to bypass the Chinese Exclusion Act, which was a congressional exclusion act that lasted until the 1940s, preventing Chinese, specifically, from having easy access to immigration into America. My parents went back to New York and found very hard times there, and there were friends from the military that suggested getting a grocery store down in Texas. And we went down there when I emerged I must have come out of the womb in Texas.

The neighborhood started somewhat mixed, but it eventually, rapidly became African American by the early 60s or late 50s. And my parents' store was situated right there in what they call the Fifth Ward. It was a cool place to grow up. It taught me something about the camaraderie and the edges. My father was very much a member of the community and very generous and very loved, apparently. After he died, I learned so many things about him and his capacity for charity. At the funeral, we were trying to give our memories of our father, and this black man in a resplendent suit pushed everybody out of the way and took the podium. He was a preacher, and he spoke of how my father had given him his first job and taught him a little bit about responsibility. We remembered that fellow as being very lazy, but it was great. Then he said something that we didn't know. He said that my father gave his family credit for food, even delivered it to the family, but would never ask, demand payment. He said they paid whenever they could, but he never would put a stop to that. "Can you go anywhere in America now and ask for food on credit and feed your family? I survived because of the generosity of Mr. Mini." We had never heard about this, but I guess it happened a lot. The preacher has a big congregation now, a TV evangelist, and he said, "Well, I've met so many people who say they're great, from the governor to the mayor, and all these people. But I want to tell you here lies a great man." This is what he thought was great. So he had been compelled to come to the funeral. I loved it when he got up there and said, "I can see I am in the minority today." Because it was mostly hundreds of Asian families that my father had also helped to immigrate, and worked tirelessly for the boat people that came through. So there's a record of just being human and not so selfish, I guess, and it was instructional. So, yes, these are my roots, the "ruts," as they say in Texas.

Maybe there's a sociological kind of directive to engage, but I don't think that's a prerequisite for being an artist. I was precocious as a child, but around age 14, I suffered a major breakdown. I lost almost all capacity to draw, and it took a year of recovery, psychologically. I had to recover myself. But it's not art, it's maybe just representing the world and trying to put order to it at a certain time. If you're gifted in one way, and then discover it could be lost very easily, that compels us to think about that gift a little more seriously.

I think by having a more organic evolutionary style, my development as an artist confronted me with situations that encouraged me to develop differently and rapidly, and to reevaluate what that status might be. That's why I say I'm still "becoming;" it's almost like I am constantly reevaluating. And even in consideration of art's historical practice and how things are labeled as art or not, or what takes prominence or not, I know that it's a very temporal thing, but time will tell whether all these actions were art or not. I've gotten to a point where I care less about its designation, I care more about doing things, and objects and actions it's no longer that interesting to me to fuss around with labels.

There were multiple incarnations to my project in Detroit. I think the only one documented was *S.P.A.W.N., S.P.O.R.E., S.W.I.N.G.*, the attempt to think about going against a conception of east side Detroit and the Devil's Night. Basically, Devil's Night was a period in Detroit where during Halloween, there would be fires within the neighborhoods. And I didn't like that conception of poor people as just dangerous people. So I went there to focus on what was really happening. There was a kind of re-greening of neighborhoods, and urban gardens were happening. I was talking to the neighborhood about what they needed. They wanted composting, and they wanted help of any kind of methods to augment that. So I thought about a worm farm, but to be economical, to compress them into maybe one piece, to create a worm farm where the whole house would just swing off its hinge to allow sunlight. That's how you sort worms, by the way, you throw them in a pile and you take them out, and you put light on them, and they'll start crawling away and you can pick them up. To make a very dramatic event out of this whole swinging house, I thought it would be cool to reestablish a surreal icon to counteract the one of the burning. I always say that one has to focus on equivalent magnitudes. One of the concepts was to create an industry of possible monetary source by selling worms for fishing. There were several houses that I had negotiated for that were wrecked by the city before we could actually do it. There were three houses that, unfortunately, did not happen, but time will tell, there's time to go back.

However, it evolved beyond that. I started thinking about how to set up something beyond me. I was talking to the University of Michigan in Ann Arbor I talked to deans of law, art, architecture, engineering, medicine – about forming a coalition to establish a multidiscipline grad school that, instead of doing their own singular projects in Detroit, would create what I called S.W.I.N.G., Sustainable Works Involving Neighborhood Groups. This multidiscipline school would engage with neighbors, neighborhoods that remain, and talk about their needs. The projects could be a sustainable school situation where the fieldwork was what participants would be compensated for. Again, that was never realized because it's very difficult to establish something if you're not going to be there.

I remember one citizen came up to me and said, "We love your ideas, but you won't come back." I was shocked, I was upset. I was there to do this. They said that their history has shown no support for people living in poverty. And sure enough, when the money ran out and the houses got torn down, I just couldn't sustain, there was no support.

I heard this again in New Orleans after we took down the Safehouse, which was this iconic structure, now dismantled and gone. I was there for two years, people loved it, but it was time for it to go to the next level. And I became very friendly with people on the street, and I heard exactly those words again, "You won't come back." This time, I said, maybe I won't, but maybe something will come back that will relieve this problem that I have discovered.

We've gone back to New Orleans post Safehouse, and now we have scientific test plots throughout New Orleans. They're quiet, not about art, rather about science. So we can galvanize and collate all these possibilities of really tackling a problem in a very pragmatic way. So the operation continues. *Operation Paydirt*, which began in New Orleans post-Katrina when they discovered so much lead in the soil, now is nationwide. New Orleans had 30 to 50 percent of its inner-city childhood population with lead poisoning from some source before the storm. And again, it's orders of magnitude. I went down there and saw something unimaginable, and I wanted to deal with this and realized that I have to back off and maybe be more clinical and go back to research. The research uncovered that this problem was there before the storm, and discovered there was absolutely zero financial backings to stop this, ever. The *Fundred Dollar Bill Project* came about because it will take 300 million dollars to salvage, to solve that problem in New Orleans. And with no money. I decided we'll make the money. It began a process to have the very people that are affected by lead poisoning, basically children, to have a voice in it, and to recognize them. The idea was that the expression or imagination of a child or grandmother could be valuable enough to be equivalent to $100 over a lifetime. We would then take the self-made bills to Congress and ask for even exchange not just for money, but also the scientific, implementable processes, which we have been working on. We moved into the scientific response, and are now moving toward the last phase, which is the delivery. So there's something to exchange for. And we've given the technology that we developed to the EPA, and it was implemented in Oakland, California, in a very lead compromised soil situation.

The project now openly talks about its childhood lead poisoning, and that we have to stop it. We are no longer skirting the issue. It's gone national. And is it art, is it social practice, is it whatever again, it no longer seems to be the question; rather, it's an action that we need to fulfill. The project has evolved so much that my position shifted from artist to delivery person. Somebody else can take the credit for it, somebody who has the capacity to actually implement it on a scale that an artist, or architect, or anybody who's a designer can't do.

When I first saw Melrose Place on TV I was going back and forth to Los Angeles in '95 for a project called *Uncommon Sense* about Los Angeles and things beyond the museum. I was at the University of Georgia at the time and I was flying back so much that I started thinking that L.A. was in the air, in the microwave transmission, all over America, and the place to work is prime time television. So the postulation was this: our world is transformed by covert business and political practice. One of the big consumption aspects of our world can be defined by television, and quite notably, Spelling Productions, whether it's Beverly Hills 90210 or Melrose Place. And the influence is more powerful and sustaining than a museum exhibition, because the season may end and maybe go away, but it is syndicated through rebroadcasts, like a virus, for the next 30 years or whatever, right? Continual, ad nauseam, if necessary, but it will be there. And that, as a potential host, is what *In the Name of the Place* became, that if we could insert concepts on that show that were complementary to character development, but would bring about issues of safe sex, of feminism, of nuclear physics, it would be cool to pepper the layer of the background and the language with possibilities never seen before or appreciated in television. Not product placement of artwork, but the product placement of ideas that could produce a more engaging life. In other words, we could create the possibility of the oscillation between something that is so unidimensional in its product and its sell that there could be a depth to it, a conception. Or, if the viewer chose not to pay attention to it, he could just follow the storyline. In a true collaboration sense, we were there actually to give the program a richer life than it might originally have.

We did 60 shows, and we did a lot of products. *In the Name of the Place* was a collaboration between the University of Georgia and CalArts. I was a scholar in residence there, and then I was a professorial chair at UGA, so it became GALA, that's for Georgia and Los Angeles, the GALA Committee. It was not hierarchical, and none of the concepts were assigned to one artist, it was a team effort. Again, here's a perfect example, create an idea that will rerun and reinstitute and reinvigorate and re-, whatever it does, and you can't control it, and it can be less or greater degrees of discovery, and may take not 30 years, it may take 50 years before people understand and start seeing the messaging and seeing what the potential is. But it's more like it was a blueprint of how there can be a generational transfer of ideas. Eventually, after we put the work on television, we sold it at an auction and gave all the money to women's charities and educational charities in Los Angeles, and in Athens, Georgia.

I returned from Western Sahara about a year ago, and I am working on a project called *The Potential Project*. It is about working with the people of Western Sahara who are stuck in refugee camps in Algeria, who have no right to self-determination, who have been locked in these camps for 36 years, to have their first currency developed, money developed, backed by the power of the sun, and, therefore, maybe they can get some recognition that way, to have an operational system and economic system based on this. And I'm in the beginning phases of that development.

I also continue to do something that may be a series. I'm buying paintings that are on eBay and things that have been discarded by their family members, portraits, and I am looking at them very carefully, respecting them, restoring them, and then I surgically cut them and rearrange them according to a new messaging, so sort of I'm doing these unauthorized collaborations. And I'm continuing to develop I just finished a body of 524 collages out of the *Funk & Wagnalls 1953 Universal Standard*. So it's not one thing I'm working on, it's several avenues that I'm approaching. And, of course, repairing and restoring and getting works ready for a 40-year review of, you know, 80 works, so so it's a good size.

My advice to students? My advice is to really examine your life and understand that the methodologies are constantly being compromised by being influenced. The definitions of what you may call art or architectural design should not be considered parameters to stay within. It's a different world. It's always been a different world, by the way. I came from an era where I was influenced by what was around me. I was very Zen-like: throw a stick in the air and follow it, you know. But it took a long time. Try to gather strength, and realize that it's not the system that you have to buck, but it's your own system that you have to buck. The life of critique, the examination of one's life and practices begin anew, it's based on everything you've learned. But sometimes you have to tackle the delusions that are piled on because of what you've learned. And it's precisely the things that were made that were not called art, perhaps, that inspire me today. So it's a field of ideas, it's wild. I'm talking of myself because I think I'm in school all the time.

There was no specific moment or person in my life that inspired me to study architecture. Growing up I was always interested in extracurricular activities. One of them was an art class. I wasn't a good artist but I was encouraged to speak about my inspirations and my thoughts, and to turn them into drawings or paintings. I learned that thoughts can take shape in another medium. Later on, I started thinking about architecture because my parents were building a house. I really enjoyed seeing the whole process, to understand that there are cables and water pipes behind the walls, that there is so much more to the structures that we are in every day. The planning process and the people behind it sparked my interest in buildings.

Karolina Czeczek investigates intricate relationships between ordinary things and the larger political urban context.

In high school, I had to make the decision about which career path to follow. It is really early but that's how education in Poland works: you have to decide what kind of exams you will take to graduate from high school. I came from a science background, so I decided on something technical, like physics and mathematics. And since I liked drawing, art, and the building process of the house, maybe architecture would not be the worst idea. But I didn't know anything about it, I didn't know a single architect. All I had was a friend who was trying to become an architect. In Poland, you have to take drawing classes to pass the three-day drawing exam. It's all about construction, perspective, lines and volumes. I saw her doing that, and I really liked it because it reminded me of my classes but it was much more structured. I thought it was pretty cool. Thinking back, I had a lot of books about the seven wonders of the world that my grandmother used to buy for me: Mayan cities, Cambodian developments, full of line drawings in the landscape of Peru. They were always spatial, always of a bigger scale, they had not only an architectural dimension but also social relations.

Even though I knew nothing about architecture I decided to pursue it. I took drawing classes and I learned more and more. I had really good teachers. By the time I was trying to get into an architecture school I was pretty set on the idea. Architectural training in Poland is quite technical and pragmatic. It's a five-year program and you graduate as an architect and an engineer. The studies comprise architectural and urban design, and that's what stayed with me. The relationship between building and planning is not as closely discussed in the US as in Europe. It's what I try to emphasize in my American practice.

When I landed the job at **OMA** (Office of Metropolitan Architecture) it was beyond my dreams. At school, we had a workshop with students from TU

Delft from the Netherlands who came to Poland for a three-week workshop. At the end of the workshop, I asked my tutor from TU Delft where I should apply for a job. I wanted to do a three-month internship and hoped for a suggestion of a good, small office based in the Netherlands. But he suggested that I apply to OMA. I thought it impossible so I didn't apply for six months. At the time I didn't know many students would take time off from school to work for somebody during the summer. I always thought one had to finish school and then start working.

I finally applied, had an interview through Skype — my first job interview ever — and they asked me to come in a week. I had obviously made sense explaining my projects. When I compared myself to other people who were there at the time I was not very well prepared for the job. I went there during the last semester of my thesis year which was intense. But I managed to stay at OMA, finish my thesis, and go back to OMA after that.

I worked in Rotterdam for a year and 1/2 and then I moved to OMA's Hong Kong office for two years. This is where I met my husband and at some point, we decided to leave OMA and start an office in the U.S. Although I had already spent five years studying architecture and had a master's degree, I wanted to go back to school. The pragmatism of my education had lacked much of the conceptual thinking or bigger understanding of the role of architecture and its future. Going back to school would be a good experience for me. After three years at work, I felt that I had some ideas to explore.

At the time I did not know much about American architectural schools. I made my choice to study at Yale because I wanted to study with **Keller Easterling**. **Pier Vittorio Aureli** was a visiting professor from the AA in London and **Tatiana Bilbao**, a Mexican architect, was also coming. These three people I could work with and learn a lot from, and that was pretty much the decision-maker. In addition, Yale allowed me to do a two-year post-professional program versus just a one-year program offered at other schools, which I thought was a little bit too short. I didn't want to just get in and out and get a diploma, I wanted to spend time in the program.

I think Keller Easterling inspired me the most, although I just took seminars with her. Her way of thinking about architecture and her spatial and political understanding of the world were very interesting. She showed me different dependencies in the connections and networks that architecture can potentially intersect with. Although my Polish education had covered the urban issues, the bigger scale was never really discussed. Neither was the theory of architecture well covered there. Keller's readings were just killers. Although I had worked in an English-speaking environment, this was my first time reading and writing. Studying for her classes was an immersion.

Architecture at Yale is very building-based - it's about the building and its articulation — and prepares people really well for practice. I took studios with Pier Vittorio and Tatiana Bilbao, but my way of thinking shifted mostly because of Keller Easterling's classes. The take-away from Yale? The understanding of a much bigger, urban scale, with global interests. We talked a lot about the agency of the projects and how sometimes very small moves and seemingly small-scale proposals affect different economies of scale, whether that's housing or whether that's food or other aspects of everyday life that intersect with architecture. I went to architecture school for two years while helping in the office. I graduated in 2015 and have been working full time since then.

My biggest problem working in the US is corporatism, which I consider the hardest obstacle to any kind of practice. There is a lot of talent, there are a lot of ideas, and they don't resurface just because people lack access to bigger projects, to bigger discussions. There is a tendency to think that the bigger the company the better the response to an architectural program or problem. In Europe, on the other hand, there is a lot of support for young architects, a lot of competitions, and government incentives based on the understanding that those young people will be responsible for our built environment in a couple years. They are supported in their learning process and trusted. That's missing from the architectural profession in the US.

My own work spans from large, urban proposals to the interior design of an underground coffee shop, and I'm happy to work in each of those scales. While I prefer the bigger, urban scale, this might also mean a building that has a bigger urban impact. The problem is that master planning usually does not result in a built project overnight. It takes a couple of years or even decades, while in the case of the little coffee shop we can quickly test ideas, materials, arrangements, and plans. As a young architect, it is exciting to seeing ideas tested quickly at a smaller scale with a smaller impact and actually built.

What inspires me generally is the world around me, and the processes I can observe. Coming from a very little town and then having lived in Hong Kong and now New York also gives me a certain angle of looking at things. I really enjoy big cities but I am critical of them, or better said, hold an alternative point of view of how life could evolve within the city. We don't always have to subscribe to the typical urban way of living, we can still carve out our own little places and should be allowed to do so. Small projects are part of our everyday life and having coffee may well be as impactful as a beautifully designed new plaza. That's all part of our experience of everyday life.

Being a woman did not affect me in a significant way. I was brought up thinking I'm as capable as a man. I did study architecture without really thinking of it as a male-dominated profession. I just enjoyed it and just went ahead with it.

OMA was very open and whether you are an intern, whether you are a man, whether you are a woman, whether you are an associate, if you are good it doesn't really matter. I was given lots of responsibilities and I never felt that I was given fewer opportunities as a woman. Practicing now I show people that I am as competent, as interested, as capable as a man. I don't even think about it. The moment I would think that way it would probably become a problem. If I ask a question and the response is not directed to me but to a man who is sitting next to me, I just ask again or respond back, so it's clear that I'm part of the discussion. I actually enjoy doing the construction administration which is usually dominated by males. If you have the knowledge and you try to make sense and you listen to people and are reasonable, they start to respect that fact. I never really had a problem with gender and hope that it's never going to happen.

I am very optimistic about architecture's future. We have to learn how to navigate a new reality. Our profession is kind of medieval; we just do one building, a one-off and it's almost like a prototype that we never repeat. Or at least not as much as other industries. Anyway, our profession is full of inefficiencies. When I look at past modern or utopian attempts I'm encouraged by the fact that architects appear to have understood the bigger issues and addressed them through new building or spatial urban designs. I think we should be doing that, too. Sometimes I get worried when I see people retreating to smaller scales or to the design of objects. Of course, it's great if someone does good work, but I think we should be claiming the urban and architectural scales. I see a lot of engineering and big construction companies trying to claim the urban sphere these days. They are claiming to know how to design smarter and better. I don't think they can. In most cases, this is very profit driven and not always in the public interest, especially in places like New York where real estate is driving the whole market. It's really hard to navigate this environment as a small player, so it is especially important to engage with these issues and to find the kind of places or areas within architecture and the city that as young architects, artists, smaller firms can still propose good solutions. But I don't think about where I will be in 20, 30 years. I hope I'm still a practicing architect and that there is work that I can enjoy doing. I'm not planning too much for the future.

I'm always interested in the reasons for a project, and that's how I'm trying to teach. I don't really want to talk about form before we identify a problem that we are trying to solve or at least tackle. It's really hard for me to judge any proposal without that kind of understanding. That's why I always start with identifying the problems that we are dealing with, and the opportunities we are trying to use. These kinds of discussions are important, even if they take quite a while. That's what I try to discuss with students. I also learn a lot from them because they bring many problems to my attention. It's kind of a two-way learning process for me and the students but I think having these discussions about where architecture can help and where it doesn't have the power to shape our built environment is really important. Not being overly ambitious about how can we change people's lives with the design of certain buildings is too. Sometimes we are just saying the building will do this, the people in the building will do that, but whether that's really the case is often questionable.

I didn't go to college thinking that I would study architecture, but I happened to be living on the floor in the dormitory where a number of my friends were doing so. Over time I became fascinated with what they were doing. I thought that it seemed much more interesting than what I was doing. I'd been interested in drawing when I was younger, making things, but when I was in high school thinking about college, I put those things aside, thinking that they were not a proper part of what I needed to do to prepare for getting into school. When I did start studying architecture and transferred into the program, I wished that I had kept up with my earlier drawing classes because I had to relearn it all. I found out later that it's a very similar story for **Peter Eisenman**. He didn't go to school to study architecture; his roommate was an architecture major. He started looking over his shoulder, and became fascinated with what he was doing. So I am not alone; I am in good company.

To **Justin Diles** architecture is an iterative process, where yesterday's mistake might be tomorrow's solution to a problem.

This was over 20 years ago when you could just go to college without a plan. Now things are often really expensive, and there is a pressure to have some professional track in mind. What I liked about architecture was that it gave me an alibi to getting a professional degree while it was still pretty much a liberal arts education. It opened my world to thinking about art, history, philosophy, all sorts of things. By studying architecture, I was able to study many things, even though I probably didn't learn them as well as I would have had I studied the subjects individually. It would be hard for me to imagine my life without architecture - it's a blessing and a curse. The long hours, the obsession that comes along with the creative process .... It would be easier to imagine being wealthier, but hard to imagine having a richer cultural outlook, having studied anything else. I would not trade it.

I don't think that there is an ideal educational structure. The ideal education of an architect is always something of a self-education. As we get older, we just continue to self-educate. The studio system is very important in that respect because you get comfortable getting up and presenting your ideas, no matter how ready you are to present them to the world. We learn that really early on. Although it is quite rigorous, the studio model will always have a place in architectural education. I've had the virtue of seeing a diverse set of educational environments, one of the most interesting being the master class system in Vienna, where high school students would be having their first architecture studio ever with **Zaha Hadid** or **Wolf Prix** and then would study for five years under the mentorship of that professor. It was quite amazing to see, and it was really fantastic for some students, and terrible for others. I don't know that there's one model that could suit everyone. It's important for there to be diverse systems, but it's also important to be aware of the weight of those opportunities each system provides. Sometimes a student benefits from slowing down and studying longer with one person; other times, it's good to sample a lot of different people, a lot of different ideas. I think we all do that in various ways in our careers, whether it is who we talk to or the issues that we work on.

At least in the Midwest, we do a good job of taking students who don't really understand the rich potential of architecture and the way it can fundamentally change the way we see and interact with the world, and we encourage them to think about having an impact on the world. We are doing an incredible job of opening students to possibility. Maybe that's a first pass, and perhaps we need to do a better job communicating that architecture is not static but fundamentally dynamic. We need to prepare students for being flexible, being able to adapt to many different situations without losing sight of what motivates them and draws them to architecture and for making sure that they feel they can tap into positivity and be comfortable with change as they move through their careers.

My most memorable moments as a student were when I was confronted with an instructor who was asking for material that he didn't know himself how to produce, and I managed to figure it out somehow on my own. Not to cast a shadow on the instructor, but rather I realized that I had the possibility of collaborating on a high level with somebody more senior than me. Especially in graduate school, we need to teach our students that it is very much about collaboration. It's not so much a top-down method of learning but a process in which we ask questions together. As a student, it was important for me to figure something out that clearly meant something to the instructor, to his own work, and his way of thinking about architecture. As a teacher, it's rewarding to take students who weren't quite sure that architecture was for them — I am thinking about two students in particular — who didn't go to the University immediately, who were a little bit older than their classmates when they got there, but started working with me in their second year. I managed to teach them every year until they graduated in some capacity or another. We ended up collaborating on projects together, traveled to San Francisco, and worked on a factory project together. They have now graduated, and are both working in New York, having completely exceeded what they thought was possible for them to do within architecture. They express how helpful I was in helping them get to that point. Little did they realize how helpful they were in helping me with moving my own work forward as well. That type of collaboration continues and is incredibly valuable and rewarding.

I feel as if I have had a very typical career as an architect. We can study architecture and end up doing vastly different things. I have friends and acquaintances who have become obsessed with rendering, producing images that have made lucrative careers out of making architectural drawings. At the other end of the spectrum, I have classmates and former friends who practice with large corporate firms. In my career, I've sampled a lot of those different possibilities. I divide my career into two phases: one before graduate school and after. I studied architecture as an undergraduate, worked for six years in the profession, working on hospitals, courthouses, lab buildings, and even exhibition design. After graduate school, I practiced a little bit with smaller firms, but then immediately started teaching, teaching more and more. As I was teaching, I began asking some of the questions that motivate my research and creative work now. And that did lead me to engineering, material science, and to some architecture. For me, it all seems cohesive.

I have had the great fortune of teaching with three of my heroes in Vienna during my four years at the University of Applied Arts. I worked with **Wolf Prix** from Coop Himmelb(l)au, taught with **Greg Lynn** in his studio, and also worked with **Zaha Hadid**. All three of those architects had been tremendously influential to my thinking. They were all quite different personalities, very different styles of leadership, of commanding attention and motivating their students. It was amazing to see people who I have grown up studying in action in the studio. Another person who has been important to me is **Neil Denari**. He is someone who works on fashioning space from new modeling techniques, but also with projection systems, mapping systems, and graphics in a way that these elements, which are sometimes not seen as properly architectural, can find their way into projects. While I never had an opportunity to work with a great architect in his or her design practice, I was able to work and collaborate with a lot of my heroes through teaching. That's been great.

I was lucky. It is quite unusual for an American architect to teach and maintain a studio in Vienna. I managed that by keeping myself open to whatever might happen, knocking on doors, and being persistent but not annoying, well, maybe sometimes annoying. I was also willing to take risks and to move forward when a lucky opportunity arose, even though it might not be perceived as the safer path. My story really starts with Greg Lynn, who was invited by Wolf Prix to take over one of the design studio positions in Vienna. That became a gateway for many young American architects to go and teach. One of my friends who was teaching there invited me to come do a workshop. Years later, a position opened up, and I applied and got it.

The program at my alma mater, the University of Pennsylvania, had prepared me well. It was, in fact, an incredibly pragmatic program, and that pragmatism is by design, something the University likes to promote since it was founded in part by Ben Franklin. There was an interest in learning by doing, having theoretical knowledge but always with an understanding or an eye for how that could be applied. Many good theorists taught at the school, **Manuel De Landa**, **Sanford Kwinter** taught one of our core theory classes, we also had a great historian **David Leatherbarrow** teaching there. There were also a lot of really interesting practitioners. **Winka Dubbeldam** from Architectonics is now the chair of the graduate program. The school tended to attract high-level practitioners who also took a philosophical approach. **Ali Rahim**, who is very influential for me, comes to mind, and also **Cecil Balmond**, the engineer, who has also written quite a lot, has a deep interest in mathematics and geometry, the behavior of national systems and self-organization. I had a studio with him — my last studio at U of Penn — and it was really fascinating to see how Cecil synthesized all these things. I think that experience has been instrumental in my way of thinking about parametrics, technology, art history, and mathematics, the way that all of these things could come together.

I am definitely interested in getting something built. The largest thing I have produced is a small pavilion, which to me was really important, but I design buildings and hope to someday soon realize a building. Not just any building but one that answers some questions that I've been asking of my design work. I think that architects always want to build more and bigger. I'm no exception.

I develop creative work on projects, installations, and designs for buildings, but also teach as part of this community of architects that is thinking about how to advance the discipline. There is a responsibility to have a specifically identifiable project. How well I'm doing that at this point, I don't know. It's a work in progress. I have been able to identify a set of issues that I think are important, not only to me, but would be useful for other people to explore. Items that I can work on with my students are an example. I draw inspiration from thinking about the way that technology, materials, and patterns can transform architecture, or how they can provide modes of rethinking even very common architectural problems like how you subdivide a large surface into smaller elements. I've begun to find some questions which others might find boring, such as how to subdivide panels, and how to subdivide a large expanse of a surface into smaller pieces.

Apart from technology, I find a lot of inspiration in history. Looking back at ways that we formerly built that we no longer build. I find inspiration from construction technologies that are less pliable today. For example, now we only build with layers of elements, so starting with a structure, a frame of some sort that we then attach cladding to, that would be the most common way. If we were practicing architecture in the 19th century, we would also be thinking about cutting large volumes and nesting and stacking them together into structures. The geometric and construction techniques were under the heading of stereotomy. We no longer use these techniques. Now we have robots, large milling machines that cut out pieces. Is there a possibility of using uncommon materials to recapture some of those techniques? I find inspiration from cutting edge questions about how technology can be applied but also very from old questions about how things are put together.

The generation of practitioners behind me and some of my peers are returning to postmodernism right now, so I don't know if we can ever go back to modernism, not in an iconoclastic sense. Still, nothing gets thrown away in architecture. Once it has happened, it sticks around. Because we look at history so much, nothing ever gets thrown away. Buildings will continue to transform and be influenced by questions that have arisen in computational design. I don't know if it's possible or even desirable, as **Patrick Schumacher** has argued, to create a single style that would synthesize everything, including computational design, aesthetics, structure, and materials into one comprehensive model capable of solving all architectural problems. I don't know if this is possible or particularly desirable, so I would say things like computational techniques, freeform geometries have been put on the table, and they will remain there, and just be reused and re-understood as new generations of architects confront them.

In the late 60s, my parents built a contemporary modern home in the outskirts of Nashville, Tennessee. It was a unique, different, playful house, and I was there to experience it getting built. Part of it was left unfinished, and I got to explore this corner of the house with open studs, frozen "under" construction. It was a construction playroom. I could go in and build stuff, explore it, figure out how things were built. Everything about the house was fun, it was creative, it was engaging, with the landscape as a dramatic space to live in. I grew up with that kind of experience, and by the time I was in junior high, I was convinced I wanted to be an architect.

I started studying architecture in 1980, graduated in '84, and worked in Boston. I had big ambitions and, working with **Schwartz/Silver Architects**, had the opportunity to do some pretty remarkable library work: first, the *Wheeler School* in Providence Rhode Island, a K-12 private school and then, the *Rotch Library*, the architectural library at MIT, a phenomenal project and an amazing thing to work on. I went out to Berkeley for graduate school in architecture and ended up working there until today. The fun has never left. It has evolved over time.

Chris Downey has more value in the profession today than he had sighted.

Out west, I worked with **Holt, Hinshaw, Pfau & Jones** doing aquariums, theaters, wineries, retail and residential work. I led a new retail initiative and ended up directing a team doing Old Navy stores. We did a hundred and twenty Old Navy stores in two and a half years, and architecturally they were probably not very exciting, but ironically it was one of the more exciting things I had to do: it was fast-paced, it was results-oriented, we got more work if we did our work well, it was very service-oriented but also very much on quality and on time on budget. Snap, snap, you're on.

Eventually, I did get a little burned out on it, even after I started my own firm. We were doing a lot of residential work at the time, custom homes and remodels, additions and things. I was getting really frustrated with how much things cost in the Bay Area, with the strain that put on clients, and how elitist residential work had become. I ended up leaving my own firm to work with **Michelle Kaufmann Designs** as the managing director of the architectural office doing prefabricated green modular homes. I was really excited about the confluence of sustainability with pricing to make good, sustainable, affordable design, less of an elitist endeavor. We did over 40 projects all over the West Coast, Chicago, Colorado, from Washington State to the border with Mexico. With every different jurisdiction, all the codes were different, so despite going to mass production, it was all incredibly custom. There was a new sort of energy in the business that I was really excited about, and I loved the people I was working with. That's when I was unexpectedly diagnosed with a brain tumor and went in for surgery to have it removed, and two days later lost all my sight.

As it turned out, I gained far more than I lost. Architects are so obsessed with sight, what something looks like. But the difference between architecture and graphic design or web design is that it's about the full human experience. It's about the body in space and time, and it's about the full physical experience, and the irony of it is that the sight of all the senses is the most detached. It has no physical connection to the thing you see, whereas touch has a direct physical relationship.

I also lost all sense of smell. Typically within the blind experience relying on that sense of smell for directionality is really helpful, especially if you're looking for a cup of coffee. All the other different senses become so much more important, and now I really think that hot, really successful, really rich architecture engages all those experiences, all those senses they track more than just the detached eye. The other senses, touch particularly, are about how your body is being welcomed and engaged within a space.

One of the more engaging pieces of architecture I have visited since losing my sight is the *Kimball Art Museum*. The sense of grabbing handrails — "Oh, what's this?" — there was a real intentional thought about what it was like for my hand to touch the handrail. Then, the sensitive modulation of the space, how I felt moving through space whether it was crossing over the travertine on the structural grid that laid out the gallery spaces, or by stepping out and hearing the length of the vault based on how the tip of my cane hit the floor. I could hear people walking on gravel out in the courtyard and beyond. There was such a richness of sensory experiences. I knew that building visually through all the publications and the books but had never visited with sight. Now I had the opportunity to visit without sight, and, on the one hand, those other senses were triggering all the visual memory of where I was; on the other hand, I was discovering this incredibly rich environment that really contributed to the experience of being there. It was so much more than the architecture of publication, composing the space for the photograph. That's not to say that a good photograph doesn't have good guts behind it. But oftentimes it's too limited. Certainly, the idea of placemaking, of welcoming the full human experience within the architectural space, within the urban space is a far more rich way of approaching architecture.

The *de Young Museum* in San Francisco by **Herzog & de Meuron** is another engaging architectural space. It was there in town where I worked, and I would run in, go to the museum shop, get something, run out; I never had the time to actually go to the museum until I had to go for a pre-op exam before my surgery and the museum was around the corner. I was looking out the hospital window to the roof of the de Young with four hours to wait between an MRI and the exam. Four hours, let's go to the museum! I went on a tour of the museum and had a chance to experience it. I have been back since and have discovered that the rich use of materials is particularly engaging. I might say that the whole skin of the building is in Braille; I could feel it. I explored the skin of the building; those who just look at it miss out on a lot. It's not necessarily something the architects might have expected someone to explore through touch, yet some surfaces are burning hot and others are cool. And they are right next to each other, and the difference is the construction behind, air moving behind parts of it, where there is a screen from the glass. I don't want to suggest that normal people that are blind would go around feeling a building, but I'm not normal. I am an architect who is blind, and I get to go around and fondle architecture to explorer it, so that's different – and rich.

There is a **James Turrell** space in the garden at the de Young that has a Sky Dome with a procession that leads down into the space and into the inner drum beneath the oculus. There are very simple concrete benches that ring a pretty compelling space. The space is clearly all about the oculus, about the light coming through. It's all about the connection to that space, that sky above, and I couldn't see any of that, the whole reason it was there. But at the same time the architecture, the form of that space, was really interesting. Despite being concrete, the bench was incredibly comfortable and relaxing. If I leaned back it actually fit my body well. In some places, I could sit in that beam of sun and could feel the sun coming through, and could gaze straight toward the oculus. The space was intimate; I could get my arms around and explore it. It is somewhat finite in its dimensions; whether I was feeling the warmth as the sun was coming through warming up some spots and not others, the details of how things were made, the sound within the space, exploring it through sound — I could always tap my cane in the space to hear the architecture around me. Sometimes I snapped my fingers to hear what was going on. It was really powerful within its limitation, an intense sensory experience, despite the fact that so much of that sensory experience was presumed to be just visible.

Another thing I really was struck by was the **Billie Tsien & Tod Williams** *Folk Art Museum* starting at the front door: I remembered these incredible door handles, and without seeing I just walked up and grabbed them. Wow, there's something very intentional about how they were crafted for the grip of the hand. The way I look at it now is that the visual stuff somehow is the easy part. I was always quick to excuse myself from the color discussion — now I can get a free pass. The harder stuff is the tactile, the acoustic, thinking about the smell, all those other sensory things. But because I know about the visual elements, I am able to include those sensory elements and have the composition work out.

The way I think of it is that the creative process is intellectual; it's in the mind. The pen or mouse doesn't automatically know what to draw. It knows what to draw as a function of thought. It's an expression of how the designer is thinking, how he's imagining, how he's construing this thing, and so the mind is incredibly active, it is problem solving. It is looking for things that are unseen, things that don't have form. The architect is trying to give it form. It is a very dynamic intellectual imaging process that traditionally takes its form through the pencil. Or through pixels on the display screen. Or within a physical model.

I started realizing that if the creative process is intellectual and I can't draw, I can't read the drawing as I used to because I can't see it anymore, I just need new tools: new ways of seeing drawings, new ways of drawing, new ways of modeling. Physical modeling; I can still do that. I don't need to see to work with clay. I don't need to see to stack materials, to build form and explore it that way.

But so much of what we do is draw things. So how do I access the drawing and how do I draw? That was the big riddle, and quite frankly, had I lost my sight 10 or 20 years prior, a solution might have been possible but not as immediate. With the advent of technology, I was lucky enough that there are things out there that made the solution almost instant. I got a large-format embossing printer that could print on a 16-inch wide roll. On a whim, working with my technology trainers, we decided to send the architectural drawing as a PDF directly to the printer instead of having someone else do the manipulations in the drawing software. The result was amazing: the drawing was in tactile form, with no intermediate steps. What's on the screen is the same PDF that would go to any other architect or a client or a consultant only it comes to my personal embossing printer and is printed in tactile form. That was a tremendous tool to work with that's really quick and required very little in the way of special accommodation. I do have to print it. There is nothing I can do to feel the screen, although there are some things underway that could possibly address that issue.

So tool one is accessing the drawing which could be a site plan, a plan of the pre-existing conditions that I am going to have to work with, or the current design of the project and working with it to understand what's going on, and the printing works whether it's in plan, elevation, reflected ceiling plan, sections, or details. We have even printed perspectives. That's a piece of work to read perspective drawings in tactile form. I've had a friend who is blind and is a specialist in tactile graphics and grew up with architects. He said, "You got to be the only dude in this world who can read this drawing."

The next issue is, ok, so I can read a drawing, but how do I participate in the process? How do I draw? Since I can't see there is nothing I can do within

AutoCAD, Revit, SketchUp, Rhino, you name it, I can't do it. But, as I often used to do in my prior positions, I can art direct my way through that. I have to communicate design ideas, and so I needed to develop an accessible way of doing that. I use these things called Wikki Stix, wax sticks, much like a kid's craft toy, but they are flexible. The version I like doesn't have anything inside it. It's just wax, they are these long sticks, and I can curve, bend, work to a sharp angle, fold it over the corner of the desk, I can come up with the angle I need and fold it to that. I can work in two dimensions, three dimensions, and the cool thing is they stick together. I can make connections, run them end to end, overlap them, and they stick to the paper, especially after I work with them for a while. The wax gets soft, a little tacky, and I can just stick it right to the paper. I realized I could draw on top of the embossed drawings with these sticks. It was like having a role of trace paper on top of an existing drawing. Instead of having a pencil I have these wax sticks. Sticking them down I can feel what I am drawing. A lot of people that are blind use them to draw, but I needed to draw as an architect, use them to draw in relationship to the rest of the space. The wax sticks became a really significant tool for doing it, and I can share my design with others who can then draw it into the computer. It doesn't matter if I'm meeting with them person to person across the table or side-by-side, we can share it that way and they can take it away in the computer. When I am working with someone remotely, I can photograph it with the iPhone, email it off to them, and say, "Like this." They draw it up, send it back to me, I print it in the printer, say, "Ok, that's good." It is almost as it was before when I was managing people, working with teams of people doing things, and just found that process for making that happen. Working off the embossing printer has been the critical element in my new phase of work.

One question I was deeply curious about was whether I would be able to continue practicing architecture. I had my degrees and my professional license before I lost my sight. I actually called California's State Architect to confirm, "I have a friend who is a licensed architect and lost his sight …. Can he continue working as an architect? Can he keep his license?" "So he passed his exam, he got his license? Oh yeah, then he is good to go."

Since then, I have ended up in specializing more in projects and situations related to the blind, visually impaired experience. I have done eye centers, training centers - and am now working with on the *Transbay Transit Center*, a four-block long multimodal transit center in San Francisco. It's hard to get intimate when it's four blocks long. My tactile drawings for that building to fit on the 16-inch wide roll of paper as long and as wide as I get it are about 180 inches long. It's all pretty interesting, and just recently, I started pushing beyond that. I have got the opportunity to do tenant improvement for an organization that's called the Independent Living Resource Center in San Francisco. It is an organization that provides advocacy, training, technology, and assistance with housing and employment for people with all disabilities. I am also teaching at UC Berkeley — they don't call it adjunct professor anymore — as guest lecturer. I just teach a semester in the fall every year and teach a class on ADA and universal design. On the bucket list is to get beyond just accessibility and universal design, whether it's getting students and faculty to embrace universal design concepts within their studios and then being able to participate in that or being able to participate in the teaching of design studios. My students have to deal with these issues in my class, having to communicate with a professor who doesn't see. That's challenging for architects, to take that into the studio setting. I have had some opportunity to do that already, but I would like to build on that. I think it's good for the students and it's something I would really enjoy.

The irony of all of this is that I have more value in the profession today than I had sighted. And I think I have as much if not more to contribute than I had before. Does that stop with me, does that stop with someone who's had experience and lost his sight?

I had a really good reason to do architecture, but in retrospect, I didn't really know what I was doing: I just did it. I studied architecture at McGill University. It was a real-world opening experience, and I had an incredible time. Part of that experience involved living in Bogota for a semester on an exchange program. After my studies at McGill in the meantime, I had met someone from France — I moved to France with her. I worked for a few years in Paris in a small architecture firm. I went back to school because I wanted to get into teaching, and knew that in order to teach, I would have to have some post professional education. And at that time, I thought I wanted to do architecture history, a Ph.D. in pure architecture history, and stop being involved in design issues.

J. Kent Fitzsimons argues that whether high end, big A architecture is relevant, is for people to decide.

I ended up at Rice because there were certain faculty members there who I thought were interesting. I had read **Lars Lerup**'s *Planned Assaults* and *Building the Unfinished* while at McGill. Lars was the dean at Rice. Another professor got me thinking about design again, so I decided to do my thesis, and then eventually my doctoral dissertation, more around issues of design theory rather than pure architecture history. I started teaching design and a bit of theory as a teaching assistant at Rice. And one day, the dean and director of the School of Architecture at Rice asked me if I wanted to be involved in a Paris program they were going to start up. They knew that I had lived in Paris and that I was bilingual, and that my wife was from France, so they thought I could help out. And, of course, I said that I would love to be involved.

While I had not yet finished my dissertation, we picked up everything after four years in Houston and moved back to Paris. And there I was involved in starting up the Paris "antenna program" for Rice School of Architecture, under the directorship of **John Casbarian**, who is the associate dean at Rice and who is still in charge of that program from Houston. That was a new, extraordinary experience, not only teaching architecture, which is what I really wanted to do, but being involved with, every semester, 10 students who were coming from Houston, but in a way from all over the U.S. and sometimes from other countries, to discover what it's like to live in Paris for a semester. I could relive the experience of living abroad for the first time, like I had lived it in Bogota, every semester. This went really well with a kind of attitude towards design teaching, including study travel and what one could call perpetual discovery, which I think is really important in architecture. Always being surprised by things, not being blasé, and being open to different ways of doing things is a stimulus for inventing new ideas and new approaches to architectural and urban design problems.

After a number of years running that program in Paris, I got involved in teaching the French system which is different from the American system, and much more centralized. The schools of architecture are not as autonomous as they are in North America. I managed to get my foot in the door, and one day I was lucky enough to go through a national recruiting process for full-time professorships, and despite the odds against me, I was actually selected and offered a permanent position in the school of architecture system in France. I was assigned to the School of Architecture and Landscape Architecture in Bordeaux. And so I commuted from Paris to Bordeaux.

I've always loved trains and planes and the idea of living in multiple places at the same time. I lived in Paris and worked in Bordeaux for a couple of years, and then we moved to Bordeaux. I now live full time in Bordeaux, but I still commute to Paris for a bit of teaching. In Bordeaux, I teach design studio in third year and fifth year, I teach a theory course, and I oversee the writing of theses. I'm getting a little bit involved in doctoral education, as well.

I always found it strange that in order to design as an architect, through drawings and model making, there was a process in my head where I imagined people moving around and doing things in order to make a program work in a building, or to communicate ideas through architecture. It was always important to me to make social change through architecture, to change people's ways of thinking through architecture. In order to do that, I had to imagine that the shapes were actually affecting people's physical experience through vision and hearing and motion. So, when designing, there were people running around in my head, going through hallways, and upstairs, and looking from mezzanines, and I imagined that that actually would have some effect on them. I don't know if a lot of other disciplines involve that kind of thinking.

One of the potentially dangerous things is that I always imagine the same kind of person, a person who can walk, who can see normally, who can hear normally, who is about the same height as I and is actually me. I'm always imagining myself, and I'm like a lot of other people; I'm a little shorter than most people, but I'm certainly part of the average kind of person. That means that most of us architects are ignoring a lot of other ways that the body perceives space and makes meaning out of the world around us.

This could be dangerous because we're cutting ourselves off from a lot of potential ways of touching people through architecture. It also means that we're probably not being very fair to people who can't see, or people who can't walk easily, or can't walk at all. This made me realize that architecture also had a dangerous side: it reduces the way we imagine the body and could lead to discriminating against certain kinds of people. In any case, the full possibilities of architecture's relationship to human beings through bodily experience might be impoverished.

I was at Rice when I started thinking about this topic for my dissertation. I was finishing my master's thesis, which, believe it or not, was about how sport utility vehicles make us mix up memories about station wagons, pickup trucks, and Land Rovers through bodily experience, and thus give us a colonial experience. It was a bit of a strange subject matter. I should probably think more about all the assumptions that I'm making about how the body experiences architecture and how human beings produce meaning. And so I looked at architecture as a discipline with an objective scientific dimension to it. We have graphic standards, we have all sorts of standards, that basically come down to the average human body. This chair I'm sitting in is designed so that it's comfortable for most people. We have all these rules of thumb and formalized standards. I researched how those rules tend to produce an average environment, good for ordenary people, but that maybe doesn't correspond to a lot of people.

Another French philosopher named **Michel de Certeau** also had a big influence on my thinking. That helped me not to be only negative about what architecture was producing through a kind of rationalization or standardization of the body. It also got me thinking about how people might actually produce fantastic worlds out of banal environments through their interpretations and their appropriations. I did a few case studies as part of my dissertation research, buildings by **Herzog & de Meuron**, and the way houses are represented in movies, and that became a dissertation that I defended.

The move from Paris to Houston was actually a visceral experience. In my first studio in the post-professional master's program at Rice, I was making a comparison between how I understood space in Paris and how I was beginning to understand it in Houston. I had never been to Houston, I had never been to a city like that. The closest might have been Miami. But I just knew northeast cities like New York and Boston.

To me, Paris space was fat space, and Houston space was thin space. In Paris, there is congestion and close proximity with other people, and the presence of noise, the overhead subways at some points, traffic, and the high concentration of people. And then I ended up in Houston where it wasn't people who were so present, but it was the humidity. We arrived in the middle of August, and it was probably 40 Celsius or 110 Fahrenheit. There was 100 percent humidity. The rest was thin: there were huge spaces between bodies, and the car was an exoskeleton that prevented rubbing elbows with people like we would do in the subway in Paris. That was a pretty radical change in how I was relating to an urban environment. And then the air conditioning in Houston, the fact that you go from 110 to 68 just by going through a door I remember the banks in particular, not that I was doing a lot of banking, but I just remember banks in Houston being absolutely freezing. I remember the first year at Rice, I always had a wool sweater on, and all the other students were in shorts and tee-shirts and flip flops. I just didn't understand it. I eventually ended up like that, too, although I never really went to class in flip flops.

I experienced a space shift years before in Bogota. I was only about 21 when I went there, yet I still can remember being really conscious of the smell of diesel. In Montreal, there's not much diesel. Also, in Bogota, the air was much thinner. Bogota is 2,600 meters above sea level. I ran out of breath a lot easier. Again, the close proximity of other people was much more present in Bogota than in other places. There were lots of extremely poor people, often missing a limb, or literally wearing rags, so tanned and burned by the sun. It wasn't very hot, but the sun at that altitude is quite intense. I would see these people on the sidewalk that I wasn't used to seeing in a place like Montreal, where, because of the climate, a lot of things are more hidden.

In Bordeaux, I did notice when I would get on the train in Paris and then be in the train for three hours working on my laptop, and then get off the train in Bordeaux, my first breath of air in Bordeaux would always seem much fresher than in Paris. First of all, because it's a smaller city, but also because Bordeaux is only about 30 miles from the Atlantic coast, and it's on a really big river that brings air in from the ocean. Maybe that's one of the reasons we decided we could settle there.

Unfortunately, I'm a little too honest about everything. One of the things I'm not so good at is lying to people and calling their bluffs. When dealing with contractors, for example, I always believed them, because I didn't like to respond to people in such a way that they might feel that I'm somehow accusing them of not being honest. I think a lot of architectural practice, at least in dealing with contractors and trying to get the best and the most, and the closest to what it should be, out of people who are doing this in order to earn a living, is to call bluffs a lot, and I'm just not good at that. I know other people who are. They're just better at that human relationship of negotiation. And I just was really uncomfortable with that. So I think it's one of the reasons I was more interested in the tools we use to conceive of architectural space, and then after it's built, how people appropriate architectural space than I was in the building phase in between.

My main question is, how does what we know about how people appropriate space help us to become better designers. I'm interested in that loop. Obviously, I could buckle down and take a few years to get better at the building phase, but I like teaching, and I like writing, and I like talking. I have had the opportunity to work with architect colleagues and my wife, who is a practicing architect and has her own firm, with an associate. I do participate in ideas competitions, mostly at the urban design scale, and now and then on a house, certain projects I collaborate with my wife's associate. My wife and I try to keep things separate.

Practice is tough, and it's a real luxury to be able to spend time reading and thinking and making mistakes, working with students who are brave, and intelligent, and generous with their ideas. I have the real luxury to be able to take all that together and share it with people who are busy with practice. For example, when I work with my wife's associate on a house project, I exchange with them so I can get a little out of them, and they can get a little out of me. Whether architecture is still relevant depends on if it's architecture with a big A or a little a. We have all these devices, but the more we dematerialize stuff, the more we're able to free up the material stuff around us for pleasure and less the purely functional aspect. Our built space is going to continue being important, or at least more and more important for other new uses. We probably will need less and less built space to be able to get together because we can use all sorts of other ways to communicate with each other. If you look at contemporary library design, for example, we're still making lots of famous libraries. Architecture has been freed up from only having to store books and make space for readers, like Walter Benjamin in the Paris National Library in the 1910s or 1920s, where there were just books and tables and people. Now, libraries are actually social spaces, and without many books, fire is less of a problem. So there, architecture continues to be relevant if it is viewed as simply built space.

Whether high end, big A architecture is relevant, is for people to decide. That's totally unpredictable. But I think we're going to keep having 99 percent of the built environment produced without a lot of thought. We'll continue to have a good one percent that is produced with a lot of gray matter going into it, for better or for worse, because sometimes that doesn't always produce the best results, but we do see a lot of good architects doing great stuff still. So, yes, big A architecture is still relevant.

I don't work on what will happen to Architecture in the future, but some of my colleagues, two sociologists, do. One of the things that they have worked on is empirical research on the evolution of the architectural profession in France. They say that people trained as architects are getting more and more involved in the professions or the disciplines that are involved in making the built environment happen. In France, for example, in order for a building to get built, there are politicians, municipalities, the State. There are engineering firms, environmental consultants, building performance, ergonomics, all sorts of people, citizens' rights groups, local interest groups, all sorts of people who now get involved in what they call this jeu d'acteurs, this play of actors, the process through which something actually gets built. It must have been like that in the past, but we do have this idea that **Frank Lloyd Wright** just used to draw up things and some rich guy would pay to have a contractor build it, and Frank Lloyd Wright would go around with his cape and his cane and say do this, do that, and the other.

It's very complex today, at least in Europe, in great part because of laws and things like this. So people trained as architects are showing up more and more in other places, not in the office of what's called the *maître d'oeuvre* in France, or the professional service provider, but as representatives of institutional clients. And they interact with the architects who are hired to design the building, in order to represent the client's interests through the eyes of someone who knows more about the built environment or more about the process, in any case, than the institutional client, itself. They are ending up in citizens' rights groups, as politicians, on commissions, on all sorts of things. This doesn't answer the question of where the profession is going, but it answers the question of where students are going or where people trained as architects are going.

Where the profession is going, that's a tough one. Architects who go into practice tend to be very versatile. Another sociologist colleague of mine wrote a book about the way architects have always managed to maintain the existence of their profession, despite the fact that there is always somebody saying you don't need an architect. They are the masters of not saying exactly what it is they do. Architects can always find a way to show that they do know something that can help improve things. So he calls that the indefinition, the non-definition of exactly what the architect does. With an acoustical engineer or acoustical consultant, it's very clear what their service is going to be: certain calculations, certain suggestions or recommendations about things. The architect is much more fuzzy, and that's what characterizes the architecture profession. It's a little bit fuzzy, and that's what allows certain individuals to succeed as really strong architects.

I've always wanted to go to Africa just from when I was four or five years old. It was something I could dream about, as simple as that. When I started architecture, I thought I could combine it with this desire to go to Africa, which definitely had a missionary side to it. You know, in Africa, people are poor, and we can do things to help and so on. And to that extent, I managed to get employed by the Institute for Tropenbau in Starnberg in Germany run by an architect called **Georg Lippsmeier**, who was at that time—and I'm talking about in the 70s and 80s—a leader in the field of tropical architecture. He published the book *Tropenbau: Building in the Tropics*.

Antoni Folkers believes that the missionary zeal is part of architecture.

In the Netherlands, there was nothing to be found: there were few dealings with Africa. We had links to former colonies, Indonesia and in South America, Antilles and Surinam, but none to Africa. We used to have links to South Africa, but at that time, there was a boycott that halted any relation between the Netherlands and South Africa. As a result, Africa was an alien place for a Dutch architect to operate in. That's why I turned my interest to Germany, and I worked for the Institute for Tropenbau for tropical building from 1983 to the beginning of the 90s. It was a research institute coupled with an architect's practice. Lippsmeier had his own, quite famous practice, with satellite offices quite around the world doing big schemes in development, aid, university complexes, hospitals, schools, local housing schemes. I worked for them in East Africa and eventually became the resident architect in east Africa based in Dar-es-Salaam in 1987. At the same time, I was also employed by the department of urban planning and geography at the University of Amsterdam, where I worked on the resettlement scheme of the spontaneous quarters of the city of Ouagadougou in West Africa, in what is now Burkina Faso. From the early 90s — I had left Lippsmeier in '91 and started my own practice with offices in Kampala and Dar-es-Salaam — I was an Africa-based architect working in the continent. Once my employees were quite capable of taking care of it themselves, I pulled out from the day to day practice. I just wanted to be more at home, a normal Dutch architect. At the beginning of the century, I left the practice I had built up and returned to the Netherlands.

But that was not the end of it. It was the end of a very active practice as an architect in Africa, but, at the same time, it was the beginning of a reflection on that period. I asked myself: hey, what have I actually learned? There is so little known about architecture in Africa in our Western environment, where cities are worthwhile as a subject of study and development. That was one of the reasons to start *ArchiAfrika* together with my colleagues. At the same time, I started reading again. I never was an academic, I still don't feel like an academic, but I started reading intensively to reflect on or to mirror my own practical experience to what was said in theory. And that became *Modern Architecture in Africa*, the book that I have recently published.

2001 was the year we established ArchiAfrika, and we started to organize the events, the conferences, we built up the website, and traveled around like mad. And at the same time, we had the practice to build up in the Netherlands. And I must admit, sometimes competitions fill gaps. You have people in the office who have not enough work, and you think, "Okay, let's go do a competition." The one on Lalibela in Ethiopia was definitely interesting. You might have heard of the rocking church, a world heritage site. The churches there start to dilapidate due to erosion, and they wanted to build temporary roofs over it. We were invited to compete but didn't win that one. Still, we had the best design. The competition was won by an Italian architect who had produced these fabulous drawings, and when they started to build it, of course they found out it was unbuildable. I can't do that. I don't like to pretend, I don't like to show things that are not realistic. I think that's a bit of cheating because the Italians probably knew it beforehand. They were seducing the world. And now, what you see, what they have done, it's quite different from what was shown to the world.

We also worked on the idea of the *Blueprints of Paradise* competition. The background is the museum of Africa in the Netherlands, which is an old mission museum, but out in the landscape, a very beautiful site. And the missionaries came back from Africa, and they brought back all these fabulous sculptures and masks and cloth and jewelry and whatnot, and they decided to make a museum. And one of the important sets of that museum is that in the landscaped area. They copied and built a number of traditional African villages, like Dogon village in Mali, and they built it in concrete. At that time, I'm talking about the 60s, it was a common way of showing Africa. We became involved in the Africa museum, we were invited to think with them, and to my astonishment, the director was thinking of extending this museum by adding yet more of these African villages. And then I told her: this is not Africa anymore, Africa is urbanizing at an incredible pace, and these traditional villages — yes, there still are a few — they are disappearing. If you are going to reproduce these villages, you're providing a wrong image of the continent. You should instead start to think about what a future Africa. Africa is in a real speedy development, and you should try to get some ideas of what it will become instead of where you're coming from. You have enough of that already. And that became the basis of this competition: to invite Africa designers, artists, architects both from Africa but also from the diasporas, and to challenge them to tell us how they think their world of tomorrow, their African world of tomorrow, should look like. We have to be very careful not to fall in the trap of this superiority, this feeling of superiority, of western technology, of western thinking.

And the Africans, they have been shy, and they have been like when our new chairman, **Joe Addo** — he's from Ghana — says, "We've just been lazy, it's time that we start to do something." It's not only in western people becoming a bit more modest, but it's also the Africans being a bit louder and a bit more active, proactive. It cannot come from one side. It has to come from both sides. We no longer look at Africa as the poor place where they need our help, but as the place where there are people who can be our business partners, with whom we can work together, and from whom we can learn certain things. And initiatives like Architecture for Humanity and a few others, they're great. That really helps. But the problem in Africa is still — and I'm talking a sub-Sahara in Africa, I'm not talking about South Africa — is that architecture training is at a very early stage. There are not many schools offering good training, and the schools that offer training are more practically directed. They are more polytechnics in which they're training people just to do things, rather than start thinking and applying an intellectual framework. Because you need to able to talk back to start this dialogue, so there's still some ground to be covered there, I'm sure.

Recently I decided to reduce my activities for ArchiAfrika — after ten years, you think other people can now take it over. But the other thing is that the coffers are empty. I've been spending all my time and all my money building this organization and now I have to make money again. I have to turn more attention to my practice in the Netherlands. I'm still doing some odd jobs in Tanzania, but that's more for the fun of it, really. And I'm developing studios at Delft University; that will eventually be more like a structural job for me. But when working in Delft, the ties with Africa will be very, very strong. I have no doubt that I am stuck to that continent for the rest of my life.

I chose architecture at 16 because I needed to take the specific classes in order to qualify for my undergrad in England. It was a bit early because I don't think I knew what I was getting into. It was a combination of arts and sciences and the built environment, as it is for every undergrad. I don't think I had a clear idea of the type of work that I would pursue in my career, but in grad school, the trajectory started becoming more apparent. Clearly, I'm not one of those who wanted to be an architect from a very young age.

During my last year at Princeton we entered the *Ephemeral Structure Competition* for Athens. This was 2001 or 2002 and was ramping up for the Olympics in 2004. The competition called for ephemeral structures in the city of Athens — deployable, temporal installations, pavilions in public spaces in the city for the Olympics. Because it was our first competition, we needed to have a name. That's where Future Cities Lab — now called FUTUREFORMS — began. Competitions are great because they are finite. There is a specific set of requirements that we need to cover, and we enjoy doing that. We use competitions to push our work and our thinking. Of course, everyone enters to win. But we also enter to test specific ideas.

Nataly Gattegno uses competitions to push her work.

The Seoul competition in 2005 was the one where we came in second. The big one. They wanted a lot of boards and a lot of technical specifications, so it really pushed us to figure stuff out. We enjoyed the process because of the urban scale. In the beginning of our work, we were really interested in urban space and public space. So for us, this kind of island in the middle of the city seemed to be a really interesting place to test out some things that we wanted to try. The competition was the concert, opera and outdoor auditorium space on an island in Seoul — on the river, in a tidal flood plain. It was a two-phase competition, and there were three first-tier entries who moved forward to the next phase. The three of us who placed second did not advance to the next phase of the competition, but we were part of all the exhibits and all of the publications that followed.

Much of our work also comes through fellowships or grants that we apply for; they're still competitive. Usually, there is a proposal, a portfolio requirement. We did the desert house as part of a Muschenheim fellowship in Michigan. One of the threads that runs through our work is the relationship between energy and form. The relationship between energies — those may be site energies, literal solar paths, or programmatic influences — and how they impact geometry and form and design. The desert house tested that to the extreme by picking an extreme environment where sun and heat are the only energies on the site to design space. Coming from Europe and never having experienced the desert, I became obsessed by it. That's how the desert house came about, and that's how our interest in extreme environments began to emerge.

The desert house was actually part of a critique of suburbia. Although a single desert house, it was seen as an aggregation of homes within a suburban condition. For us, it was urban as in a kind of alternative American urbanism, especially for Phoenix, where that project was sited. We gravitate toward extreme environments because of our desire and need to limit parameters. Extreme environments are useful because there are only one or two things that are extreme, and those become the parameters that influence the design. That necessitates figuring out how to work with a more limited data set, while ultimately wanting to bring it back to a more complex data set, or urban environment. Later we did a proposal for the situated technologies competition that was for an urban proposal in Union Square, where responsive technologies such as indexing and infrastructure that we're currently working with were applied in the urban environment. We use extremities in order to figure out how we can actually control the data, and then we try to feed it back in, constantly understanding that data sets are complex, and they're as complex as are urban environments. The scalar jump isn't one that we've totally figured out yet, from installation to city, from city back to installation. We are working on it ....

Competitions also play a role in my design teaching because they have a very clear brief, whether it's a conceptual argument that's given from the competition committee, on the one hand, or a successful proposal and submission with a very clear conceptual and design argumentation embedded within on the other. For students, this is very, very useful. I'm currently involved in the thesis curriculum at CCA, so I teach thesis prep and thesis studio. This is a yearlong studio. We just finished our competition charrette this past week. It was the first week of the semester, and we essentially asked thesis students who worked last semester on all of their thesis development work to literally put a single board up that took one aspect of their huge thesis proposal, and extract a little piece of it and put it on the board and design it. They had to make a competition board that made a clear argument that showed and embedded design methodology, and that needed no explanation. We call this quick fires or crash test. I think this time we called it crash test. As a way to just test an idea, what better way than a competition?

Being a juror is different because a juror doesn't get the dialogue. I don't get asked questions. I don't get to figure out what the designer really intended. I might read the things I want to see, or I would read it into the boards. I've judged a couple of competitions, chair competitions and furniture competitions, for example. I enjoyed the Moon Capital competition a lot because it was very provocative. There was neither standard nor baseline to limit what could be done and what could not, because I was an architect and the rest of the people on the jury were astronauts, and engineers, and someone else who I think was a designer. It was an interesting flip to be on that side, considering how many competitions we've entered. But I definitely enjoyed it.

Our dream competition? We've recently applied to a competition that's in the art field, more on the installation or exhibition side of things, which we've never really done before. In this case, we've applied to be considered for an in-site, on-site installation, and submitted an RFQ. That's been an interesting trajectory that we didn't think we would be following. But in terms of what kinds of competitions we would enjoy doing, I would really enjoy doing another urban scale competition because we haven't done one in a while. It takes a lot of time, and it's a lot of work, because there are so many parameters involved. But no matter what comes next, we take a competition and use it for what it gives us.

My trajectory is fairly atypical in architecture. I was working for **Asymptote Architecture** in New York, 2007 to 2009, and that was when the financial crisis happened. Most of those projects were either put on hold or stopped for various reasons. We were working on a project in Abu Dhabi called the Yas Viceroy Hotel, and I had the opportunity to go to Abu Dhabi and work on that project directly, but I chose to stay in New York for various reasons; I particularly wanted to stay closer to the design's generation. Afterward, I regretted that decision because I still haven't been to Abu Dhabi or Dubai; it could have been a nice experience. So when I got the opportunity to work in China, at **MAD Architecture**, a firm similar to Asymptote, I went. People always ask me: did you want to live in China, and were you really into Chinese culture? At the time, I wasn't, but I am now. It was an opportunity and I liked the work, I liked what MAD was doing. They were just starting to build these bigger projects, and I thought my specialties and my interests would align with theirs. And they have.

Six months after **Daniel Gillen** had lost his job due to the financial crisis, he moved to China to work for half of what he had earned in New York.

I had a great education. I studied before computers were really ingrained in academia or even in practice. I was educated through drawing, and in that regard, it was fantastic. But I was one of the few people in my class that were even considering digital tools at the time, and I would have liked to have learned a bit more in terms of the technical aspects of tooling and software. That was the only part that was really lacking. From a design methodology and a design strategy perspective, the education was fantastic. I learned how to think through problems, how to work through iterations, how to think creatively, constructively, practically, and to balance that with fantasy. I thought it was great. I had great instructors. Nowadays you're expected to come out of school running, there's not a whole lot of tooling-up time. If you want a job, if you want to be competitive, then you need to have certain skills. You need to know AutoCAD or Rhino, 3-D Modeling, and 3D-Max coming out of school. We expect our youngsters to teach us the software. That is how it differs today.

Working in China is exciting. The number one thing is the pace of work. This is enhanced by the way MAD works, which is very rapidly. Architects do continual iterations of projects and designs to get them right, to refine them, to make them better, to include more ingredients without disrupting the concept too much. Architects work rapidly as it is, and then add the pace of China on top of it, and the overall effect is extraordinarily fast. In China, things happen very quickly, and you have to be able to adapt to that. It is not the case that buildings are getting more time here. Clients across the world don't want to wait for the buildings, but in the US there's still a certain cadence to the process that is accelerated in China. Everything is manufactured in China, so all of these pieces are at hand and people are mobilized to work immediately. And, if you need a lot of people, you can get a lot of people.

Based on the work I've done and the offices I have worked with, I wouldn't necessarily say I'm the best judge of what is standard. I have been lucky enough to contribute to some special projects over the years. Working with Asymptote and working with MAD — they are not very similar but similar in intent - there's a heavy focus on design. I'm very familiar with the workflow that Ma Yansong, creative director and founding principal, envisions, what he wants to get out of the projects, what they mean to him. It translates to the U.S. as well, because it is the same creative entity that is coming up with these ideas. Maybe how that interfaces with the consultants and the rest of the team in the U.S. is a bit different in terms of procedure.

Here we live in a very litigious society, so a lot of things have to be vetted legally for insurance, responsibility, and liability before things proceed. This vetting tends to hold up the process. Risk aversion also very common here. If something is atypical, then it takes a little longer to make sure that everyone is okay with it. In China, there's more of an interest in getting it done, and there is less of a fear in terms of what is being built. There's also a lot of public opinion in the US that can guide projects in good ways or not. In China, there is more a top-down approach, for better or worse.

I had the luxury of teaching in the US as well as in China, and there are two sides to that. There is a discipline in China, and there is a curiosity and a questioning in the U.S. — I was taught to question everything — and I think that if the rigor on one side and the challenging on the other side could be blended, that would allow for a really prime design. You have to be critical, but at the same time, you have to work hard. The more critical you are, the harder you have to work. They don't operate independently.

Do I experience culture shock? Definitely. I am American, and I grew up here. It was really beautiful to see what China was doing well, and then on coming back, I want Americans to do all those things well and more. I was more critical of the US coming back, which I think is good; it's why we are lucky to be able to be in this country. We have the freedom to be critical in the US. I also experience culture shock with regards to infrastructure and public transportation. When I spend a lot of time in Asia, I see how rapidly and how accelerated their infrastructure is, how advanced, which is quite nice. Lessons from China? Recycle, do your best to protect the environment, and, as architects, do more in terms of our industry's contribution to the earth. We are smart enough as a community of architects to acknowledge that we need to be more proactive in solving earth's problems. We see urbanization on a major scale, a scale that's unknown to most. Everybody has to do their part, that's the number one lesson. Our quality of life multiplied by 7 billion is not sustainable for the planet to live on. You see it first hand in Asia, unfortunately.

I have the luxury of working in a creative land in a world where we facilitate creative ideas and are open to any sort of stream of creativity. I am inspired personally by everything from art to nature to humanity to aeronautics or to automotive design or to anything that I think is fashion. I can draw inspiration from everything. The work I do tends to lean on different industries a lot in order to pull solutions or pull ways of doing things from other industries. Architecture is an aggregate of so much, to be able to pull from lots of inspiration sources is really important.

My story starts with art. This probably goes back to my graduate studies, being at Columbia in the 1980s when prominent artists like **Barbara Kruger**, **Martha Rosler,** and **Jenny Holzer** were doing some extraordinary work. I remember something that **Bernard Tschumi** said not too long ago: when he first came to New York in the early 70s, maybe it was 75, he came not because of architecture, but because of what was happening in the art scene, the New York art scene. When I worked for **Stephen Holl**, every Saturday afternoon, we had to take a break, and Stephen would say: okay, go visit some galleries, see some art. And periodically, Stephen's friends like **Vito Acconci** or **James Turrell** would come through the office. So I am going to start with art today because that is what I have been looking at in terms of how artists translate the political, social, cultural issues through the various media in which they work and construct discourse. Most of the architects who were mentors to my generation, I mentioned Tschumi and Holl but also **Liz Diller** and **Ric Scofidio**, their early projects were with artists doing installations or working on their own doing set design. There is an affiliation between art and architecture, and that is really what I am interested in And even now still, on Saturday afternoons, I go out and I see art in Chelsea. And if I am in the office, I will take a break. And invariably, I run into Stephen Holl or run into Bernard Tschumi and other architects who are out looking at what is going on and seeing what is fresh and what is interesting.

Mario Gooden does not do watercolors when he gets up in the morning.

Working for Stephen Holl and **Zaha Hadid** had a big influence on me. But when I worked for both of them, it was actually quite a different time. For example, when I worked for Zaha, it was 1989. There were six of us in the office, not 250 people. This was pre-digital, it was hand painting, hand drawing, ink on mylar, and Zaha was very much involved in the production of the work. It was very experimental just in terms of space. Similarly, with Stephen, there were maybe eight of us in the office. This was in the early 1990s, '92 and '93. Although superficially, they might seem to be quite different, I think they are actually quite similar in terms of their investigations about space, not form but space. And both of them speak very forthrightly about space being the issue. For Zaha, it was and still is about extending the project of modernism, not as a formal project but as a spatial project. For Stephen, it is about the experience of space. There are other similarities; both of them began their process through painting, Stephen with watercolors, Zaha with acrylic paint. For both of them, there was a connection between art and architecture. I think they are my primary influences.

Stephen was a teacher when I was at Columbia. I never had him as a teacher. I decided after I had graduated that I wanted to work for him. With both of them, with Zaha and Stephen, I was interested in the way that they thought and wanted to understand how they went about their process. I think at some levels both work intuitively, but I also think that decades of research have had a big impact on their work. Zaha did research through painting and drawing, and thinking about the multivalency of space, and occupying space from many positions. Stephen would produce a few watercolor sketches every morning, not necessarily based upon any program but just experiments with space and light, and a sense of materiality. It was my experience with their thinking about the experience of space, not just the theoretical discourse, but the active perception of space. I really enjoyed being in both of their offices and think of both of them as my mentors.

I don't do watercolors in the morning when I get up. I still have a sketchbook. This is probably old fashioned since everything is digital, but I still have my sketchbooks from years ago, and I still buy sketchbooks every few months, and I still do drawings. And lately, I have been documenting things that I'm interested in, photographing works, and collecting them. Some could be works that I am engaged in, let us say linguistics practices. Some of the early work of Barbara Kruger was very much about using language, so it wasn't necessarily about the form or even about the image, but using language sometimes with image and then let the viewer read the work and interpret the work. That reminds me of another lesson by Bernard Tschumi: if architecture is the materialization of concept, then we have to think about how architecture is performative. So it is about what it does, not necessarily what it looks like. I am paraphrasing him. For me, the interest in art is not only the drawing. It might also inspire me to write something about an idea in my sketchbook, or how an artist is using language, or maybe about a juxtaposition that might appear in an artwork. Usually, the kinds of works that I am drawn to are installation pieces, photography. I am not so much interested in art as the formal object or the aesthetic. Yes, aesthetics matter, but not in terms of sculptural form, but what is it saying, what is it that one reads, and what is that subject-object relationship that the viewer has with the work.

In the office we use digital technologies from the very beginning in terms of the research. We are using parametrics or scripting but not necessarily to generate form. When we were working on a project for a shipping terminal, we looked at the numbers of people that came through the terminal throughout the seasons and throughout the year. We tracked the number of vessels per week and their schedules. So we developed a script to see the space of flux in terms of movement at the terminal and to find out how we might respond architecturally. This is part of the process of how we think about relational relationships, relational conditions. We use technology that way.

I find it absolutely as inspiring as the old media. I am not the technology expert in the office; I am kind of the coach of the students that I sort of work with, and I can say: we want to do this. How do we do this? So we all sort of work together in terms of conceptualizing what the process is, not necessarily knowing how it will look in the end, but thinking about what it should do and what our research process should be.

I worked for my partner Ray for about a year and a half in 1990. He originally had an office in Charleston. Then I moved back to New York. That is actually when I went to work for Stephen Holl, lived and had my own practice in Gainesville, Florida, for a few years, and then in '97, Ray and I formally established the practice Huff and Gooden as a partnership. We have two offices. We have an office in New York, and we have maintained a small office in Charleston because Ray is the director of the Clemson architecture program in Charleston. Most of the work is done out of New York. There was a time before the office started growing when I was going to Charleston just about every week. And now Ray comes to New York periodically.

Why not LA? At the time when I finished my undergraduate degree at Clemson, New York was totally at the opposite end of the spectrum: Clemson was in a small, rural town in northwestern South Carolina, and New York was the most urban place that I could think of to go. Two weeks after graduating, I moved to New York in preparation for attending Columbia and really just fell in love with the city. Even when I was just living in South Carolina, I was spending some time in New York about every other week because I was also teaching at Columbia. It is a city that fits me very well. Now we are doing some work on the west coast, so when I visit the west coast, I think about living there, in Los Angeles probably.

How do we collaborate? We start working on a project together, and we have done that consistently with every project. That has been really important to us. Of course, once we get into late design development or construction documents, we cannot afford for both partners to have the same role. So one of us will take the lead in terms of construction documents or construction admin. But it is important to us from the beginning that we are bouncing things off of each other to push the design along. Sometimes one of us may produce a few more sketches than the other, but it is a give and take; we really work in tandem.

I think we complement each other. Sometimes we come at it from the same point of view, sometimes we come at it from different points of view, but they are actually complementary. It is nice when that kind of synergy of thought occurs about a project. We really begin all of the work by asking a series of questions. We usually start with the same questions, questioning the project in terms of its cultural issues or political issues. Part of that has to do with having a practice in South Carolina, in Charleston, which is very culturally and politically charged. There are lots of ironies and lots of things which seem contradictory, and we are really interested in those kinds of juxtapositions, things which seem like they shouldn't coexist but they actually do. And I think that is perhaps what drew us together, although initially, there was just attraction in terms of the kind of work that we were interested in doing.

Our most challenging commission is probably the California African-American Museum. Over the past fifteen years or so, the design of museums has been about creating the iconic image. Most museum clients wanted the Bilbao effect, wanted the powerful, sculptural, iconic image. The California African-American Museum was a project that we approached quite differently. One, it was a very contested site in terms of the buildings which neighbor it. There is an existing building that was designed and built in 1984. It is about a one and a half story beige, brick building near **Frank Gehry**'s air and space gallery that was finished around the same time. There is a **Thom Mayne** school that was finished a few years ago that was nearby. The USC Coliseum is just south. The California science center is just adjacent to it. And its hemmed in very tightly on its site. However, no one knows it is there. It is virtually invisible from the main north-west street, Figueroa, and not visible on the Exposition Park campus until you get up to the building. The challenge was how to create an iconic building there that competes with the air and space gallery, which has a plane cantilevered off the roofs. It also has an exterior exhibit that is a DC8 jet about 15 feet from the corner of the existing California African-American museum. There is another spy plane in an exterior exhibit that is also pointed toward the building. How did we respond to this? Was it a matter of being loud? Or did we need a forceful presence for the building instead of building a tower? Of course, we really didn't have the budget for a tower, but we felt strongly that the building needed to speak its presence to the site, that it needed to say: yes, I am here. We designed a building sheathed in a glass scrim that enmeshes words and images which appear and disappear. The panels of the glass scrim are at different angles so they reflect the environment. They reflect the daylighting, so at some times of day, the images and words are very strong. Other times, they fade out, and so the building is there, it is not there. It is kind of a ghost on the site. But how to render that? That was the most difficult challenge. We finally produced some renderings and built some models, and the client really appreciated it. We wanted the building to be about how it performs, and not so much about what it looks like because it is still almost impossible to see the entire building from anywhere on the site, because of the proximity of the other buildings. So it was not going to be Bilbao; it was not going to be the Disney concert hall, which exists sort of monumentally with nothing else around it. But it has been a very interesting project, and I think it is going to be quite nice.

What drives our design process is cultural, it is theory. Each project starts differently, with its own set of questions. The California African American museum was about identity, its physical identity on the site, but it was also about African American identity in the western United States in California. For other projects, for example a theater renovation we completed in Charleston, which was a historic building, the questions were about the relationship between the past and the present, or the past and the future if you will. We are not preservation architects or even restoration architects, but that was the world that we entered. And actually, it was a very interesting project that turned out to be quite successful. And underlying that, we had to deal with issues of performance, theatricality, the procession and seeing and being seen, and the gaze of the observer. So there was a little bit of theory there. Each project is about the layering of many different issues.

I don't think we approach architecture differently as an African American owned firm with two African American principals. It would not be 100 percent truthful if I didn't acknowledge that we are probably more aware of certain conditions or situations. For example, with the California African American Museum, we zeroed in right away on the issue of identity and the invisibility of the museum in its current condition. We focused on how to address that and how to think about African American identity in terms of being visible and being invisible. Our own cultural experiences certainly play a role in how we approach some projects. But I think that doesn't preclude that we couldn't design another kind of cultural museum, a Jewish museum, or a Native American museum through our usual processes of research. I think we would still want to ask pointed questions, no matter what the project.

Color is not really an issue, but the size is. Small practices, in general, have problems with the accessibility to larger projects, the kind of projects that we are interested in. And that is not necessarily dependent on the color of our skin, but it is more so related to economics, to whom you know and whom you don't know. Really it comes down to that.

I teach because I am obsessed with knowledge and learning. For me, teaching is about imparting what I have to offer to students, but it is also for selfish reasons. I learn quite a great deal from my students and the kinds of things that I ask them to do. The kinds of questions I ask them I am also asking myself. Teaching gives me a way to complement the practice by asking more in-depth questions. Often projects don't allow for this, either because there is no time in the schedule, or because the budget is limited. And teaching gives that opportunity. And it keeps both Ray and me fresh, keeps us on our toes not only in terms of technology and research but also in terms of thinking. It keeps us sharp because the same questions that we ask our students we ask in our practice: to be clear about your concept, to be clear about what it is that you are doing. For me, teaching and practice really work together.

Fifteen years ago, however, academia was perhaps more on the leading edge. Then the profession caught up. In some ways, the profession has overtaken academia, and at times it seems as if academia was just producing professionals to work in offices instead of propelling the profession to move it forward. How does the student work look today? It doesn't look like anything in particular, and I think that might mean that we're getting a little bit smarter than the profession now. At least I hope that means that we are moving back to being on the leading edge in terms of the questions that we are asking the students, and the projects that we are doing at the school.

Our profession may be in the midst of introspection at the moment. Over the last ten or fifteen years, cultural projects like museums were interested in the iconic image. Architecture became consumed by its own image, by its media image, by the sexy rendering, and the media came out with the term starchitect. So architects became this kind of personality, almost a caricature of what architects actually do. Now, architecture is still in the midst of a recession. Architecture is at the lagging end of economic cycles because it is only affordable by a certain percentage of the population, maybe the one percent, maybe a little bit more. And because governments have been strapped as well, even public projects have been few and far between. But this gives the profession the moment to be more introspective. Maybe we can become a little bit smarter while emerging from the recession, and hopefully, that will mean that we are not consumed by the image, but get back to thinking about architecture's performative qualities. It is not just the image to be consumed by a certain percentage, but it has an effect upon the space of the city, it has an effect upon the built environment, and other contexts. My optimism is that we will emerge smarter. But I think we are all in the midst of emergence now, sort of figuring out exactly how to go forward.

I don't think I look at design as having to make a choice in the different cultural setting that I've put myself in. Landscape architecture was the first, and there was a kind of going home after architecture school. It felt like that was the best place for me. Architecture seemed too hermetic, too closed off, where landscape seemed to have more possibilities. I'm much more of an urban thinker. Landscape just seemed to somehow provide that context. Why not planning? Planning died. Physical planning is dead. Urban design doesn't deal with landscape. Urban design is just architects making boxes. Landscape, to me, has become a place where I can talk about culture, ecology, and many other things, and it still has a bearing on what I do. When you can talk about these things in making a building, it really doesn't have a lot of meaning. Landscape is a broad place where I can ask these broad questions, and can actually work with the broad questions. At least that's where I am now. Who knows? Maybe as I get older, I'll go back to the box.

Walter Hood wants people to see that they are part of a larger story, no matter who they are.

Most recently, I finished a degree in art at the Art Institute. I was pretty lucky to be in the right place at the right time with a well-known curator who knew the stuff that I was doing and asked me to join a group of artists working in Charleston, South Carolina, for the Spoleto Festival. This went on for maybe 30 months. I really enjoyed working in the context with artists. I had worked with artists before, more in a kind of professional relationship where the project needed an artist, but this project was open-ended, speculative. We were invited to come to a place and to think about it, collectively, and then make work, collectively. Just being with artists and seeing how they think of making work is pretty damn eye-opening. We are trained to be very formal in our thinking — what's the problem, how do we set it up, and then how do we attack it; the artist is empowered from day one, from a kind of personal empowerment to cultural empowerment. I really loved it. I understand the schism between architects and the artist, or landscape architects and the artist, and it's not jealousy, but it is that freedom, that freedom to be able to say what it is you mean versus somehow putting it into jargon, or the terms that the culture accepts. It actually freed me. So the last five years have been a complete renaissance, as far as how I think about work, how I think about practice, and how I think about the things I've done. It's given me a really interesting frame of reference to go back and look at things in a clearer way that really gets to a lot of the questions that I was actually asking. I just didn't know how to understand them, because there's so much stuff on top. Just getting to the basic stuff is freeing.

Some of my clients are amused at my returning to school, and some understand because they've seen the evolution. Some components of art have always been part of my work, whether through drawing, or through making, or telling stories, but I could never find a place for it. It was always oh, we don't need that on that project right now, or why are you thinking that way, we're doing this. Some of the clients expect as much, and some question why I want an art degree. The typical thing that I get from a lot of architects and landscape architects is now that I'm an artist, I think I can just do anything. They don't understand that if you put yourself in a different cultural setting, it becomes a richer context for work. It's not that I want to call myself an artist, or call myself this or call myself that, it's just I enjoyed being in that realm, and I still enjoy being in that realm.

I have always been about telling stories. Stories are very personal, and they can be true or false. They can start anywhere, they can end anywhere, they can stay open-ended. It is an experience that one shares. To me, that's architecture, that's design. We each have these experiences, and we're sharing them with one another through our work, and it just happens to be architectural, or it happens to be landscape, or it happens to be art. I'm a true Southerner in that way.

I was lecturing in Mexico City a couple years ago, and afterward this guy said, "I understand now. You're a storyteller, you're from the South." It made a lot of sense to me. I'm really interested in weaving a chronology of events, of spectacle, of mundaneness, all that stuff that makes up our everyday. The task is how to make projects that embody that. In the end, hopefully, they will show meaning. They will show you that I live in this place. And that, to me, is the really beautiful part of it. Most people can't read the story, can't hear the story, or don't even see the story that they're living.

As environmental designers, we're actually creating the backdrop or prosceniums for people to see that they are part of a larger story, no matter who they are. To be able to articulate that in a lot of different ways and in a lot of different places has been a lot of fun. It's not always the truth, man. Some of it are really good lies. Sometimes you have to spin a yarn, just to get people to sort of understand something.

When I started to work on the *de Young Museum* the parti was there, but the skin wasn't complete. I'm writing stories of every project, as part of this book I'm working on, and it's a three-part thing. There will be stories, there will be a landscape grammar, and then there will be the actual transformation of the grammar into some narrative. I was writing the story of when I first met **Pierre de Meuron**. We visited the *Ricola factory*, and a storm had just hit. We were throwing ivy strands off the roof, and that was my first introduction to Swiss landscape. They were able to get ivy in these long strands just to come off the side. I had never seen this before. These are the guys that I'm working with, so that's the context of the story.

Another story with that has to do with **Jacques Herzog**'s telling me that he has a hard time reading landscape drawings because he looks at them and they look very busy. And then when the landscape is done, it's not busy at all. Through those two moments in time, I then had to figure out how to script the story of making landscape with this building. I imagined green courtyards that had a kind of wow landscape to them, but a very dumb landscape kind of emerged. The architects had always talked about the building as a place to see the park. And I then started thinking, well, how could we see the park in the building? And the idea was just dumb. So I just took plants that were within the context of the museum, the larger area, and just took the most non natives and put them inside. In one part are ferns, and in the other are eucalyptus trees. And that then became the story about the culture inside the museum. Again, the architects' parti allowed for that story to emerge.

Every time I work with architects, I try to be very clear about the fact that each one is different, and working with anyone is different, and that I have to find a way in. I'm not the kind of person who is combative or trying to come in declaring, "This is the way I need to work." And a lot of it is cultural, but a lot of it is also just how do we feed off one another. And that one was easier because I had only dealt with the architects inside the building. Another part of the challenge was to deal with donors outside of the building, which is a completely different story, right? Donors, they don't want anything to do with the architecture; they want to deal with themselves and the money they're giving you to make their things.

I've been lucky to have really good people working within the city government who believed in certain projects. Particularly in those early Oakland projects, there were just two people, and they're not there anymore. And if you don't have people like that in government, you're just not going to get good projects. The great thing that's happening in New York with all this good urban work is that there is **Amanda Burden**, the city's chief city planner, and the mayor said, "Anything you want to do, I'll stand behind you." But projects need that kind of leadership. And if it isn't there, it's just impossible.

We just finished the *Powell Street Promenade* in San Francisco, and Audi gave the city a million dollars. Thank God, they had this program in place, the park work program, where the money could come right into that, and we could do it. We just ran right over the public works people. Of course, they were pissed off, but it got done in four months. I'd never seen a project get done in four months. Over three city blocks! You've got to have good programs and people in government, and a lot of cities don't recognize that. It's really hard to do good work in L.A., it's really hard to do good work in Oakland now, and it's impossible to do this kind of work in Berkeley because there's just no one there, there's no advocacy there. I can leverage the work I did in the past, but it still comes back to the people who are going to implement it. Right now, a lot of the projects are implemented through public works, and they are engineers. It just so happened that I've gotten to know them, so my 7th Street project actually got built. And the engineers knew that they had to build it, and they were freaking out. But it worked out. Still, you want advocates there, because otherwise it's going to down to this really awful stuff.

20 years ago, people didn't have iPhones and Facebook. Now people are just unaware of their surroundings. The public realm in America is the worst it's ever been, a far as patronage is concerned. I was just in Frankfurt. People had been telling me Frankfurt sucks. I looked on the map, and there was a green thing around the old city, and I went for a run. And I was just blown away by how amazing their public realm is. And I don't mean just clean, I mean, people there are tinkering with it, messing with it, cleaning it and doing all kinds of things. There's an expectation of the public realm to give something back.

The machines have allowed for our advocacy to disappear because now it's in the box — I even watch people walking down the street, crossing the street — it doesn't really matter anymore to them, to a certain degree. If you're out advocating for better sidewalks, no one cares, why should we pay for that. In a way, it's taken us away from what's real; instead, we're more and more preoccupied with the virtual world. And I see myself doing it just a well as other people. But I do think that when we have the opportunity to show people where they are, it trumps the virtual any day. Because if we do it in a prophetic way, it will get people to notice they forgot. What's really driving a lot of my work now is trying to find just these simple things to say, like look, this thing is here, and all you have to do is dust it off a little bit." There's not a lot of money needed to do that; it's just that people have to be open enough to take the ride and see where it goes.

My most personally successful commission? That's hard because they're all — all the projects have their moments. But I would have to say the first project, Courtland Creek, probably would still be it — it's been 20 years. Actually. I noticed three weekends ago, there was a 20th year anniversary, and they were doing a cleanup. I went there, and they're still cleaning up, but all the stuff is 20 years old. And I know what it cost, it cost like 300,000 bucks, and people are telling me stories about what goes on there. And there's something really fulfilling about that: to make something with very meager means, and to stay connected with a place for a long time, and then go away, and then to have them call and you go back out there. The bones are still there, some more frayed than others, but I would say that's probably the most fulfilling.

Someone was asking me downstairs. "How many people do you work with?" I answered, "Six." "How do you do all these projects with six people?" There's this mentality that big is better. That you can't work in an incremental way. Courtland Creek reminds me that it was just me, and it was very incremental. We just forget that as projects get bigger and budgets get bigger, we risk losing the original design.

Lots of things influence my design work. I don't think there's one thing that rises to the top. The nice thing about lecturing — and I lecture a lot — is that it allows me to think. I mean, what the hell am I going to say? And every time I say it in a different way. I might be talking about the same work, but I'll talk about it differently, depending on the audience, and there's always something that I learn along the way. Working with communities — communities are different, and that is something that refocuses the work, pushes back at the work. And then there is art, or making things, which is part of an internal logic that requires constant dreaming. And that's the side that I try to feed a lot because more and more today, it's really hard to dream. And what I mean with "dream" is to be faced with the practical context and still be able to speculate. It's really hard to speculate. I was talking to the students, and I was trying to get them to talk about speculation. It was really hard. I don't think they understand it. They're talking about BIM and all this other stuff. And I said, "While you're learning that, you can still make things and come up with things." But that's the side of us that we don't train. Right now, I'm teaching my students CAD in the first semester. And they have a drawing class one day a week at night, five hours, and that's the side where we're speculative. But they cannot automatically just bridge it. And I keep telling them, "You have to let go." Instead, they compartmentalize these different activities. But they both need each other.

Teaching forces everything to become entropic. I've got to teach, I've got to pull it all together. I have to do my research. And if those areas are not feeding each other, I am pretty lost. It's taken me 20 years to really make sure all of those things are actually feeding one another, which is fantastic.

Doing the art program only made it better. I've taken over our first-year curriculum — we have these two programs, landscape and environmental planning — and I've decided to put them together. If I hadn't done the art thing, I don't think I would have taken that on, but now I do see the synthesis between environment and landscape. One is more scientific, but it's the medium that's more important - it's landscape. If we could understand that it's an amazing medium in which to work, whether you're a scientist or a designer, we're both mining the same thing. In a lot of cases, scientists, even engineers, look at the landscape completely different from designers, and I think we have to look at those things as being the same before we can mine them. It takes this multidisciplinary way of understanding all the pieces, which is really hard to do.

I don't make long-term goals anymore. I don't have that much time. Over the last 20 years, I've had these six-year periods of enlightenment. The first six years, I was working on the Urban Diaries. And the second six to seven years, I went to Rome and found palimpsests, which give me another way of telling the story. I'd never gone on so many archeological digs in my life. But, they allowed me to come back and have a very critical kind of eye for landscape. That second group of works is really into digging, and telling stories through digging.

The last five or six years have been influenced by the Art Institute, where the cultural idea really shaped. How we work with people, how we look at ourselves in places, and how we gain momentum from those within the work proved to me that the practice has always been cultural, not from a landscape/architecture point of view, or from geography, but in the sense that people are in a place because they want to be there and that they change that place based on their values and attitudes – and that makes a landscape. Whether they liked what happened there or not, it existed, and people existed, and that's important to the story.

So how do you work within that logic? I've broken it into three major areas; the everyday and the mundane, life-ways, and commemoration. Through these three ways, we say something about who we are. Commemoration really talks about who was here before. I don't think we're really good at that in this country. I don't mean making a sign, I'm just saying look at who made the thing before, and respect that in some way. Life-ways is not community design or urban design, but respecting how people choose to live in a place based on their values and attitudes. Some people want to live in familiar household relationships, some people don't, and I think that's what gives the urban landscape its vibrancy. The everyday, the mundane is kind of like everything else. It's that stuff that we just don't pay attention to; there is just so much of it, and we spend our money on it. And that, to me, suggests a way of working.

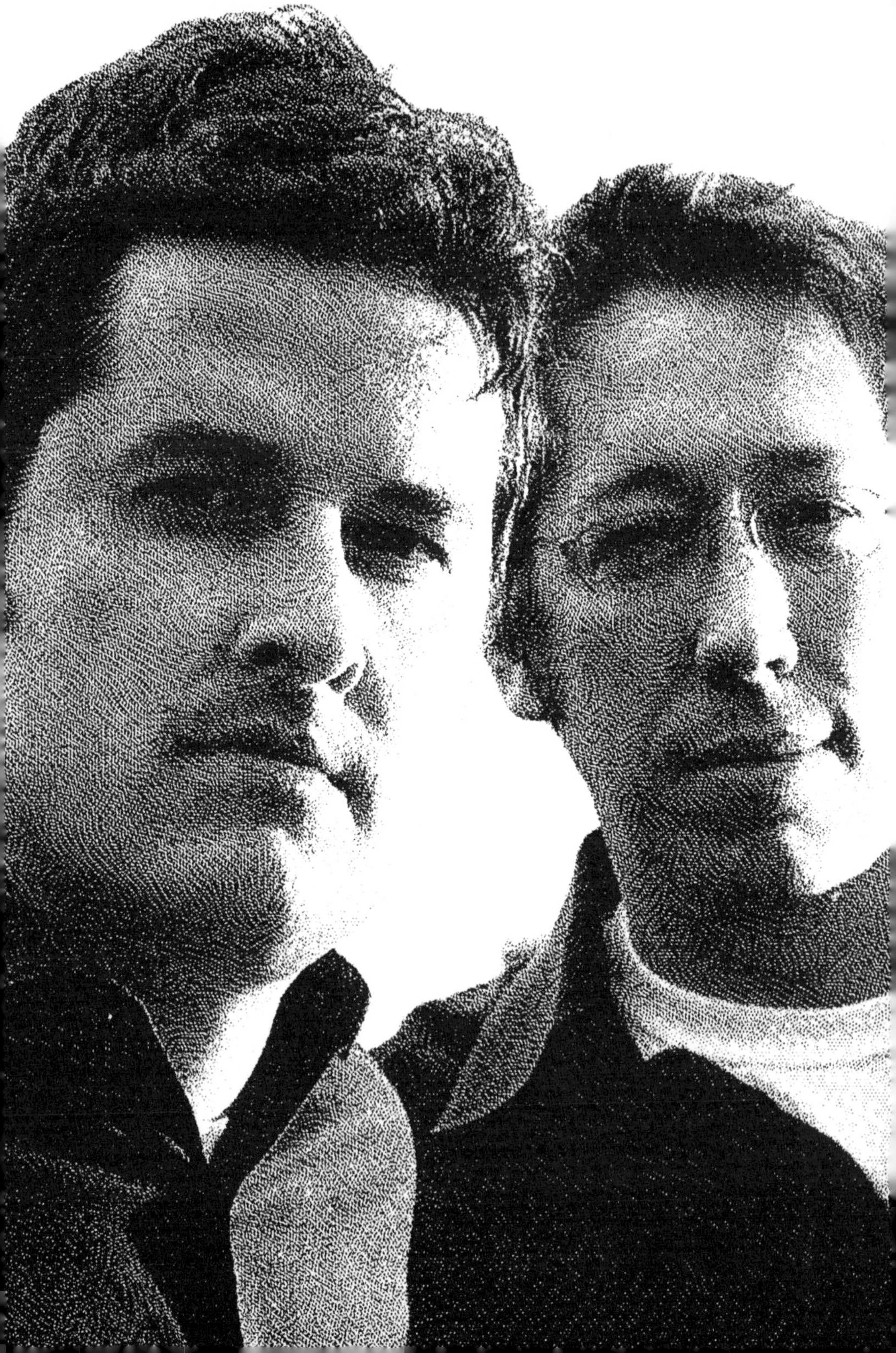

BS: One of the reasons that Marc and I connected is our shared, often unhealthy interest in popular culture. We invest in a lot of things that many of our academic colleagues might see as too central or low-brow. We both play video games. We both watch sports. We both are very interested in movies for reasons ranging from production to narrative. Another commonality, neither of us took a direct path to where we are in practice. I didn't start out in architecture at all. I was going to be an industrial designer. Then I was going to become an animator. I arrived at architecture after a few false starts. But I think we both bring many of those earlier interests with us. All of our baggage remains, and as a result, I think we view the world through different lenses. It has become a strength.

Marc Swackhamer and **Blair Satterfield** are avid gamers and chat about design issues while trying to kill each other in VR.

MS: We are also grazers. We tend to find interest in a lot of different things, and a lot of those things are interesting novel ideas that arise in different disciplines. For example, we might talk about a shirt designed by Nike that changes its weave pattern, becoming thinner where your body sweats or thicker where you tend to wear through your shirt. This becomes a driving idea and starting point for a project (the perforation pattern on a homeless shelter that we designed in this case). Adopting the strategy allowed us to respond to the program in an incremental way. We draw from interesting ideas in other disciplines and synthesizing them into our own work.

BS: Our work is also very tool-focused. We are as interested in what we are using to make something as we are with the product that's being made. This also comes from our upbringing - my dad is a biologist, Marc's is a mechanical engineer. We both inherited an interest in process and systems from our parents. We also come from heavy making backgrounds, so the equipment we use is fair game for investigation. We understand the correct tool use, but we are also interested in figuring out how to productively misuse tools. We have found that clever misuse might net something positive and interesting. We don't always accept the package of equipment that we're given. Our approach is to challenge the process, through the equipment that we're using to get to the end product. We are keen to see if there's a way to innovate in that space. We can always redraw plans, but if we rethink the way we cut a piece of timber, we might make more efficient buildings. Innovation is not just about the big formal move, yet it seems to be where a lot of architects focus. We're interested in the whole process. As a result, a lot of our work takes a long time to come to bear fruit. We work at it. We're not shy about revisiting ideas either. We have projects that we've been working on for several years. I can't tell you where the endpoint is for them. As technology evolves, the ideas evolve, the way we can fabricate things evolve, and we follow along. We surf the process as much as we drive it.

MS: Right now we're working on an adaptable vacuum form. It's a table that has actuators and pistons that independently move up and down. We can get multiple panels out of the same table. We don't have to make very expensive formwork for each piece or resign ourselves to the same shape over and over again. An adaptable form means we can make an infinite number of shapes out of the same formwork. We haven't seen this done before, and we are working with an engineering colleague at Minnesota to develop the actual machinery to do it. I think we're getting more and more interested in developing the front end tools, taking that on as much as the design project itself. This adaptable vacuum forming strategy presents a nice opportunity to adapt pieces to specific existing conditions. We can adjust different panels to accommodate existing geometries in a really interesting way.

BS: Another example of our approach can be seen in a project that we have been working on called Hometta. Hometta is a house plan company that's virtually based. It's an online company. The mission is to expand access to architectural services for the tier below those that currently engage architects for custom designed homes. The Hometta team recruited a pool of renowned and quality architects and asked them to create builder sets for a single-family house. These will be made available for a set fee. We became interested in novel ways to shop for a house. We built a sim-based island of homes where an interested buyer can select an avatar and walk around. A virtual showroom. It's something that Marc and I plan to develop for other work. Playing with tools and playing with market environments are the same. Being open to both begins to draw work in new directions, and maybe even re-defines or expands the role of the architect and the designer. The more we get specific, the broader the practice gets. You know, it's the classic counter force idea.

MS: We really look up to **Charles and Ray Eames**. We have always appreciated the way that they used gifts to other people as a way to test ideas about furniture. Those gifts became production models that ultimately find their way into their work. We've done that several times with people we know. We've designed and built furniture, or small interventions, like this wall system that we're making. It's a nice vehicle for testing ideas.

BS: We also are participating in competitions; in fact, we are hosting our own.

MS: And we are going to do it again, only a better job of it.

BS: One of the things we learned is that with anything like a competition, communication is key.

MS: Just as the deadline hit, we heard word from all kinds of interesting people who were like, "Oh, we were going to enter the competition, we just found out too late." Next time we need to do a better job and solicit responses.

The competition was designed to crowdsource ideas for our Open Source Wall project (OSWall). We were looking for novelty, so it wasn't necessarily about finding the best idea. We selected three, and we gave them money to build prototypes and do drawings of their entries for an exhibition we had in New York. The pie-in-the-sky idea that we don't really have the infrastructure or the funding yet to do, is that OSWall as a system could exist as a platform. It is intended as a literally a framing system that one would buy into. We make the analogy to a smartphone. The consumer buys the piece of hardware (the wall). Everybody's piece of hardware is essentially the same, or standardized. What personalizes the phone and makes it more functional and useful are the apps that are put on the phone. OSWall is our hardware. The modules are the apps. We proposed the competition to solicit lots of ideas. The long-term goal would be a marketplace for wall apps. If you lived in Arizona, you would look at the arid, dry category of apps, and select those optimized for that kind of a climate. If you were in Minnesota, you would look at the upper Midwest apps because you needed stronger insulation, and so forth. Through an open crowdsourcing strategy, all these voices could come together to create a patchwork of different components that could be curated to respond to different needs, just like the applications on a phone.

BS: There is a T-shirt company called Threadless that uses this model. You can submit a design for a T-shirt, and when that shirt design hits a critical mass of orders, they produce the T-shirt. The popular ideas rise to the top. The more people are interested in it, the more you sell. We started to envision this type of ecology of applications for this wall.

MS: I think ecology is the right word. Competitions are handled as events. We've won competitions, but it's the competitions we received honorable mention or didn't place at all that have had a bigger impact on our progress. Our approach is to revisit a project, especially one we didn't win. We develop a new version of a proposal that we cross-pollinate with another project, perhaps entering it into another competition, or running with it as an independent research project. We don't look at projects as isolated and bookended. Our production is fluid. I think the iPhone is a competitive ecosystem. Basically, everybody has access to the system, some rise to the top, some don't. It is a competitive environment that way. It's an interesting way to think about work because it lets the system course correct and tune itself to feedback from the environment. It makes work less about a preconceived approach. Work becomes responsive.

BS: Hometta is the exact same system in my mind. The more I work, the less interested I am in the "self-preservation" posture that I see practice taking. To survive, practice should be far more about an open-source environment, and less territorial. We should broaden the footprint of practice. The medieval guild system was basically a mechanism for protecting intellectual property. It was inflexible; it couldn't progress as fast as the world was progressing. It lost pace and therefore lost out. I worry a little about architecture (the profession) in that way. When we spend so much time defending our position (or worse, a title), we shut down opportunities to actually grow that position. We should continue to think of ways to increase access to our services. We should allow everybody to have a stake in the enterprise. I think architects can have relevance in the future, as synthetic system thinkers that other people need. Collaboration is a form of synthetic thinking.

MS: I think you're right. We need to expand what we do and where our bread is buttered. The idea of doing these one-off buildings for very wealthy people isn't tenable anymore. The music industry has gone through this, and bands are much more likely to just give away music because they have found other mechanisms for making a living being musicians. In some cases, they might just make their music more affordable. In other cases, bands give away music to build familiarity. They make money when people come to see them at a concert. The financial model has changed. Consider a band like Girl Talk. Girl Talk is a guy we really like. He samples and mixes different existing songs together to create new music. When he has a new album, he just gives it away. When he performs his shows sell out. People know him because he just gives the "product" away. He rethought the financial structure of the business. I think architecture could stand a little bit of that. Like you said, we're good at synthetic, complex thinking. Architects could find new areas where we could be of value and maybe get our work out there a little bit more.

BS: There is so much architects could influence that is left to other people to design. I don't see any reason why we shouldn't be participating in more types of work. Look at big four consulting firms — Deloitte and those places — they've completely usurped the green movement. Architects are the experts in the built environment. Architects are responsible for building design. Yet if you go onto the websites of all those big four firms, you will find entire environmental consulting divisions that are taking over the whole process. They are focusing on the metrics and staffing teams with engineers. These firms focus on how companies can make themselves environmentally responsible as a system. Architects spearheaded this movement, and many are better equipped think of how one might handle a work environment that is simultaneously humanistic, holistic, and synthetic. But we're so worried about maintaining our limited position that we miss the opportunity to lead. A lot of talented architects that I know see that they can have more impact and make more money by not being architects. They go to work for these types of institutions. Their skills translate, but the precious title "architect" and old business model do not. That is a bad position for the profession to be in. I worry that nostalgia and fear get in the way of opportunity and evolution. I don't think architecture's going away. I do believe the guys who have a stranglehold on the business models and the professional body might be going away, but that's probably alright.

Architects don't really make buildings, right? We design them and then we draw drawings, documents to show others how to make them. And the more complex a project gets, the more collaborators you have. Even in the simplest project, you are still going to have a structural engineer; you still need to deal with the mechanical. You don't necessarily need an engineer but at least a mechanical contractor. You are still going to need to deal with a contractor, a builder. You deal with sprinklers, lighting, acoustics — a lot of things. And the more complex things get, the more you need. Really good projects happen when these things coalesce. The architect is meant to be the person who understands this greater scope and understands how all of this fits into a design. But it doesn't always happen that way. While architects understand all of these things, we aren't doing the calculations, and we're not performing the simulations. We need to just understand what they look like. The field of architecture keeps getting broader in that more and more disciplines and fields are involved in the making of buildings. And it keeps getting narrower in the sense that they are becoming ideally more integrative. There are some really great examples out there in the world where air flows through perforated structures for example, or facades are dynamic and form the skin of the building but also affect the environmental performance of it. There is much more integration potential; that seems to be the future of the profession. But only great architects know how to make great buildings. And you can be really good at a lot of things and talk about architecture, but still not be able to be a good architect. We should train people to be good architects.

Lisa Iwamoto finds conceptual art fascinating. It impacts her design.

To do this, we have to be able to do building information modeling to communicate more effectively with consultants. The big hindrances in all of this so far are the contractors. I've been to a number of symposia, and what I have seen is that in this country, the really high-end work is done from façade engineers and window manufacturers from Germany or Canada or Japan, but not from the US.

My own education did not necessarily prepare me for practice. The kind of structural engineering I did was so different. It was analysis, completely abstracted, and the design was a single line diagram of steel frames and foundations and stuff like that. That is pretty different from what it takes to put a building envelope together. Do I feel prepared in that I can figure it out? Yes. I absolutely feel that I can figure it out. Have I done it before? Some of it. I have worked in offices, and I have work experience where I specifically did focus on detailing and construction documents. So yes, I feel prepared in that sense. But I still think it is different from having gone through an education where I was armed with every tool I needed in my tool belt. Instead, I think what I was armed with was a certain kind of confidence. I feel I could figure it out if I needed to.

To become a licensed architect in the US you have to get a professional architecture degree and do a three-year internship after you graduate. If you are in Spain or Switzerland or Germany or Japan, and you go to schools there, you can design a building and stamp it and do your preliminary structural calculations, do cost estimates. That is the only thing you need to do to get that building built the minute you graduate. We don't have that model here. In America, you work for a little while, then you take eleven licensing exams, and you are able to do those things; you can actually call yourself an architect. It seems to me that the more professional education became in other countries, the less professional education became here in the US. We focus far more on conceptual, intellectual understandings or just framing of architecture than those kinds of schools in Spain, Germany, and Switzerland. That's good and bad. It is bad because we don't get to make great buildings coming out of school. But I think it is productive in the sense that we are a leader in leading-edge design, in computational and other techniques and form and concept. Some people come here to get their education and then go back to the country they were from and are able to build, to become a leading architect because they have had an education in the US. So I think we are doing some things right. Does it have to be at the expense of professional knowledge? I don't know. I haven't really seen it working that well. I think we picked a side, but it would be great if the two systems were more combined.

What impacts my design is that I really enjoy conceptual art and art practice. One of my colleagues told me that whatever invention is in architecture, artists have done it twenty years before. I don't know if that is true or not. I wasn't keeping track. But I certainly find the world of conceptual art really fascinating. I find it fascinating from the 1950s and 60s too. My partner Craig and I enjoy looking at and studying the work of a number of people like **Eva Hesse**, **Tom Friedman**, **Ann Hamilton**, and **Gerhard Richter**. We enjoy art and this influences our work. On the other hand, things that influence our work are things that are just cool, like things just out in the world. And a lot of the things that happen in the front yard are often more interesting than the really high design building next door. We like to keep our eyes open. Well, I cheat because it's Craig who discovers a lot on the Internet. If I could calculate the hours . . . He is an avid collector of not just art but a number of things. It is just in his personality. If he was not an architect, he would be collecting information of other stuff: music, motorcycles, cars, cute animals, art work, picture of nature, tons of stuff. We have been together for 25 years, so he knows what I am interested in. He shows me things that he thinks I will be interested in. So I have a very easy person's way of looking for things. But I would say I look more when I am trying to find something. I research more focused. I am not a general collector of stuff.

Craig is really easy-going. Whereas I might see there is one way to do things, he thinks there is a ton of ways to do things. And if it is this way, it could be really great because of that, and if it's this other way, it could be really great because of that. I met Craig when I was still an engineer. I hadn't started studying architecture yet. And then we overlapped in school together, and then we had overlapping work where I was interning at **Morphosis,** and he was an employee there, and then we worked in different firms for a while, while we were living in Boston, and then we started teaching at the same institution, at Michigan for a while, and then formed our practice. But now we are teaching at separate institutions. So we have a big part of our lives that is also separate and always has been in some way.

I definitely don't think we separate work and relationship. We sit across from each other at the office, we have plenty of talk at the end of the day, we have plenty to talk about during the day. It is pretty seamless, I have to say. We get along really well. We find a lot of the same things funny and interesting. We find a lot of the same things stupid. And we are also complementary. Work and relationship are really intertwined. I would imagine it would be hard for an architect to be married to a non-architect. But maybe not.

We are not each 50 percent on every project. It is equal on the whole, but not every project is equal. But it's not 90/10 either. I would say it's like 60/40. Both of us are involved in every project. And we have very similar design sensibilities. I don't know if that just happened because we grew up together architecturally or because that's just who we are. But sensibility is a really important thing because a judgment about how you want something to be or look or be designed is something that is sort of ... you can't change someone, right? So luckily we have very similar design sensibilities. If Craig is talking with one of our people who is working for us on something, I am comfortable not having to go over there too. And vice versa. What I would talk about is going to be similar to what he does. Now our office doesn't always think so. They say, "Well, Craig said this and you are saying that." But the differences are quite minor. Yes, it may mean that you may have to redo that thing or that has got to change a little bit. But it is never by a very big degree. We are quite interchangeable. Actually one of the things we complain about is that we are too similar because we don't have the business partner or the marketing person or the production manager. We both like doing the same things like working on the design.

We would happily practice in Los Angeles or New York, and if we were from another country, we would probably go there because it is much easier to build good buildings, especially for a more boutique practice. But Craig and I both grew up just a few miles from each other in north Berkeley. Our families were friends from when we were very little. We didn't know each other then. So it was home. We both have a degree from Harvard. I got a position teaching at Berkeley, and now Craig is involved in the California College of the Arts, which is a very great school. That is why we practice in San Francisco.

Our most challenging commission was one I didn't work on at all. It was a house for Craig's parents. So we'll just stop the conversation there. What is the second most challenging? I think that would have been a really early residential project that we did. Back then we weren't confident in what we brought to the table, and we hadn't had as much experience with client management. Although we ended up with a really nice design, it was very difficult to convince the clients that they needed to spend money on specific elements to make the project worth it. We would constantly be out-voted by the contractor, who wasn't great and finally just kind of did the project. We aren't 100 percent sure how it turned out. I'm sure the basic schematics are there but in many other ways, it probably didn't end up so well. Now we have clients who trust us a lot more, and we've earned that trust too. Most of our clients are repeat clients. Some are small scale developers and some even residential clients. So we've built up a relationship.

We really want to get the bricks and mortar part of our practice going. We've done a little bit of work, but we really need to do more work. Yes, we did the Edgar Street Tower — a parametric design — but that tower was not getting built. We mostly explore parametric design through installations, as smaller scale work or even a small part of a bigger project. It's not whole buildings for us at the moment. We're not **Frank Gehry**.

We want to get stuff built. And so houses are definitely a part of that, a part of doing that kind of work. We actually have a fabulous project that we haven't even started yet, but the client is just wonderful. And so we think it is going to be a great project because they think like we do — that design is a value. Design is an added value to a project.

It is important to recognize that where we are born has a profound influence on what we become. Costa Rica is an intense place. Its nature is raw, and it is powerful. Perennial rains saturate and ravage the built environment. People are highly aware of the fragility of what they build, that is, the temporal quality of buildings. An enormous effort is made to build the best way possible with limited resources. Still, as it happens in most developing countries, we do not build our cities well, we waste substantial amounts of energy and materials in the process. It is the opposite of what happens, for instance, when a tree falls in the rain forest. A fall advances the ecological sustenance of the whole place; it does not turn into a tragedy or a waste of resources. It becomes a new engine of activity and production, a constructive future that benefits all species inhabiting that ecosystem. In our contemporary cities, we plan and build for future waste as our buildings become either paper-thin or irrelevant in order to sustain an indifferent, ruthless market. We understand time as a formulaic response to present wants, oblivious to time's more beneficial lessons already cast in the past as they are also cast to the future.

For **Carlos Jiménez** it's not about the myth of starting over because we can't escape the past.

I see architecture as an opportunity to understand the value and investment that time brings to the work. Time is as marvelous a material as light is in shaping and informing the life of any work. Architecture builds time as it releases an awareness of its countless lessons. There is a simultaneity in this release, allowing us to inhabit a place constructed by the past, the present, and the future. Sometimes I talk about architecture in terms of light, in terms of materials, in terms of the city, but if pressed to define what architecture is, I would define it as building time. This awareness affects how I design, how I build, how I try to make something last, not solely at the level of durability, but for the work to be enjoyed, projected and transformed in time. An architecture that reflects only a single tense of time has a short, limited duration. I have been exploring these concerns through the ongoing construction of my house and studio — a work that is altered, added to, subtracted from, learned from, that is, a work that grows in time. It doesn't have to be demolished to its foundations to make something else happen. After all, it is the arrival of each day that is truly new, and all I need is some corner in my studio to sit, think, draw, or simply just look out the window. This is my place to get lost in time, or as **Aldo Rossi** intimated, a place where one can forget about architecture, a paradoxical condition that transcends any given spatial circumstance.

I lived in Costa Rica for almost 15 years. It was a wonderful environment to grow up in, a fusion of landscapes from industrious rainforests, mountainous coffee farms, to primeval seashores. It was a world that my parents harnessed as hard-working, enterprising coffee farmers. My father died suddenly in a tragic accident. I was only three years old at the time. I have no memory of him, but I do remember the many things that he built on the farm: a wood-framed house here, a market shed there, even a small, delicate church wrapped in zinc sheets. My father loved building things. I was not told of his accidental death for some time, or maybe I blocked it from my memory. I heard in a whisper that he was traveling somewhere or something to that effect. As time went by, I would trace him in the things that he had built. I became fascinated by these objects in the landscape and their connection to a person's will, memory, and action. Every summer, I would engage my younger brother, nieces, and nephews on small construction projects, from tree houses to small farm buildings, claiming our modest stake in the intense tropical landscape that otherwise would overwhelm us.

Eventually, we moved to the capital city of San Jose. Growing up in the bustling city in the mid-60s and early 70s, I was fascinated by the large signs that I would see at building sites, large perspectival drawings of the structures that would soon emerge from this or that other site. I was further intrigued by observing their gradual construction, one floor at a time. Watching this building activity as if it were a live theater performance made an indelible impression on me. I moved to the United States soon after I turned 15, finished high school, and started studying architecture. I graduated from college and soon after I started building my house and studio in my adopted city of Houston. During this time, I did things impulsively and with an open grain of naivety. I got myself into some financial trouble by building my first free-standing project using several credit cards at once. In the end, it all worked out, and I began to work with my first client, and then another, and another.

I have been very fortunate to work from one project to the next as a continuum as if following a natural set of circumstances. Sometimes I turn down some work so that I can maintain this pace of work, sometimes at great risk as the project might be postponed or canceled. I start with my client's narrative foremost in my mind. I follow it with a reciprocal interview, they interview me, I interview them. I ask many questions that go on for some time. I seldom talk about fees at this stage, I do not want fees to be a factor of such a consequential decision.

I work first with intuitive concepts through sketches, drawings, reflections, and study models, to sense and establish a common endeavor with all aspirations related to the work. Once I begin to feel the workings of a mutually supportive and reciprocal relationship, I articulate the project in more precise ways. I rely on and trust my intuition not only at the initial stages of a project but as I develop the work in the studio.

We recently finished a large art school in Philadelphia, a challenging project on many levels, primarily due to the fact that we did not have an advocate in the institution that commissioned the work. Their indifferent, removed attitude pervaded the process, which caused me a great deal of anxiety. I considered withdrawing from the project several times, but I was so taken with the artists, our true client, that we kept pushing, enduring on their behalf. I realized that though we were not working in the most ideal situation, our withdrawal would have added further detriment to an already difficult project. That is why it is so critical to have an advocate, a steadfast client for any work of architecture, regardless of budget or constraints.

I often ask my clients to imagine their project 10 years from the moment it is built, and we may be sitting in their living room, or their library. I then ask them what they would like their friends or relatives to remember about their house, something they can take with them like a memento or a postcard. It often turns out to be a view, a vista into an intimate or vast landscape, the feeling of light discreetly dancing in the space, a sound, or a texture, fragments, interludes, moments, ephemeral yet lasting images of architecture. I much prefer an architecture that invites you to ask questions. A work is always more interesting when it reverberates with questions. Why is that window placed there? Why is this door so narrow or so tall? Why choose this material and not this other one? The answers are not as important, and the questions vacillate from casual to significant. It is a liberating process that allows us to be curious, observant, and less likely to overlook architecture's nuances. It is akin to the moment one reads a poem, and a few words construct an indelible set of images.

I like to see my projects growing like a tree, nurtured, and being cared for. I get enormous satisfaction when I see people taking good care of their buildings. I think that sometimes architecture is much like designing a shoe. The pleasure of the shoe resides in how it fits its user, not its designer. A brand is the least interesting thing about a shoe. Perhaps at the beginning, the shoes may feel tight or slightly uncomfortable, but if they were designed with walking as the critical consideration, they get softer, easier to fit or to run with them. They even achieve beauty when resting at night, or as they weather or wrinkle with use. I desire these qualities in my architecture, the full experience of the work as it unfolds in whatever amount of time it is to last. A few years ago, I visited **Alvar Aalto**'s *Villa Mairea* and stayed at a guest house nearby. During my stay, I felt an overwhelming sense of happiness as I was able to experience this bountiful work of architecture, a marvelous house that could have been designed one hundred years ago or one hundred years hence. I could feel the indisputable presence of its designer, but Aalto never gets in the way, it is more like he is there quietly narrating the multiple experiences that the work unfolds. Villa Mairea demonstrates how much a generous work of architecture communicates about our common humanity, who we are, what we do, and how we engage and participate in the world to do our best and beyond.

Architecture is not an easy undertaking; its pursuit is riddled with as many complexities and contradictions as there can be. Yet, its objective remains always clear and direct: to make our lives better. Architecture is also a frame that enhances our experience of the world. Lately, we have become quite proficient at producing architecture as "merchandise" as a friend likes to call it, as its material and social and spiritual value decreases from the moment it is built. It is not just the explicit whims of the market but also the insatiable capitalism that now consumes our planet. We are all caught in the consequences of this brutal appetite. I often tell my wife Clare that under this all-consuming reality, one can never stop fighting for one's freedom. This is a freedom that we earn daily through our deeds, accountability, and generosity to others. Understanding and appreciating the virtue of limits is another way of countering the state of our conflicted times. We do not need much to be in the world, and the most valuable things in life cannot be purchased. I am reminded of the 2008 financial crisis and its devastating effects on our profession. My studio for one lost a wonderful project in Spain just as we were starting the working drawings. Yes, I was disappointed, but mostly I felt so grateful for the many experiences I had already acquired: from traveling to Valencia several times to eating the most exquisite paellas, having memorable conversations about the medieval Valencian poet Ausias March to meeting the most enthusiastic community leaders. I had become richer and wiser in knowledge from a project that suddenly lost all of its material capital. One has to survive and transcend these turns as they will always come to be, and it is never easy for anyone. When a tree falls in the rain forest, it is for a reason, or to paraphrase Leonard Cohen, "That's how the light gets in."

I think I discovered a love for architecture when I fell in love with a boy who was an architecture student. I had been very involved in music; I was in a conservatory and had been very focused on that. When I decided that I didn't want to do that anymore, all of a sudden, not having this thing that I had been so focused on meant that I was a little unsure of what to do, and I found a lot of things interesting. At that moment, I suppose everything was interesting, but architecture had a little bit of a bonus. I was a student in New York, and architecture was not at a very interesting moment in its history, not really. Things were ending: the *Institute for Architecture and Urban Studies*, for example, was on its last legs, and Columbia was a very sleepy and quiet place. And when architecture started to kind of rev up again, it was very interesting to witness because it seemed like it had a long way to go, it had a steep learning curve, there was a lot to do, and that was exciting.

To **Sylvia Lavin** the word is everything.

I certainly think the romantic model of the architect as a solitary, self inspiring creator of immaculate ideas has been replaced. Architecture, as a discipline, came to that image late. As a historical figure, the architect earned the right to think of himself as an artist much later than others did. The architect had to work harder throughout the long history of modern architecture to maintain that image, and, therefore, is more reluctant to give it up. Some architects are really struggling with the loss of that self-image. But, no man is an island. It's been a very useful fiction. I think it's being replaced by other kinds of fictions that have to do with intelligence in relationship to technology and social forces and other kinds of inhuman systems of which the architect is a part.

"What makes you tick?" is actually a common question to an architect, and it's that kind of question that is part of the apparatus that produces the idea that the architect operates in the realm of talent and imagination, which is to say something that begins with an intuition, and that its becoming architecture is a process of that private thought's becoming public. I think that would be the way to understand the trajectory of architecture. And so in some way, for the figure of the architect, to be asked personal questions is not only not different from what he does as an architect, but is reinforcing to the way he presents himself as one.

I come from the perspective, not the architect, but the historian, and historians and critics are generally not treated that way. They are generally not thought of as operating through talent and genius, they are generally not thought of as having an inner personal life that becomes public through their work. The cliché is that historians and critics are dealing with facts and the feelings of others, and that any betrayal of their own personal feelings — or any registration of their own personal feelings in their work — is a kind of betrayal of the architect, in fact. I hadn't thought of the relationship of the critic/historian to the architect in exactly that way, but I'm now thinking about work that's happening on historiography, which is to say people writing about writers, and thinking about whether this kind of question then will begin to unfold also the way we think about the history of writing in a new, maybe more or less personal way.

I am relentlessly fascinated by the moments in which architecture appears or maybe more explicitly, can be made to appear in unexpected places. In some way, I am a product of the post-Eisenman universe and, therefore, I cannot not think outside the concept of the discipline. The distinction between the discipline and the profession is like the air I breathe, even though I understand it to be historically constructed. But because I understand that my "truth" is itself a fiction, I feel that it's interesting to look at those moments in which the facticity of the discipline and its fictional nature collide. That I find really fascinating because it's both affirming of the discipline and diminishing of it at the same time, which I think is an appropriate response.

One of the things that makes me most like the typical architect is that I consider myself to be a hunter of interesting phenomena in popular culture, and I use those phenomena to rethink things about architecture. Right now, I'm working on real estate speculation and how it affects architecture. Now, of course, real estate speculation has always affected architecture, but these days, it seems to me it's affecting it in a way that really gets at the core of the discipline, in ways that make it impossible to maintain the difference between building and the discipline, and I find that super interesting.

My interest in hoarding, curating, it didn't seem so hard to get to that question of how much is too much. I think that that might be a question that we could ask of many institutions today, architectural institutions, which have expanded. When you think about schools, they're huge in number, with satellites and global outreach, and they're collecting students. I think there are reasons for collecting students, not all of them have to do with educating more and more people. Schools are being asked to run more and more on their own independent economies, and students are resource units. So I think it's an interesting question, when is enough enough? And so hoarding, for me, just opened up a whole series of different kinds of questions. It's part of a strategy that I hope I have found ways that are repeating in other areas, even though they may or may not look anything like hoarding.

I also do work as a curator. The discussion of hoarding came up in the context of a conference on curating, collecting, and museums. And so it has been interesting for me to think about how we show work. There really are mandates about how we show work, and things are framed, and they're separated from one another, and they're seen according to a certain visual object. I think it's important to start showing work not in that way. And that could mean a couple of things. It could mean, for example, changes in the actual display strategies of an exhibition.

I can give an example: Jeff Kipnis did a show of Wolf Prix's work, and the installation amounted to a very large table, and very high for someone my height. I'm short, and I almost had to go on tiptoes in order to see it. For a person of more normal height, it would have been more at eye level. But on this giant table were all Coop Himmelb(l)au's models jammed together. So, without super careful attention, it wasn't easy to tell one project from another. That was an example of hoarding, but one which, on the other hand, produced quite an extraordinary effect, wherein all of those buildings produced a city. They produced a hypothetical city, a city that Coop Himmelb(l)au will never get to make, but that made it very clear that the interpretation of the Coop Himmelb(l)au's work was that it imagined a new kind of urban fabric that were it possible to produce, would look something like this. It was a kind of speculation that a more traditional form of curating wouldn't have been able to produce. The use of the concept of hoarding is part of a change of ideas.

Another has to do with showing and thinking about objects that people don't usually look at as objects, such as working drawings. Working drawings have a very uncomfortable, if not to say, invisible relationship to disciplinarity. There is a line in the drawing set that you can mark, generally speaking, this way, that this part of the drawing belongs to disciplinarity, and this part of the drawing belongs to building construction, the professional apparatus, et cetera. So it would be part of my strategic interest in crossing that line by looking right simply at the one just above and the one below and interrogating the differences there.

And that is even though it's not about excess — a kind of hoarding view in the sense that it puts something that belongs, that is not intrinsically wrong, but it puts it in the wrong place. This is the thing about hoarding that I found so incredibly interesting that 10 frying pans in the kitchen are reasonable if you're a chef. And if you're not a chef, and the frying pans are in the kitchen, something else has happened, so that it's a placement and program issue. To take a working drawing of a certain kind and to look at it as though it were art would be like taking the frying pans and putting them in the wrong room, and seeing what they do there.

I have written on a wide range of topics in very wide ways, and in very wide settings, maybe with more diversity in tone, in topic, and structure than most of my colleagues. Whether that's a failing on my part that I do a little bit of everything, or whether it's because I believe in being adaptive to changing circumstances, but I would say that the world changes and we risk becoming an intellectual police force if we don't adapt to current concerns.

The translation from one media into another always produces fascinating incidental transformations. My experience of that is probably more as a teacher, which is to say that I make concepts available to students, and then it's often not recognizable what it is that they do with them. Sometimes they get better, sometimes they don't, but the process is always interesting.

With writing, oh, my God, I would feel that writing is always way too much. I would never feel that it's not enough. Writing is like a vindictive master, it's always out of control. I, of course, think the word is everything. Inventing, making the concept available is, for me, a more profound or more generous, maybe, act than using it. So I would definitely hope that I make concepts available, and that's what I make. It's not that I don't make and others make; that is what I make, the form takes that.

My exhilarating experience with architecture? Oh, that's very tough. I generally like to be positive and enthusiastic, and I will say I have recently become a little bored with the field. I feel that there are interesting things that I'm sure are about to happen, but I just don't totally feel that they're happening now. So I would have to go back, which is kind of not good. The most exhilarating... No, I actually think I can't say going to see a new building, having a new idea, hearing a new idea, they're all little moments of exhilaration. I have moments, still, and historically have had moments of radical transformation. I'm just trying to think that it starts to like feel like a repetition kind of thing, so it just seems so depressing to say that there is no exhilaration after youth. That can't possibly be the answer.

But I remember, when I was a student — my advanced degree is in art history — one of the most interesting things that were happening was the rise of women artists. Artists that we now think of as the foundational cadre of a certain form of postmodernism, photographers **Sherrie Levine** and **Cindy Sherman**, and people like that. It was just a coincidence that I took a course on Vienna's art history. I was at Columbia, and there was a Viennese scholar, and because it was largely an art historical program, I sort of took anything that had some architectural component. There was a lot of architecture in Vienna at the turn of the century, so there I was. I had learned a little something about **Egon Schiele**, and I was downtown one day, and I idly walked into the New Museum, and I came across some Egon Schieles. And I thought, oh, well, isn't that interesting to find these here when I happen to be taking this class. And as I started looking at them in an art-historical way, I looked at the label; maybe I'll have to say which of these are on a test. And they were all labeled "Sherrie Levine." What is going on here? And as I worked through this strange concatenation of phenomena, the world really was not the same for me after that day. It was a radical re-understanding of what a work of art was, what a museum was, what identity was, what a woman was, all of those things. It was very important to me.My worst encounter with architecture?

Oh, my God, the world is full of shit of all kinds. I mean, if we started paying attention to all of it, we'd throw ourselves under a bus .... The worst would have to be something in which I had expectations that it would be better than it was. Expecting the worst and finding it is not much of a surprise, the worst is expecting the good and finding disappointment. If I look at a hotel online and I get there, and the sheets are shitty, and I am very disappointed. I mean, there would be that kind of building of expectation that's based on certain kinds of images, and I guess I would say that I'm probably a good enough of a researcher that I don't go if I'm not interested already. I protect myself from those kinds of disappointments. Here's the thing: The disappointments are many and constant because we can't control what we have to see in daily life. But in moments of focus, I go where I'm already interested, so I think I probably don't get all that disappointed. Yeah, I would probably avoid it.

I grew up in New York and in Rome and went back and forth a lot. And this makes me think of two things. One was that I have a very strong memory of seeing the Harlem Globetrotters in Rome, playing basketball in the *Palazzo dello Sport* by **Nervi**. I remember this with an incredible intensity, not only because the basketball was insane and crazy and kooky, and what were these giant black Americans doing in Rome in the first place, but it was almost as though this kind of neo Frank Lloyd Wrightian, organic, hyperbolically structured building itself was like the basketball players. And having the sort of quotidian experiences like going to a basketball game framed by an intelligent building, and to do that without even being aware of it, I think that that's an incredible thing. I feel the same way about the **Saarinen** *TWA building* because I spent a lot of time in that building as an airport and as a pre architectural critic; in other words, not with the focused view of a formalist. And, indeed, the plane trip began in the building, in a way that it absolutely does not now. And so the special building as part of everyday life I think is an extraordinary thing, and is one that relatively few people, including me, don't have.

What is a good architect? I mean, those questions of value are very tricky. You can have a good architect that does an uninteresting building; you can have really interesting architects that don't do much building. It really depends on what your criteria are, and I don't think there is any one stable and systematic set. We have to ask when, and why, and under what circumstances. Lots of people are becoming interesting now, who were not thought of as interesting then. Lots of people who were thought of as very interesting then are becoming not so interesting now, and that will again change. For me, because of what it is that I do, an interesting architect is somebody I can make a good argument about.

When I glimpse into the future of architecture, I see a table of Wolf Prix's models becoming the City. I have to say I'm a little bit sad to say this right now, but for the next little while, I see a lot more architecture, like a lot of design, there's a lot of design going on. Good design is becoming commonplace in a way. It will be interesting to see whether the becoming commonplace of good architecture is a realization of the modernist's dream of good architecture for all, or whether the problem with architecture is that it is a cut in the commonplace. I think that's a real question, and I'm interested in witnessing the unfolding, but I don't know who will win.

The church is what got me into architecture. When I was an undergraduate in English literature at Washington and Lee University, they only had housing for freshmen, so after that, you had to find off-campus housing. And I bought an old church. Don't ask me why. I just came across this old, abandoned church, and I thought that seemed kind of cool. And it was ten thousand dollars, and I talked to a friend of mine, and Bill and I bought this with our savings, convinced our fathers to sign the mortgage papers, and then we rented it out to friends, and pretty much lived for free for three years.

Olle Lundberg: The Church made me do it!

I had experience working as a carpenter's helper and road crews and I had been involved in the physical end of building as a high school kid. I enjoyed it. So, the design side came out of the sculpture. The sculpture was really a result of just finishing my English major about a year early. I needed more credits but didn't really need more English courses, so I decided to get another degree in sculpture, which was fun and got me more involved in visual arts, composition, and things like that. And that, combined with the experience of the church, led me to Virginia, the architecture school, which was a great program for me. It is a good program for people with diverse interests but not necessarily a lot of experience in the architectural field because they are fairly patient and value the differing perspectives that unusual backgrounds give to the university. So I went to school there then worked for two years for a firm called VMDO in Charlottesville, which I think now is the largest firm in Charlottesville. And then I decided I didn't want to do brick buildings anymore, so I moved to San Francisco. They do have the Jeffersonian curse there in Charlottesville.

Here we have a four thousand square foot shop for metal fabrication as part of our office. It is in a neighborhood in San Francisco called Dogpatch, which is one of the few neighborhoods that is left that still has a fair amount of manufacturing and residential still in it. So it is perfect for us because we can make noise. Nobody really complains. The MUNI yard is right behind us, they make way more noise than we ever will. The Hells Angels are right next door. Their Harleys make way more noise than we do. It is a good neighborhood and we are very fortunate to have bought the building when we did, which is about fifteen years ago because honestly, that amount of shop space in San Francisco would no longer make sense. I would make way more money by renting it out than I do by having it as a shop.

The shop is both the literal and the functional center of the building. And it is a great space. The shop occupies really the middle of the building. It is one floor below the office, but it is a double-height space. The office is at the front of the building. The shop is really in the middle, and then my apartment is in the back. So we kind of surround the shop. It has become critical to us as a design firm. It is what I think defines us from our competition. But also defines how we work.

We use the shop in a variety of ways. I think the most obvious way is we use it as a laboratory for ideas. We are materials guys. We love new materials, different materials, combining materials, detailing, all of the things that get us involved in kind of a materials science. And the shop allows us to experiment with that. I find that the process of building things will inspire design. Some people see it as the opposite. I don't. I find that when you understand how things can go together, how they can connect, how you can resolve these intersections, new ideas spring up. And also, the nice thing is they are ideas that tend to work because you can actually test them and make sure they work rather than something that you kind of draw on paper and then hope something can actually make it happen. So I think our buildings are technically very sophisticated, I think that we pride ourselves on good detailing, on interesting and innovative use of materials, and I think that the shop as a laboratory is invaluable for that. The other thing is that we use it for is marketing. You know, a lot of clients hear stories about architects: they are great visionaries, but you try to build a building and nothing works. You have probably seen a few of those in your day. I have too. You walk into our building and see a shop there, and you know that that is not going to be true of our buildings. And it is not. And honestly, I don't know anybody else that is doing this. This lets us stand apart. Architecture is a competitive field, and this is one way for us to be noticed.

I think there is one other thing about the shop that is really important. One, since we are not really a design-build firm, we are building signature pieces for our projects. But there is always a contractor on board, and we are always working with that contractor. The shop encourages, first of all, a more collaborative relationship between us and the contractor. And we can help them out sometimes when they run into problems. And of course, there is a quid pro quo. We can get them to help us out when there is an issue we see. Having that kind of close relationship fostered by the ability to actually make things can be invaluable when you are trying to do essentially perfect work, which I think our detailing often demands. The other thing is that when you build something as opposed to designing something, it is a gift. No matter what you charge for it, you are handing something over that you made by hand. And this notion of craft, and introducing craft into our work, and making that craft almost an object as a gift makes the work very personal. That is how we connect with clients, and that is what we are trying to do. We are trying to give them a work of architecture that, at the end of the day, they don't think anyone else can give them.

My favorite project is always the one I am currently working on. But we have had a couple that have been extraordinary projects for us. The *Ellison House* changed our practice forever, and I will always be indebted to Larry Ellison for having hired us at a time when I think everyone in the world thought he was crazy to hire us. I think that the Hourglass Winery in Calistoga that we finished a couple years ago on some level is one of my favorite projects because my thesis was a winery when I was at UVA, and I have always wanted to do a winery. I have always thought that the relationship of the landscape to the building in a winery is unique. It is unlike anything else. It is so literal. The product is coming out of the land. It is just this very geometric landscape that then flows into the building and then flows back out of the building. And it is this amazing combination of science because there is all this laboratory stuff and stainless steel and all that, and art, because at the end of the day, if they all knew how to make good wine, they all would. And there is this component of magic that nobody quite can quantify, which is a great opportunity for an architect. The interesting thing about *Hour Glass* is that we ended up talking the client out of doing a building. It is really more of a shutter and roof that a building itself. But that was a good solution for that project. And then *Slanted Door Restaurant*, which was the first restaurant that we did for Charles Phan, the first restaurant we did for anyone. Charles this year is up for the national James Beard Chef of the Year award. For Charles to have hired us when we had never done a restaurant before, I mean he was a rock star then, he is really a rock star now, but that was again an extraordinary leap on behalf of a client, and I will always be indebted to Charles for doing that one. And since then, we have done six more restaurants for him, and we are doing one more now in New York. The one in New York now is certainly one of my favorite projects. We are also doing a house in Hawaii, which I think is going to be an extraordinary project. It is a very well-known client in the tech world, and we have a nondisclosure agreement so we probably won't get to publish it. It is an amazing project with an amazing budget.

But the challenge when you are doing projects with that kind of budget is: how do you edit yourself? Because the immediate temptation is to do everything you wanted to do, right? That is really bad. And we have all seen architecture like that, and it is not good. So on Ellison, that was the first chance we had where we had really had no budget and I thought we were very good. The best thing we did there was editing ourselves, and I think on this one, called the K96 project, we have edited it way down. It is a simple, elegant, very Hawaiian house, certainly inspired by the site and the client, and I think it will be one of our best projects yet.

Our firm tends to be the perfect example of where architecture is not going because we tend to instinctively rebel against anything we see as sort of mainstream or a general direction. I think that architecture is just becoming more and more specialized. Firms are becoming experts of particular building types, and they market themselves that way. At the end of the day, architecture is about marketing. How do you get work and how do you market your firm? It is standard that firms try to set up these areas of expertise and then push those. We are always going after projects we have never done before. We have been reasonably successful at it. My goal is to do one of each before I stop doing this. I probably won't get there, but we have been surprisingly successful at it. And we just try to market ourselves as designers. We say: well, if you have seen a building that you like, and you want one of those, then you might want to go hire that guy. But if you actually haven't seen the building you like, maybe you should consider us. Of course, after we do one, then we say we are experts and then, you know … but I think that unfortunately, architecture is going to go more and more in that direction. It will be interesting to see if, at some point, there is a reaction on behalf of clients to maybe not choose that because a lot of the work that you see from the expert firms starts looking a lot alike. And I think that is — I am not really blaming them — I think it is almost inevitable if you are working on the same kind of problem over and over: you know there are solutions that work there, and you tend to recycle them. That is the great thing about houses and why I think we will always do houses is that they are the one building type that is infinitely varied, and they are very personal, and they are fun for that reason. For the same reason, they are often a bad idea from a business point of view because they take a lot of time because there is no solution at hand. You have to find out what that is.

What else about architecture? I think one of the things that we are seeing is that as a culture, there is an alienation from our buildings on some level. There is a loss of a sense of craft, of the handmade, of the personal object. And it is not just in building. It is throughout our entire lives. We tend to be surrounded by objects that everyone else has as well. One of the things we are trying to do is keep that notion of craft alive in our buildings, not only to encourage the craftsmen but also because I think keeping those crafts alive is an important thing in our culture. I think if you go through your favorite pieces of architecture in the world, most of them have those pieces in them. And it is funny, I just think that that is going to continue to be important and I think maybe more firms will embrace that a little bit even if it is just for the signature pieces. I recognize that you can't do that on an entire building without an extraordinary budget. Fortunately, sometimes we get those budgets. But certainly, we also do very inexpensive buildings as well. Even when we do those, we are always looking at the opportunity for that one little gesture that will make it give a touch of the human.

I would love to do a water treatment plant because they are very sculptural. They are not bogged down by the typical constraints of a building, like they don't need windows. They are mostly sculptural forms, and there is all this water and all of this stuff. I think they are often an underutilized opportunity. And of course, they have to do with landscape, and site, and grading, and all of that, because they are very much tied into the flow. So those are kind of cool. It would be nice to do one of those. I have always wanted to do a golf clubhouse because I have never seen a good modern golf clubhouse. I am not sure there are enough cool golfers in the world that need one. But you never know, maybe. Golf, you know, is becoming cooler. For a while, Tiger made it cool. Now, not so good, but you know. So that would be sort of interesting. But, you know, I like any kind of building. With the right client, any kind of building is good. The wineries are still ... I would like to do more wineries. The Napa area is really remarkably traditional. They are mostly these faux Tuscan things. There is just not a big market for modern wineries, but I am hoping we will get another one at some point. Maybe this time we will do a real building.

For me, it was architecture, architecture, architecture, from the time I was five. In fact, I have a friend who was always setting up crazy things for us to do, and we went to this guy, Michael Lutin, who writes the horoscopes for the New York Post, and he had his horoscope done. When I walked in, Michael Lutin looked up and said, "You get up for architecture, you work for architecture, you do it in the morning, afternoon, evening. That's all there is, there's nothing else out there." Well, at least I chose the right job.

I'm in that mindset all the time. If there were anything that I would have possibly done differently, I would have tracked more into the fine arts. That's also why I ended up in so many artists' studios. There is a split that's occurring within my practice, because initially, my studio was always in artists' studios in New York, which is where I feel comfortable. At a certain point, my partner demanded that it be in an office building. For me, that's like death. I don't want to be in a space like that.

Victoria Meyers got one thing - Architecture. It's the only thing out there.

For the same reason, I feel that the kids at architecture schools that have been all prettied up don't do good work. If you want to make good work, you want to be in a big, empty factory space with good light, roll up your sleeves, and start making stuff, and not be worried about getting stuff on the floor. Fabrication is a key part of what architects do. There can be no fear of getting the place dirty. I don't really know what it's like up at Cornell these days with their new building. For me, the old building was great because it was just an old gun factory. All the critics complained about it, they all thought that it just wasn't fancy enough. But I didn't want fancy. That was where people made things. It was perfect.

I did my undergrad in civil engineering and art history. The civil engineering studios are not pretty, because that's where they do slump tests, they have these big vibrating machines to sift things, and they have huge machines for pulling stuff apart. These are big concrete rooms with 25-foot ceilings, like a factory. I felt pretty much at home in those as well. Mine wasn't a typical progression, especially, I think, for a woman. I've been on job sites since I was about 17. I'm not sure whether the profession has come to terms with women, but I feel that women have taken the reins in a way in which space has changed. A lot of the spaces of early modernism are really uncomfortable. They are way too dogmatic. Space has become more comfortable, less dogmatic, and a little bit softer, without being intellectually compromised. That, I think, is positive.

I remember going to the University of Illinois at Champaign Urbana, giving a lecture, and staying in this gorgeous modernist house. It was uninhabitable:

it was winter, it was freezing. Some floors were carpeted, but other floors were just raw pebbles. I just remember walking around on these pebbles, and thinking it was a nightmare. The shower hung out of the building, and it was completely uninsulated. Standing in the shower was like standing on an ice cube because it was in the middle of winter. The house was beautiful as a diagram, but who could live here? Obviously, it was designed by a guy.

I have a friend who moved into a very Kahnian diagram I helped her out with, in Washington, D.C., and it was so funny because, again, it was a really dogmatic diagram. It was a cube, and then it had a rotated cube inside, that penetrated the outer cube. The guy didn't have the money for windows, so he just put plywood panels where the light could have come in. My renovation consisted of taking all the plywood off and putting in the glass. Now the house is really beautiful and soft. I just tipped it over into that sensibility.

Most of my friends are pretty much in the arts, which is how I've done so many collaborations like the Bruce Pearson Sculpture Installation. Bruce is probably one of my closest, oldest friends. I would say he is the one person living today who probably has the closest approximation of the personality of John Cage, always smiling, always sweet, always nice, always funny, always intellectually stimulating. My whole group of friends in New York was so great.

I came to a point where I wanted to finish *DWi-P* (Digital Water i-Pavilion), a very important building for me. Partly because it's a culmination of a 15-year argument I had with composer Michael Schumacher. Michael is my sound collaborator, a very close friend, a brilliant person, a composer, musician, and like all artists, slightly crazy. I wanted to get that building done because I had done the book about light, and I wanted to do a book about sound, and I felt that I needed a piece that was big enough to really fill the book. Together with WaveLine and Ojai Festival Shell, I have enough pieces now that I think I can fill it out. I reached a point where I was at a dividing line, and I needed a year in academia to look at the book. Not that I have made much progress in the book, for I'm always getting sidelined.

I look at New York, and it's just not what it used to be. Every day I used to walk by an original neighborhood with the flophouse where Patti Smith lived with Robert Mapplethorpe. They couldn't pay their rent, and he was sick with AIDS, they didn't know what was wrong with him, and their landlord was going to evict them. So Patti Smith put Robert over her shoulder, dragged him through the window, they went out the fire escape in the back, and then she carried him up four blocks to 23rd Street, walked over with him to the Chelsea Hotel, went up to the manager and said, "Look, you don't know who I am. I'm Patti Smith, this is Robert Mapplethorpe. I'm going to be a famous rock 'n roll star, and he's going to be a famous artist, and we need a place to live right now." And that's how they moved there. That was my neighborhood, and I felt like I could walk around, and I felt that stuff. But that is really getting scrubbed out. With gentrification and all these really, really rich people moving in, we no longer have little cubbyholes that artists go into.

For me, the whole issue is about making space in architecture. I'm always looking to make a space so empty that you can't really even put your finger on the fact that there's something there. It's so empty that it's got to be architecture because nobody else could empty it out like this. But that's my goal. And my other goal is that no one ever looks at any of my projects and gets the whiff of any kind of style, trend or fashion statement. For me, that's nauseating. I was not a postmodern person. I always felt that what I should be doing as an architect should be above the style. And that's why today, I like **Louis Kahn**. As a student, I went to see Kahn's building at Exeter. It was funny because I was at Harvard, and at that time at Harvard, they hated Kahn. They all talked about the fact that they thought he was an idiot, a loser, not a good architect. I got there, and I had to walk around the building two or three times to find the front door, and I thought, what is that? Why do I have to walk around the building three or four times to finally find the front door? I went in the door, I stumbled around and I found this main staircase pointing at the glass wall, and I went up and I went into the room and I felt very confronted, and very upset. I hated him, I hated him. And I went through this thing with Lou Kahn of five years of total hate, of waking up in the morning and almost the first thought on my mind was Lou Kahn is an idiot, and I don't know why anyone likes his work, I hate his work. It was so infuriating going into that building. It was five years of a wrestling match, right? And I woke up one morning and I started my Lou Kahn routine, because this was a daily thing, and at a certain moment, I came to a full stop. I did this complete flip. Oh, my God, I love this guy's work.

Good architecture is very emptied out, like the work of Louis Kahn. The first thing he ever did, which made it for him was the Bathhouse, and there's almost nothing there but space. It's great. I also love that he used really poor materials. Except for the British collection at Yale, of course, there he used better quality materials. I'm much happier using bad materials myself. I'm much happier using the cheapest thing I can get my hands on because I have so much more freedom. First of all, the client isn't as stressed. As the budget goes up, the client gets angrier, gets more stressed, and becomes more aggressive. And it's not a good equation for the architect. I don't like working with that much stress. I like relaxing into it because then I can think better. And if I've got a client on the sidelines who's gritting his teeth and sharpening his knives and telling me he's going to kill me, I have a hard time relaxing.

When we did the master plan for the Pratt campus, our whole deal was to say, look, buildings are facing out, let's make them face into the campus. Our

Pratt Pavilion was the first building in that effort. We forcefully took these two other buildings that comprise over 200,000 square feet of space, and with a 10,000 square foot intervention, turned the buildings around. Ours was not an easy building to get built. When **Steven Holl** did his building, the architecture school, which was done right before we started our building, Pratt had a really good person running buildings and grounds, and he was allowed to hire Sciame Construction. But then the school decided to bring this other guy on board who they hired from NYU. He was a nightmare. He basically hired a contractor who had only built concrete block shopping centers and strip malls in New Jersey, behind our back. And that for a highly, delicately detailed building with very special metal panels on it. At the end of the day, for the contractor, it was a bad deal because he ended up developing heart problems from the stress of trying to get the details right. He didn't know how to build this little pavilion in the air, which it had to be because the site was so tight, and we were having to knit these other two larger buildings together.

This guy did everything he could to destroy the project. He fought with us, tooth and nail. He decided that he would not allow us to clad the buildings in metal because he wouldn't give us the money for that. Not even the cheapest metal panels, he said it has to be Dryvit. Then Bruce Gitlin, a board member who owned a metal fabrication plant in Brooklyn, stepped in and donated those panels, which are actually extremely expensive hand-rubbed panels. That's how the building got clad. Then the builder started building a plywood construction in place of our glass entry to the building without telling us. He was going to block off our entry into the building and have people enter into the plywood shed that was already halfway up when I discovered it. My partner, Tom Hanrahan, then handed in his official letter of resignation at Pratt and demanded that either this be fixed or he would be out of there. Finally, they got the guy to back off. That's the difference between the experience we had and the experience that Steve Holl had with Sciame. Had we had Sciame, it would have been a dream. But it's funny to see the difference of how things go with these projects.

When it was done, and the plywood shed was gone, we opened. I finally have gotten this building of some note, which is a public building, built, and there was someone standing next to me and he's taking photos of my building. I told him I was the architect. He put the camera down and said, "Oh, you're the architect. I bet you think I'm taking photos of your building because I like it. I hate that building!" And he said, "I actually am faculty, and I work in that building, and I'm taking photographs because I'm complaining about the building." And he proceeded to become more and more revved up and chased me off the campus. That was a really bad experience. But then I thought about how I had reacted to Lou Kahn. Architecture creates a reaction, and I got a reaction.

The way that it always worked was that we worked on everything together, and if one person dropped the ball, the other person was there to pick it up. There are certain ways in which I like to form things, and I pretty much know when I get it there, but sometimes Tom will do a better job with it. I always know when the cake is baked, but he doesn't. When the cake is baked, I basically put my foot down. And then there is a tug of war because he may want to make changes, but I say no, it's perfect. I think that's a really important skill to have.

When I graduated, I went to New Orleans as a civil engineer for three years, between undergrad and graduate school. What I got from that was less about the technical knowledge, and more about acclimating to being a woman alone in a man's business, a woman alone on a job site, and always feeling like that was my place and that I could stand in my place. I feel I can go into any job site, and the contractors know that I know everything that's going on. I'm not a stranger; I'm part of that crew. I might be a woman, but I know what's in the tool belt. That's a skill set that a lot of women don't get.

Architecture is still a medieval guild because the toolset that the guy brings to that job site today is almost exactly the same toolset that the 13th-century guys brought when they built the cathedrals. But we're in a moment where the guild is broken; computers take away weight and gravity from the visual stuff, which has removed a lot of discipline. One of the difficulties about practice now is that recent graduates will come into the practice and not know things. I'll try to tell students the difference between sandstone, limestone, marble, granite, and they don't care. It's a meaningless conversation for them. And yet there is a claim by so many students that they are so involved and so keen to be involved with sustainability. Well, where do you think that comes from? Understanding materials. They are so in love and enamored with the computer and the gibberish that it lets them produce. At the end of the day, buildings are big objects, and they have to stand in the landscape, and they have to perform.

There's a nuclear arms race amongst critics. I notice, particularly when I go to the schools who are at the top of the feeding pile, the conversation that's going on in the studios is so purely academic that the students are terrified to even make things, and the last thing they want to hear about are the realities of construction, the realities of materials. They just want to impress these critics who are speaking in the most esoteric terms you've ever heard. And they're having a conversation, and a very intense argument amongst themselves, which has absolutely no relevance to what's happening on the ground. There were plenty of times when I got booed out of reviews at various places like Columbia, where all the kids were doing what they thought was very avant-garde, but it was unbuildable. I started having this conversation about how you're doing something like **Frank Gehry**. Frank Gehry is a good builder, and everything he builds is a trabeated post and beam system, and the curves are decorative panels that are attached to that structure. And the kids went berserk and started booing me, and I had to leave. It really takes standing up and talking about the emperor's new clothes and telling people how the stuff is really built.

We did the *Tenth Church of Christ* for the Christian Scientists, with a lot of curves. But this was a client who had a very tight budget. I never would have put the curves in because of their budget. But they wanted curves everywhere. I was working very hard to tone it down and had very difficult arguments with them because they didn't understand the money. And at the end of the day, I ended up bringing the project in at 2.75 million dollars, which was pretty low for what they got, and they were still completely devastated. They had a six-story building and were going to sell off the upper stories to a developer to pay for the work below. In the course of the project, they blew through most of the money that they had, and now they're having a very hard time, they had to lay off staff.

The whole reading room in the front initially had all stainless steel panels again, because the client wanted the stainless and then as the budget crunched, the client rep asked for alternatives. I suggested hot-rolled steel. It's a beautiful material. I prefer it to be stainless. Not as cold as stainless, less than half the price. But the client had a hard time giving up on the stainless. The floors were just raw concrete, which, to me, is beautiful. They wanted something more refined. At the end of the day, they got more church than they could afford, and yet in that case, I don't feel remiss. I think Steven Holl had a go at that church before I did, and his version came in at 5.5, with a contractor that bids at 50 percent of what he's planning on charging you. So he was really at 10.1 million. I came in at 2.75. It's always a shock for the students to find out they're going to have to understand numbers. It's somebody's life savings. It's not free.

I think that as an architect, you have your own toolbox. Color is another thing. Take **Canaletto**, who did these amazing scenes of Venice. Many people did scenes of Venice, but they didn't become famous. Why, what made him different? Canaletto, when painting these scenes, would always choose one or two little spots, little, tiny, minuscule, almost molecular spots where he would put this dollop of canary yellow or crimson red. And when you're looking at it, your eye would always go to that spot, and you could never understand why. But if you get really close, within an inch, you see the dot, and you know why, there it is. With a lot of my work, I put that dot where I want people to look, where I want their mind to go. I'm always playing with those things. If I feel like it doesn't have a spark, it's not crisp enough yet; I want to be able to pull Canaletto out of my pocket. It's a difficult art, too, because you can't do it without building things that cost millions of dollars.

And, unfortunately, there aren't that many people who get to do it. And you can't get better at it unless you are given that opportunity to make things, which is a privilege.

JD: I've always been interested in architecture and visual arts together. And as an undergrad at Harvard, I ended up in Visual and Environmental Studies, an interdisciplinary undergraduate major, really a studio art major, but it included environmental design and film-making. It really was a broad-based visual education, but I'd always had the intention of going to architecture school after that. EB was maybe a little less direct.

EBM: Oh, way less direct. You're like the guy who wanted to do it since you were a little boy. I had originally thought that I was going to do pre-med and be a doctor, but I had always liked art and had drawn quite a bit when I was young, all through high school. When I got to college, I went to Brown, and Brown had this very easy cross-registration with Rhode Island School of Design, so I started taking classes in art and discovered that maybe I didn't want to do medicine. A friend of mine suggested architecture, which I had never thought about. I took an undergraduate studio at RISD, their intro sophomore studio. That was horrible, it kicked my butt. I was hooked, so I did end up double majoring in art and architecture, a lot of architectural history and studio art at Brown, and then decided to go to architecture school. We always wonder about other things we might have done. I think I suffer from that masochistic architecture complex much more than Jeff does. But architecture's been satisfying in a lot of ways. I don't think we can really complain.

E. B. Min and Jeffrey L. Day collaborated using phone and fax machine.

JD: We both went to graduate school at UC Berkeley and worked on some competitions together. After graduate school, we were employed by separate firms, but we occasionally collaborated on projects. And in 2000, I moved to Nebraska to start teaching. Soon after that — we were still collaborating on things long distance - we decided to set up a practice. We really have never had a practice located in one place. It has always been split into multiple locations.

EBM: Most of my experience comes from working for a design-build landscape architecture firm - **Topher Delaney** and **Andrea Cochran**. And after working there for about two, three years, I started getting a couple of projects through them. So Jeff started helping me on the side, outside of his regular job. And then he moved. That was when we first really talked about whether or not we should try practicing together. This was pre-internet, the internet wasn't a big deal yet, nobody had DSL, everything was still dial-up, there was no shared anything, and so everybody thought we were crazy. But we thought that Nebraska would open up opportunities. Especially being young architects, we were looking for opportunities. We thought it could be really interesting.

JD: Collaborating has become easier, fortunately. Certainly, the logistics of running a practice are easier with broadband internet pretty much anywhere you want to go. Storage online is easy. Everything is essentially shared online. All of our business management software is online. Location doesn't really become that important. Contrary to that is that our offices are very material and messy, and they're full of models and stuff. Although the practice tends to operate virtually, there is still all this physical stuff that is located in our spaces.

EBM: But when we started our practice, it was just the two of us. So it was very easy for us to communicate because it was mostly phone and some emailing. We would do sketches, print our drawings, and sketch over them, and fax them back and forth. That was when people still used fax machines. When we started hiring staff, things became a little more complicated because the ease with which Jeff and I could communicate - we'd known each other for so long - definitely changed as people were brought into the practice. The building that we're in in San Francisco could not get DSL until 2004. It was very late. As our projects have gotten larger and more complicated, it has become harder to communicate because it's not just Jeff and me, it's everybody. I think it used to be that all the clients would know both of us, now that's not the case. One of us is definitely the lead, and the other may never speak to the client, maybe, but we'll work on the projects.

JD: Our favorite commission was one house that we really like. We had a really great client relationship, and we did all of the interiors as well as the architecture.

EBM: That was sort of ideal. They were fantastic clients with a beautiful site and an interesting take on the vacation house program.

JD: It's the *House in Okoboji* in Iowa. It's not the only project that we like to promote. There are a lot of other things, smaller projects, which are pleasurable for me on more limited issues. That one's a very comprehensive project, and we were just fortunate to build it and work on it, in a lot of different ways. But I don't think we've had a bad client. We tend to be careful in selecting them, as I'm sure they are in selecting us. And fortunately, we have not ended up in a bad situation with anybody. Most of our clients are quite happy with what they receive.

EBM: But I think it was a big project for us in our development. A lot of ideas we had, we were actually able to implement. And the client was sophisticated and had a great attitude. There was a landscape component to it that we had to work out; it was a really good project for us because it utilized our entire range of design skills.

JD: Now we tend to manage different jobs. What happens is that we typically work as a team designing most projects, but the client may only interact with one of us to make it simpler, so they don't have to figure out whom to call for certain questions. We've done things where we'll have Skype meetings in both offices, have two or three people sitting in front of a computer, and we'll hold drawings up. It makes it a little bit easier when we can do that. We don't do that on a regular basis, but it happens project by project. It's not very sophisticated in terms of using virtual tools. We could design at the same time on one project, but we just find that the scrappier way that we do works fine, and we don't need to change.

We do occasionally have projects where we don't collaborate very much, and that's just due to logistics. Either they're very fast-paced projects, or they're small, and it just doesn't make as much sense, or we've got a lot of things going on, and so there's a need to do a split. In particular, we do some design-build projects that I manage as the alternative practice FACT with students in the Midwest, and those don't usually involve people in the San Francisco office. The Omaha office will work on them, and once the students get involved, it's really just me working with the students.

EBM: What aspects of architecture interest me the most? That's a difficult question for me to answer. Right now, I really enjoy teaching, I enjoy the social aspect of it. Right now, what I find interesting is the process, how long it takes to do it, and I don't mean how long it takes to build a project. That's a whole separate issue. But just how long it takes for architects to train and become competent in what they're doing. I feel that we've grown a lot in the last few years, but I'm just amazed by how every day I'm still learning something new. It's surprising. Every day I feel that there is so much I still don't know. I feel that architecture is a constant, consistent education. And that is why it's still very satisfying to do it. I think that's why a lot of people stay in the field, despite the fact that there's no money. The financial rewards are not present, but there's this constant feeling of evolving.

JD: The reason I'm interested in architecture more than visual arts is that architecture is a way of communicating and commenting on culture in a really direct way — as opposed to the way an artist might engage culture, which is removed from everyday life. I also like the fact that as an architect, I'm performing a critical role in society, performing a functional role at the same time, and applying my critique by making things in the city. That's really enjoyable.

EBM: That's absolutely true. There is something really pleasurable about doing architecture where you are solving problems. There's a high level of design in it that takes a lot of skill and a lot of thought. Not everybody appreciates it. We understand that. But there is a lot of pleasure derived in that, at least for me.

I'm also on the board of the AIA San Francisco, and the role of mentors is something we've been talking about, and I feel this is something very important to my career. I've had personal role models who have been my mentors throughout practice, and without them, I can't imagine what the practice would have been like. When I worked for Topher Delaney, I learned how to speak with clients, understand how to get interesting projects done, how to develop source material, and how to invent my own details. Everybody asks: how do you figure these things out? How do you make these things happen? You have to have somebody in your life who has done it, so you see that it's possible. And it didn't hurt that they're both women, and it was an amazing experience to work for them. And I think it gave me a huge foundation that I still draw on today. So they were certainly very influential, not in terms of the way our work looks, but in appreciating and being open to different materials, color and texture, scale, landscape, and the way landscape should interact with buildings. All of that has been incredibly valuable.

JD: I look a lot at contemporary art, and I'm interested in artists like Robert Irwin and the way Irwin would modify a space in an extremely subtle way that it has a profound effect on how somebody would experience that space without knowing why they're being affected. In some of the projects we do, we'll put a tremendous amount of energy into something to make it so that someone doesn't see it. They'll understand, it'll create an experience in a space, but the device that creates that experience is elusive. And part of that goes into just techniques for detailing the spatial situations that we try to create.

Landscape is a really important part of our practice. I'm actually now on the faculty of the landscape architecture program in Lincoln and so even though I'm technically not a landscape architect and I have to make sure that's clear to those on the faculty, I'm really interested in how landscape as a process can be used to make architecture. A few years ago, **Mark Cousins** said in a lecture that landscape is not something you can see at a distance, it's something you're always in. You can get outside a building, you can appreciate it as an object, but the landscape is something you're always inside of. That's a productive way to think about architecture. It gets us away from thinking about the building as a well composed object, like a sculpture, and to think of it as an environment that's somewhat continuous with its surroundings. When we do design buildings from the ground up, we try to design them in such a way that there's a bit of an ambiguity between site and building, that they start to perform with and against each other. And even when we work on interiors, that tends to happen — think of the interior of an existing building as a site. Often in our engagement with that idea, there are ambiguities; there are things that are clearly built and inserted by the architect, and there are other things where it's not really clear where the project begins and ends. I think that's a derivative of looking at landscape.

EBM: When we look at interiors, we don't perceive them as a collection of objects on the inside. We see an interior landscape, interior conditions that are landscape like. We do make references to lots of natural phenomena and landscape features in our work, whether it's interior or part of architecture.

JD: Furniture is another area that we are really interested in. Typically, all of the furniture we have designed has come out of larger commissions. But in one case, there's a piece called the Stones Table, which we actually sell as a product. It's still custom made, so someone has to purchase it before we build it. There are actually three of them in Cincinnati right now in Proctor and Gamble. We haven't seen them. But we do like working at all scales, so working on furniture projects is sort of enjoyable; from the physicality of making something, we can control all of its aspects. We're not designing chairs yet. We're a little afraid of chairs. They're so particular, and there are so many good chairs out there that we don't want to add a mediocre chair to the world. So we tend to do benches and tables and semi built end pieces. Some of the furniture comes out of FACT, an academic/professional collaborative design lab. We're doing a set of modular tables for an art institute in Kansas right now. They are pretty interesting - they are supposed to be delivered tomorrow.

Where does teaching end and the profession begin? It's an interesting situation because there is a range of logistical, ethical, and creative boundaries that one confronts when practicing and engaging students in practice. I teach at a school that does not have a cooperative education program like Cincinnati, so the students may only get summer internships. They don't all have that kind of experience, and so my belief is that having a design-build pedagogy engages students with the physicality of making things. And the logistics of actually getting something built—I'm less interested in the kind of design-build where the students do everything from digging foundations to putting a roof on. I'm more interested in students engaging the project like architects, so they're talking to fabricators, but they're not doing all the fabrication themselves. And it ends up being very collaborative. We use FACT as a resource for the office to allow us to engage in pro bono and not-for-profit projects because, as an office, we can only do so much pro bono work before we can do "pro us" work.

EBM: I'd say too much pro bono work!

JD: Yes. Some of the rent doesn't get paid, but it's a win for the students because they're getting a really good educational experience. And it's a win for the clients because a nonprofit client is able to build an interesting project. We focus more on creative clients, art organizations, and so on.

EBM: I'm much more in the profession than Jeff is. Jeff is a full-time educator. I really enjoy teaching, but I only teach one semester out of the year. And I teach a master's architecture class, a studio. I see teaching as a release valve or an escape form practice and a thing that helps complement our practice. If both of us were teaching it would be really difficult to run a practice. And I really love engaging with contractors. I love the whole building, the whole project, designing, working with clients. But the lovely thing about teaching is that it still reminds me why I like architecture. I get to use part of my brain, which I only use maybe 5 percent in practice, but I get to use all of it in those teaching hours. That's really great. There's this big obligation or feeling in architecture that you should give back the things that you've gotten from people throughout your education. I feel that it's important to teach, if possible, to do just that.

I'm just struck by how much more students have to know than when we were in school. The amount of skill that they need to acquire in the same amount of time is astonishing. They have to learn how to draw by hand, but not well. None of them do. Then they have to learn all of the computer programs to make sure that they know how to do the work, but also that they're employable later. Plus, all the other courses we weren't required to take. Sometimes I think that the program should be longer because it's still only three years for the same program we went through. I don't really know if it means that there's not enough time to be spent in just thinking. The other part I've noticed is that there's a lot more tendency to do collaborative projects, to do team projects than there was when we were in school. Obviously, that's the way the industry works. I don't necessarily think that's a bad thing.

JD: Like a lot of state universities, what's happening at my university is that there's a state mandate to allow undergraduates to complete their degrees with one hundred and twenty credits. Because we had a hundred and thirty, this meant we had to cut out three classes, which works against the need to give them more time to actually achieve the level of expertise that's required. The unfortunate part about this is that those credits come out of electives, so the students have less time to be creative about their own education. A higher percentage of their time is now in required course work. A lot of studios now move towards a more design-research studio culture, where students are really working on problems. Some of it is team-based, some of it is individual-based, or, as in the case of the Architectural Association (London), the studio inquiry is going on for maybe a year or two years, and the students coming out of that can deal with bigger concerns. My school has become very integrated, so there are a lot of interdisciplinary studios and courses where students from landscape architecture, interior design, and architecture can work together. I think that's encouraging, and it does help prepare students for working in a more integrated professional environment.

EBM: Like many architects, we have no marketing ability. That's probably our greatest weakness. But it's true, bigger projects are more interesting to us. We'll always love to do residential work. I enjoy it. But there's a sort of fineness of scale that residential has that just requires an incredible amount of concentration. And I would like to spend some time on things that have different issues. So we have been working on some commercial TI (Tenant Improvement) projects. And that's been really interesting because when we design residential, we're worried about the detailing, everything. And in this commercial world, if it's fifteen feet away, I don't care about that. We need to care about a bigger picture, bigger read, bigger idea, not about whether that's a perfect trim joint or the reveal there. That's not important. A change in scale, and a change in approach, I like that a lot.

JD: TI projects often have very strict budget limitations. So they're challenging, and we try to make some substantial but fairly inexpensive bold moves with, for example, a project that is really all about carpet and lighting, and the furniture is all off the shelf. There's not a lot of money spent on fine-tuning things, but a lot more energy goes into thinking how a company works. What's next? I think that for both of us, we really want to start working on larger and more public projects. As much as designing the House on Okoboji was really satisfying, it's still a private house, and it serves a very limited number of people. Not everyone can visit it. So right now, we're trying to strategize to make public projects at a larger scale happen, whether it's through competitions or just doing RFPs or begging.

In 2018 Min|Day reorganized as two independent firms, E.B. runs Min Design in San Francisco, and Jeff runs Actual Architecture Company in Omaha. Jeff still directs FACT at the University of Nebraska.

My father was trained as an architect, and I have a twin brother who is also an architect, whose first job after college was actually helping to edit a book on this building [**Peter Eisenman**'s College of DAAP], which I'd never seen. But my interest in architecture was always opportunistic because I entered college to study the sciences. I had never imagined entering the family profession at all, but when the finer mathematics of quantum mechanics revealed themselves as not for my brain to adequately encompass, I became really interested in architecture as a container for all of the things that I was interested in: thinking, making, being concerned with the questions of the city, for how things actually work versus how I imagine they work – for all of these things.

I have had a really great time doing all of those things and being able to call myself one thing, which is part of the nature of architecture as a profession from another time. Really, it's a kind of time capsule in a landscape of increasing specialization that affords an almost unique ability to do things. In the last 10 years, I have worked on some buildings, done some exhibits and installations, designed software, and published a book on the history of the Apollo 1 spacesuit. I don't think I would have been able to do all of those things in any other single profession. Sometimes I get exasperated by the profession, as I think we all do, but I adore it for its flexibility and for its uncompromising quality. In a landscape increasingly defined by the commercialization of all kinds of space, there is a space within architecture to come to a building like this one, which is a difficult, somewhat exasperating building and couldn't be anything other than an architecture school.

Nicholas de Monchaux does any kind of architecture they let him do.

I find inspiration in many things. Intellectually, I am inspired by things I don't understand but that seem interesting, and I am inspired when I see a thing that's well done or well made. I'm inspired by my son, who is seven and interested in any number of things in a most exciting and curious way, and is a treat to have around. I'm an urbanist, quintessentially, and so cities inspire me very deeply in terms of how they actually operate and survive and thrive, and how little we know about how that all works. That's very exciting. A street corner in London, or New York, or Tokyo is always very inspiring just for the sheer complexity of everything that's going on and its ability to happen, often despite architects' best intentions, not because of them.

The spacesuit book is about all of these things. Like many children interested in space and science, I wanted to be an astronaut when I was a boy. You never lose that. But then, in graduate school at Princeton, I did a paper for a wonderful professor, **Alexandra Ponte,** on architecture's relationship to the desert and how extreme situations reveal the truth of architectural relationships. After that, I was in a seminar with **Georges Teyssot** on domestic space, and I didn't want to write about bathrooms, so I tried to think of the most extreme domestic space I could. I had a really interesting time. I thought it would be a question of just reading what people had already written about that ubiquitous 20th-century artifact that we see so readily produced, but no one really had written anything, so it was a lot of weird research and strange facts. The spacesuit was made by an offshoot of the Playtex bra company and was made of 21 layers of different fabric, all taken from different earthbound contexts. I didn't know quite what to make of it, so I wrote 21 short papers or 21 one-page papers about a series of facts and decisions, and that was it.

I had just started teaching as a teaching fellowship at UVA, and, through my thesis at Princeton, started a relationship with the Santa Fe Institute, a high-end research center in the sciences. I was invited to give a lecture, and I was quite intimidated because the people lecturing were people who had discovered DNA. I thought, well, at the very least, everyone loves spacesuits, and it's also a great way to talk about the way in which my work overlaps with the mission of that place, which is all about understanding complex relationships between manmade and natural systems. The lecture was a big success. It grew into a project which I thought I would finish in the summer, and then it took nine years, as these things do. It was actually surprisingly difficult to get to a lot of the original sources and materials, and I was very insistent. I became a research fellow for a year at the Smithsonian in 2005 2006, and that really let me get at all the primary sources. I even met astronauts, not because they wanted to necessarily speak to me, but because I discovered that they regarded the suits as part of their own bodies. Everything else to them was a car or a vehicle. When they came to Washington, they actually visited the suits in the storage facility at the Smithsonian and made sure they were well taken care of, as you would a part of your own body extended. Just by being there, I got to have these amazing conversations.

Having all of that information, I wanted to do it justice, so it took another couple of years to put it together as a project. In between, I became a father, went to Berkeley, did a bunch of other stuff. And were it not for the arbitrary clock of the tenure system, I might still be working on the book because I enjoyed the material so much.

Until I took this dive into the story of technology in mid-century, I didn't really realize how many of the tools we take for granted, whether it be JASC or CAD software, or how deeply and directly all of the software comes from that one particular military-industrial moment. Even today, the assumptions and the predilections of that moment are embedded in these tools; we use them, and we don't think about where they originated. We are in a profession that is being transformed yet again by technology and media, and tools. That recognition led to the more design-oriented work I've done since, whether it's exhibit installations around questions of media, or the software that I've been developing at Berkeley, or things which are actually very grounded in that spacesuit work even though they might not seem to be.

As an architect, I occasionally find myself in a room full of people who aren't architects, and someone asks the very sincere question, "Oh, you're an architect. What kind of architecture do you do? Is it commercial or residential?" I try and answer that honestly, simply saying, "Well, I do any kind they'll let me. We are not masters of our own fate." When I was working with the **Hopkins** office in London, or in New York with **Diller & Scofidio**, I did larger scale building projects. I also spent a month designing the bar stool in the Brasserie, and then the next year, everything was suddenly much larger again.

Architects are lying if they won't say they'll take any good, juicy commission that comes their way, but I am very, very lucky that the teaching, which I love to do, also affords the privilege of choosing my work judiciously. I have tended to go towards work that's either at a large urban scale — I've done both consulting work and research-driven work — or work doing installation exhibit scale work. In the last year, my work at the Open Museum or MCA in Chicago afforded a level of attention to painstaking detail in the craft and construction in a venue that was robust and engaged lots of people.

Unfortunately, the Bay Area is a very difficult place for architectural practice because it has that particular quality that slightly smaller cities, historic cities have. San Francisco is a deeply conservative place that is incredibly convinced of its open-mindedness, which is the worst of possible combinations for architecture or for making. I've done the odd house addition and things like that. But if somebody came down the pike tomorrow and actually said, "I would like you to design a house," I would ask: Really, what kind of house? And I'd give it a try.

Why teach? I would say I experienced a combination of good teaching and bad teaching. The good teachers I had, whether it was someone like Liz Diller or my great undergraduate teachers at Yale, like **Alexander Purves**, or people who are really strong, like **Esther da Costa Meyer**, were great. It was a privilege to just sit there and be a hungry mind. At the same time, the nature of American research universities is that there is a surprising amount of really bad teaching, too. I suffered through a bunch of that, as well, and one of the things I do really get from this family of architects is if you're going to do something, do it well. When I started teaching as a graduate student, I realized that there was a deep craft to it like there is to anything, and if you're going to do it, do it well.

I didn't necessarily set out for a career as a teacher. I took a one-year teaching fellowship at UVA when I wasn't quite sure whether I was going to go back and do a Ph.D. or go back to London and practice, but nothing challenges you more intellectually than the right kind of student, in terms of shaping your own sense of what you're doing. The particular luxury of the American research university affords you a really interesting perch to speculate and think about what architecture needs to do, and I think we're at a historical moment when there's actually urgent speculation that is very necessary. That's why I teach.

I remember talking to Liz Diller about teaching when I was a graduate student teaching for her. She said that the only courses that she regarded as really worth teaching as an architect were the very introductory courses and the thesis at the very end because they were the ones who forced you, on a daily basis, to question your own deepest held assumptions about what you're doing. I have become more appreciative of the deep craft and responsibility of the teaching that's in the beginning and the end because I do really feel like it's as much a service to self as it is to the student. Will I spend the rest of my life doing it? Maybe, you know, but it certainly seems to be working so far.

What challenges lie ahead of architecture as a profession? On a global scale, we are building as much urban fabric in the next 35 years as we have in the previous 10,000 years of human history, and doing it at a time of great uncertainty over issues of climate and resilience. The slightly less apocalyptic view of that is to say that once another three billion people move into cities in the next 35 years and we get to a world population of nine billion or six billion in cities, we'll build that much city, and then we'll stop. Because if we are able to do it right, all those people will be educated, have fewer children, and will stay at roughly a population of nine billion or so the forecasters imagine. All that city that we build in the next 35 years will be the city we live with for quite some time.

So it's either a terrible, or an interesting, or an amazing time to be an architect. And, of course, most of that urban fabric won't be built by architects in any conventional way. But as a time to think about the building, making cities, there's literally no other time like it in the history of our species. It is also an important moment in terms of the impact of build form on issues like climate change, emissions, and where we build. One thing I have learned by looking at history is that every moment in history simultaneously seems like an insoluble crisis, and yet gives some degree of reassurance that the current moment is soluble and is really an interesting moment in history. If the profession manages to grapple with this growth and becomes a leader in the sustainable and marvelous making of cities and buildings, then, great. It's almost a bit like the human race itself: if we manage to make it through the next 35 years, I think the hundred after that could be a little bit easier.

But the interesting thing is that the effects of technology on the profession are at once deeply corrosive and deeply empowering, especially the enormous pace of change and the lack of reflection about what those changes mean. There's no reason to believe that there aren't technologies now that involve database information-driven techniques of construction and rapid prototyping that will make the profession we know as architecture as destabilized as journalism. If we think about what we do, we are basically users and producers of media, just like journalists. We have a bigger landscape of liability, which makes the pace of change much slower. Still, fundamentally, we are manipulating and processing information, and then, at the same time, controlling the disposition of matter, which is also being radically changed by technologies of stereolithography and the rest. I have the luxury of being part of great groups like the Center for New Media at Berkeley, where we get insight on the pace of transformation and demolition in any information based profession, of which architecture is fundamentally one. It's not the most glamorous or sexy or fastest changing, but that's still who we are. We don't actually make things; we make informatics tools that other people use to make things. And that has been the case since the 15th century when the master builders stopped being at the job site and started directing the flow of information about the job.

Still, I'd say there's no better time to be an architect because these fundamental questions are all being asked. If you were an architecture student in 1962, or in 1890, you would have been beholden to an orthodoxy about what the profession was and how you should go about doing it. They were different orthodoxies, but in their own way, they were very much the same. One of the best things that might be happening now is that the students know the most about the way the wind is blowing and have a sense of architecture as something that is open for a range of career paths, a range of different kinds of practices. I hope that we don't settle into yet another orthodoxy and totalizing system.

Especially in the landscape of the city, there are moments for total transformation and absolute creation, and then there are moments for adaptation and fashioning. Intellectually, the spacesuit book, just to bring it back to that, is called *Fashioning Apollo*, because it was at great length about clothing and architecture. I fell in love with the word "fashion" because fashion, especially in architecture, has these connotations of something that's temporary and momentary, which, of course, all architecture actually is, but in architecture, the temporary nature of it is taken as a negative, if you're just doing something that's fashionable. But then fashion is quintessentially of the moment, but it also is this word that means an adaptation or a turning around. So you fashion a hammer out of your shoe, or you fashion a spacesuit out of a bra. The urgency and timeliness in which we need to act in the heat of the moment doesn't allow for the time to invent universal languages, as beautiful as they are, but it does allow for some spectacular fashionable moments to be had, nonetheless.

I am the principal of Alibi Studio in Detroit. It's an "alibi" that ebbs and flows, generally, because of the location of the site, or how much work is needed. I generally work on my own. Alibi Studio is mainly I and wherever I am. For some of my really important projects — the *Once Residence* series, the installations of all the abandoned former houses — my father is the person onsite with me the most. He says, "I have a daughter, she works in Detroit on these sites that are often in really contentious spaces, so she's not working by herself. I'm a retired kind of general handyman for the thing." So he became the one person who would be on site with me all the time. When the project comes along, its needs dictate how many people are involved, what type of people are involved in terms of theirs their skill set, how long they are there, or if they're right there with me or not.

Catie Newell does not like buildings. Her work is not about fixing problems.

I'm a maker. For me, it's hands-on making. I don't trust drawings alone to facilitate the things I'm after. I am very responsive, very nimble and super observant to spaces because I obsess over issues like light and darkness, and I can't do that in drawings, I have to do that through making. I get inspired by odd things that happen accidentally or weird, kill-your-ideas because something's going wrong, or there's something that is seemingly destructive that is actually productive, or something bizarre that happened because of some moment, some very time-critical instance.

I would say in a lot of the work I do, the initial steps are somehow on instinct and trust that something will come of it. After I start following something and things start resonating together, I study the effects that are actually happening, or I research the cultural contingencies that are brought up, or the legal issues, or something similar. Once something grabs me I spin off on trying to absorb information about the knowledge base and things other people have done, but also I'm just experimenting, experimenting, experimenting. There is an instinct when it comes to something drawing me in, to work with it, study it and its many connotations.

The best spaces are ones where absolutely everything starts to resonate together. So if you're doing something on site and all of a sudden you realize how the sun hits during sunset you have to change this whole area. When it rains, you actually realize what the water is doing, you are starting to raise the walls to make more water happen. It is very much observational, but it's also a kind of a game for me, and that's what I like to do. For me, there is a simultaneity between a really interesting site that has peculiar things going on. Whether it's the shape of the site or something odd about it it — it used to be a house, and now it's not a house — it's under some sort of contentions, somebody wants to tear it down, the city is angry with it, or somebody broke the law to do something, or a fire hit it or something. There is generally a site that grabs me and then a material study that I'm doing the exact same time, and it's trying to build a relationship between some sort of commentary I am trying to give on the site.

I don't like buildings! My work, my installation work, is not for fixing problems, it's generally not something that is fully occupied, but it is actually something that ends up being completely of that time, ephemeral because it is making a commentary on that exact moment. More so, it is giving us a substrate for discussion about what's happening. Our field needs to be more responsible to the spaces that we have. You don't have to answer everything with a complete building. There are other things particularly at that scale, particularly for someone as a maker, that that size and installation as a medium lets me go through conversations faster and more immediately when there's an urgency involved or when something needs a comment or a critical eye right away.

For me, it definitely comes down to understanding space making. I'm completely dedicated to ideas of occupation, not just in terms of considering something spatially and how a person uses it. I'm also deeply committed to what the space and the installation can say about larger aspects of our world, such as social aspects, legal aspects, cultural aspects, and that's something that can get really lost in buildings. My work can be seen not so much as a commentary on architecture but a commentary on these issues. A lot of my work is also a commitment to existing spaces. So much of architecture deals with building from the ground up, completely new. We got to a point in our cities that so much is built, especially in the rust belt area where we have all those things that are empty or vacant. It is part of our field to be capable of being responsive to those.

I applied to The American Academy in Rome because I was tagged as a Detroit artist which made me realize I had to make sure that I could do projects beyond that city. I wanted to take something that was crucial to my work on darkness and apply it to another city. When I went to Rome, I had a five-minute presentation to express my interests and intent. I gave my presentation about darkness for five minutes, and the deputy director put her hands on her head and said, "You are studying darkness? We assigned you the brightest studio!" This was true, but what happened was that I loved my studio, and I loved the Academy; it is a sociable space, and I have already mentioned that I am an introvert, so I have to excuse myself from things just to go be calm in my own space once in a while.

I have heard stories about **Louis Kahn** at the Academy. He would stay in his room and watch how the light would change the room and the space, and not too long after he came back from the Academy he did the Kimball Art Museum. The chase of darkness and the brightness of the studio also taught me to become more attuned to light and darkness than I had been before. I have become really particular about every bit of lighting and how it's working.

I really adore darkness as something critical to a space and as something that I like to respond to. There is something in it that just jars me. I also took with me the darkness I knew from Detroit, which is more a kind of scary darkness, a little bit more like not wanting to be out in the dark. In Detroit, a building is dark because it is boarded up, or it's seedy. Rome taught me that darkness is its own thing. It taught me that it can be very calm. It can be experienced in different ways. I held on to studying it, everything, from fear to urban characteristics to working with it as a material. I developed this series of photographs trying to capture darkness, which I brought back. Every time I go to another city, I ask what the city can teach me about darkness. It sounds like such a simple task, but living through it and doing it I think I really have opened it up. I think Rome, just the experience of Rome, taught me to open up all my definitions that I have for everything.

Thankfully my most glorious failure turned into an eventual "figuring out." It was for the Venice Biennale, actually the 2012 Venice Biennale that was curated for **David Chipperfield**. There was a group of five of us who were all fellows at the University of Michigan, three years or two years prior to this commission. We had taken over a house in Detroit, and each of us used a portion of that to fulfill our research for our fellowship. Five individual installations, five different practices, five different ways of thinking. One of Chipperfield's curators who was a friend of a friend of one of the fellows had gotten word that Chipperfield was looking for more Midwest representation and maybe a younger group. He asked us to revisit those projects and, because Detroit was very hot, to curate a show about Detroit. The greatest failure came at that moment when we were trying to figure out how we were shifting our projects, how we were ghosting and taking this house, and how we were moving it over to Europe. I realized that this is a massive collective group where we were trying to figure out how to think together, but everyone still wanted their own project. I mean, this is the Venice Biennale; we all want to say, "This is my piece, this is my piece, this is my piece." My first design, which I held onto for a really long time, was trying to fit into the collective group conversation, which I now realize I didn't agree with, just talking about how does one respond to Detroit or bring things to Detroit. I knew I worked in a different way than my fellow fellows, we all worked differently, but as somebody who was a maker and not a drawer, I was trying to draw through something that could be constructed over there. They offered to build our projects if we sent them plans.

I brought on an assistant too early because we were all panicked about time, but when I don't know what I'm doing, I can't really have a helper. I am an introverted person when it comes to creativity and energy level. I have to do a lot of thinking and messing with things before I am capable of actually handing off something to somebody else. So I had an employee, I had an idea that I didn't feel good with and we worked with it for a really long time. We did material experiments, and it still wasn't working, still wasn't working, still wasn't working. It was one of these moments where I wasn't true to myself. It took one of my friends to ask me what else I really wanted to do. So I gave myself two hours to draw something else, and that sketch carried us through for the rest of the project. I didn't care if my project was a lot less now. I just sketched something that I really wanted to do, and there was our design, and we were off and running, and we pulled it off.

My heroes? People do, of course, bring up **Gordon Matta-Clark**. He becomes kind of a standard. Some of my heroes fit more into the art realm, the art installation realm: **Anish Kapoor, Cornelia Parker, Damian Ortega**. I am always curious about what I can learn from **Ruth Asawa**. When it comes to architects, when there's a really strong material sensibility, this is the range from **Herzog de Meuron** to **Peter Zumthor**. My mentors, I was trained at **Office dA** for several years, so I have strong mentorship from **Nader Tehrani**. He is probably the best architect as an influence on my work in terms of his obsession to detail. People I also look at are **Robert Irwin, James Turrell**, and **Olafur Eliasson**, where there is almost an envy. How they are getting commissions that are $3 million dollars. Darn it, I am working with $271.

I feel I am in a fortunate position. I have been teaching in Ann Arbor, Michigan for six years, and now I start to have classes where I can design them myself. That has forced a little bit of clarity trying to explain my work. I try to talk about the way I see things, or how I see a city, or how I might pursue the city in my teaching. It strengthens the need to have to be able to explain it, but at the same time, I often wonder, if I may be more effective teaching them how to get through a whole building instead of trying to teach them to see a site and see it strangely and work through trespassing and vandalism, and destroying the site to remake that site, and how the exchange of give-and-take works. It is a messy blur, but I find it is easiest for me to teach the things I know: materials and making. This is how I approach architecture. And some students cling onto it, and some don't.

I hope that there's a way that as a profession, architecture can be embraced more by the public, either by teaching people the value of real quality spaces or by making really quality spaces that immediately teach people the value of that. I do feel like the world has too much developer and quick building contractor spaces that are not thought through. I truly believe that our spaces have to do a lot with our happiness; everything from the rate of illumination to having the right colors in the wall to getting the right view and still seeing trees out of your window really has an enormous effect on people. And so my hope for the discipline has to do with a stronger outreach to the public that encourages the value of the field. For making the world better, for using it as a way to attend to our spaces and attending to our cultures and our histories — as opposed to how fast can I make it, who can make it the fastest, what's the most innovative material right now. How can I care for this community, how can I care for this space, how can I care for this individual room through architecture? I want people and architects to want that too.

I was always around building, and that's what drove me to architecture. And when I got to architecture school and realized that there is so little building connected to it, it didn't matter. I reveled in the design aspect of it. It seemed kind of odd to me, but I never looked back and just continued in the design world. I married my high school sweetheart, we had a family at a very young age, and I graduated from school and started teaching to avoid the draft because the draft was bearing down on everybody. So I found myself teaching and starting a family on a school teacher's salary. I was a little worried, so I started building because I could do it and was pretty good at it. I just kept it up. I went to Kansas in 1980 and built for other architects for a couple of years until I could begin to attract clients to my own design interests. I'm good at being able to figure things out; therefore, I can produce designs that I like to imagine as being somewhat fresh, and maybe things people haven't seen before. They're not store-bought designs. They're from what I call the presence of the hand. They're made by people.

Dan Rockhill talks budget in the design studio.

Rockhill and Associates have restored most of the Kansas historic sites. There are nine sites that are administered by the state. We have restored six of them. So, I know a lot about preservation, and I've had my hands in all of those buildings, and I respect them. I don't want to be cavalier about the importance of preservation. But I also want to make it very clear that time moves on and to have both feet mired in the past is foolish. There can be a rich, eclectic mix of historic and present, and at that, we really have to work hard. That's the hardest thing. Making restoration accurate and historic, that's easy. The hard thing is not ignoring that there's a future and trying to find a creative way to recognize that and integrate that. That's hard.

I think to just gussy up these old houses just for the sake of preserving them is a mistake for any number of reasons. One is that the social structure of families, the way people live today, is very different from the way they did a hundred years ago. Energy is probably the single greatest reason. Many of these homes weren't even insulated. How do you get an R-50 or 40 in a wall that was never insulated? I don't think it's smart to imagine that preservation is going to continue on its own as it was as if time had stood still. We do need to find creative, interesting ways to work with the past, show respect for proportion, scale, and rhythm, but we need to do it in a contemporary manner. And we've really pursued that with enthusiasm when we saved the Benedict house from demolition by having new construction on the site pay for preservation. From the preservationist standpoint, they're glad to settle for at least having the building and whatever they can in the environs maintained. Yes, it changes the environment that it was originally placed in. I do not see the world as standing still, and I take exception to those people who do.

Teaching has tremendously influenced my career. Teaching is learning. I doubt I would be even close to accomplishing what I have if I hadn't been teaching. Being around young people, despite all my grumblings about them, the constant interaction with them is what I owe my entire career to. There's a freshness to it. And that's why I teach. There's a pleasure that can be derived from that. So that clearly comes back and influences what I do in the practice. It's a good thing. I love it.

Studio 804 developed because so many interesting projects simply aren't in anyone's budget. One of the reasons I do what I do in Kansas is that when I get a phone call about a possible project with Rockhill and Associates, my associate is quick to say: it sounds great, but what's the budget? Within the first two sentences, that has to come up. And within the first conversation, I will always ask the client. The single greatest thing that is never talked about in the studio experience is the budget. The budget has a huge impact on what we can and can't do.

I was teaching architecture 804 to students who would graduate. They would take 804 in the spring semester, and they would graduate that May. So I was really the last studio. I really felt that I was blocking them. I was standing in the door, keeping them from moving on. They already knew it all. I couldn't tell them anything. They were working on their portfolios. And it was not a comfortable studio, but I taught it for a couple of years. I did a great job, but somehow there was something wrong with it. Coincidentally, Rockhill and Associates were asked by a local preservation group to do a project out in the country. We couldn't do it — it was timing, money, all kinds of things. So I thought maybe I could get out there with a couple of students. I said something to the studio, and they said: yeah, we'd love to. During the three or four weeks, there was the most remarkable transformation of the students I'd ever seen. I couldn't get over it. They would be pulling their cars up around the building and working under the headlights late at night and working on Sundays. They were drunk on the experience. I couldn't believe it. Clearly, the opportunity for them to get their hands in the concrete, and to synthesize what could have been a five or six-year educational experience, had never really appeared before them. Given the opportunity, they were quick to grab hold. So I did one or two additional projects the following Spring just to confirm in my mind that this was indeed something I was going to want to do. As the interest continued, I realized I was on to something. In fact, the students were saying to me, "What are we going to do when our time comes?"

I went to the city of Lawrence and said that I've got some eager builders, and you have an affordable housing program. Why don't we get together? They agreed. Since then, we've done one house every year. In fact, we just did a university building. That aside, for the vast majority of all the work, it has always been housing. And I do it because I could not only see the difference in the students at that level but how young people today are denied any connectedness whatsoever to building or making. You can't even have a tree fort in most communities. Those kids are denied the chance to handle a board and to try to cut something. I do this to make them better architects and to give them the chance to see what's involved in producing a building. I'm not the least bit interested in making them builders.

When we do the sewer tap, students are standing in the street, and their eyes are wide open. They can't believe it. They can't wait to see how it works. I can remember the first house that we did. We were standing in front of that house, talking about the drainage. I used to teach the big lecture courses on what we call BTech, building technology. An easy, guaranteed way of putting everyone to sleep is to talk about drainage. Who gives a shit about that kind of stuff? But in front of that house, talking about the drainage, I remember one student turned to me and said: I had no idea how little I knew. That's when the light came on for me. I said, "This is important. These kids have to have this experience." So I've been doing it ever since.

Studio 804 is a not-for-profit corporation. I'm completely independent of the university. I don't need to ask anybody at the university what I should do, what I can do, unless I want to. In fact, I have an agreement with the university that basically said, "We know you're doing something that is different, and we don't want to know any more." When that agreement was written up, my feelings were hurt because after the first couple of houses I thought I was some kind of hero. But in the end, it was the best thing that happened to me. I've run the not for profit corporation like a business. I go to the CDC's (community development corporations), not unlike the way I did with the first house, and say, "You have an affordable housing initiative, I have needs here for students in building." Now we have a track record, so it's pretty easy. What I want is basically for them to front me money. So they give me 100,000 dollars for four or five months, whatever it takes me to get through the project, and I'll give them a percentage. I might give them six percent, so they'll get 6,000. They're always going to get back what they would have had if they banked it. But they also get a house in their jurisdiction. And they're all about housing so they get a house, my students get the experience. I also tell them, "I'm going to sell that house for as much as the market will bear." And if I sell a house where I borrowed 100,000, I give 106 back. But if I can sell it for 150, I'm keeping the proceeds. I've got to operate like a business. And now I'm in a position where I don't really need to grovel to those CDCs. I do it on my own because I have enough money in the checking account. We've been shaving enough money off in those projects that I've described, that now I have enough money to be my own developer.

Do I pay the students? No, they get course credit. First of all, the students aren't worth a damn. They should actually pay double tuition for this experience. Quite honestly, if they went to — there's a school called Yestermorrow School as an example — they would have to pay money to go and have that kind of experience to do a building. So the whole idea of students getting paid is just nonsense as far as I'm concerned. They're a liability quite honestly. That aside, I don't know how else to do it. I purposely seek out crappy neighborhoods. We put the buildings up, and we sell them at whatever — I mean, if I sell a building for 155,000, I bet if I added labor, I'd have 250,000 dollars in it. So whoever gets that house is getting a hell of a bargain. And we have no problem selling the houses. In the end, I think the students are enormously satisfied by the experience even though it takes a while for them to realize that.

Mod1, the first-ever student project to win the Architecture Magazine award in the professional category, was the first house that we prefabricated. I really used prefabrication to my advantage. Up to a point, a lot of the design work became arguments with students, and I was just weary of arguing with them about design. I have a very strong design interest. And of course, students are fresh out of studio, very idealistic, and don't realize that subtlety in design can be effective and that making a beautiful box that's beautifully proportioned and very simple could win awards. But we did with this project.

Students are incredibly pampered. We deal with a culture now where you sign up for soccer you get a trophy. That's what we're dealing with. Computers have screwed us because these kids, even in their freshmen or sophomore year, are showing their mom and dad these amazing renderings. Their parents think they're **Frank Lloyd Wright** and their boyfriend or girlfriend just think they're amazing. And of course, in the totally pampered society that we live in, even the studio instructors say: oh, sure, that's great. Nobody ever says: god damn it, that just sucks, that's awful. Maintaining a very firm undercurrent about design and the importance of design is the most difficult aspect of what I do. And trying to get everybody on board with that and respect it is probably the first and most difficult thing that I have to get myself through. The first month or two with the students is the make or break aspect of the project. From there on, it takes a life of its own. We know what has to be done and what's expected and how much work needs to be done. I go through everything with them. But keeping these very fragile egos in line and getting everybody working together is the challenge. Most of these kids have never really had to work together on a design in studio, and of course, that's the model for the real world. That in itself is a very difficult thing because everybody has their vision. And I treat it like a shell game. I just keep moving stuff around, and pretty soon, they're tired of it. They cave in and give in to the direction it should go.

I like to think that as professionals, we are quite capable of integrating our projects into the neighborhood, the region, and I take exception to these design-by-committee emphases that I see where we're going to get together with the community and we're all going to have a big group hug, and we're going to get all the likes and dislikes, and they're going to tell us exactly what to do. I'm sure we've all heard this. But I don't tell my attorney about tort law or my doctor about neurology. At some point, there must be respect for what professionals do, for better or worse. There's ample evidence out there of bad design. But still, I fight very hard to maintain design quality. I know the pressure points. I know what I have to do before even going into it. In the last house we did, I knew going into it that I had to do a pitched roof on the house. If we didn't, we would have a big fight on our hands. So we figured out a very creative way to put a nice pitched roof on that. On another house, the one before that, is a combination of a pitched roof, and we pushed it back off the street and pushed it down to bring the scale down for the thing to work on the streetscape. And prior to that, I felt that when we did a lot of flat roof projects, I was on the fringe of these neighborhoods, and it was acceptable to do it on those edges. So even though we work in communities, I'm very protective of design.

The profession has been quick to embrace design-build, but that's project delivery. It's a very different beast. There is a whole design-build institute. That's not what I do. I respect it but carry it out differently. When I see it in other schools, it's literally just having your hands in the concrete and making it work. I don't think that'll ever happen in the sense that it would become institutionalized — in other words, somehow engaged by the AIA — or further legitimized. I think there are people like me who are disgruntled with the current methods of delivering architecture and who will choose to say: pick up the hammer. It works for me, but I don't romanticize the building aspect of it. I'm good at it. But there are a lot of other ways, and many different models for practice, and mine happens to be one. In the end, the building has to stand on its own or be on its own. Nobody really gives a shit who built it or how it got built.

I really take exception to having a watered-down design. And we show by example modern design. We show a sensibility to sustainable issues. We do Leed platinum buildings and so on. I think we should take a leadership role in building. But we are doing such a shitty job of explaining the real world to them that students come back saying: man, why didn't you tell me? Through the studio setting, we idealize all the wonderful, intangible qualities that we bring to design. It's a wonderful experience for students. But it is also an idealized view of the world. And so when I say that students would come back and say, "Why didn't you tell me?" It's because all they're going to do is go sit in front of a CAD machine and move a mouse around all day long. And sooner or later, after a couple of years, they're going to look out that window and say,

"This is it? This is what it's all about?" It's almost frightful when you see what happens to them when they're out there for the first couple of years, and they see what it's like. It's pretty grim.

Our faculty are still arguing over whether we should teach BIM or offer BIM courses. The world is changing. I've seen it change. We have gone to Revit in our practice, and it has changed the way in which we do business. I can't believe the amount of time we would spend on the front end developing design — which is always important — but how long it would take, and how quickly today we can do it in Revit modeling. It has transformed the way we operate. Get with the program, really. A lot of it is that not that many faculty practice anymore. The need for these Ph.D.'s and the over-emphasis on the faculty's need for higher education is always at the expense of some connectedness with practice. You're not going to get a Ph.D. and pursue academic pursuits and, at the same time, be able to practice. We just do not have the strength with practicing faculty that I think we need to have. Nobody practices anymore. When I started teaching where I am at Kansas thirty years ago, I was in third year, and every one of them practiced. Now, I don't think any of them do. The whole thing has changed terribly. It shows up in the classrooms. The studio culture has been diluted.

We've become so bureaucratic, so expensive, so layered, and so mired in codes, and insurance and litigation. In the end, there are no buildings, no good buildings so to speak, or there are so few of them, you can count them on your fingers. What have we gained as a culture? Very little. If through the studio 804 experience, some light comes on and some guy picks up the hammer on weekends and starts doing a little bit of building for relatives, in the summers and vacations, and pretty soon gets enough traction and confidence to take that alternative method on himself or herself, great! Anything that we can bring to the table — in my case it's studio 804 and doing building — will remind them, when that time comes in their future, that there may be an alternative. Whatever it is that we can do to find different ways of practicing architecture is important to the growth of the profession.

Early 2009, journalist Michiel Hulshof and I founded the *Go West Project*, a research and design studio focusing on the emerging megacities. The reason for this was our interest in the unknown megacities in China. We figured that there were tens or maybe even hundreds of cities in China with millions of inhabitants that were pretty much unknown outside of China. We were very curious about how these cities were emerging and how these cities were changing. We decided to explore them.

After three years, we produced a book, *How the City Moved to Mr. Sun*, and that is the starting point for new endeavors and new research, and also for architectural design in China and in Europe. From architecture and design to research, and now finally back to design.

When there is a crisis, **Daan Roggeveen** starts to write.

Why write and not build? Apparently, when there is no work, architects enter academia or start writing. With me, the opposite was the case. Over the past four years, I've been based in Shanghai, and have been working in central China, which is the fastest urbanizing area in the world and an area where lots of construction is going on. I felt like a child living in a candy store, yet forbidden to touch what I like most. So it was almost therapeutic to start writing. My ambition was to try to understand what I was part of in China, and to go beyond general observations. By writing, I start to understand the context, and therefore the architecture. So we did our analysis upfront, and now we can do the design. And that was maybe the hidden agenda of what we're doing.

I think that the bottom line of our research is that Chinese cities are very much about top-down versus bottom-up systems. On the one hand, there's this notion of the Chinese city as being very much planned top-down, very strongly, with a lot of force, and a lot of money, and a lot of power, with its advantages and disadvantages, obviously. And at the same time, the lesser-known stories are the bottom-up forces of China's economic miracle. In an economic sense, they are maybe even more important than the top-down forces. These forces are small entrepreneurs, small farmers, building a shoe factory or building a tee-shirt factory, workers coming from the countryside to the city to build up a new life. Where these top-down and bottom-up movements clash, it is very interesting.

The second thing that is very typical for Chinese cities is that they are based on this idea of build first and then program the spaces. They create the physical conditions first - roads, railroads, airports, residential areas, museums - and then they fill them. And especially the soft side of the city, how these areas are being filled up is something that we are very interested in. How are cities that are physically ready, that look like a world city, how do they develop their soft side, how do they develop their human content? How do people behave, how do people transform into urban citizens?

Some of our work is very much about migration. The exhibition or the performance that we did for the Shenzhen Biennale was about taxi drivers coming from the cities of central and western China to Shenzhen to tell stories about their hometowns and to take the people of Shenzhen around the city in their taxis. That's very much about migration, it's very much about local culture versus generic culture, it's about language, it's about telling stories, sharing memories.

For the *About a Minute Project* (2010), we connected people from cities of central and western China with a phone to a gallery in London. This idea was about unknown world cities being connected with a "known" world city and about the difference between the two. How do people communicate between these two places?

Architectural projects should be a plea for the bottom-up movement, a plea for a smaller scale and finer meshed urban planning vis-a-vis the top-down forces and powers that be. People are the software to how museums, galleries, concert halls are being filled in with exhibitions, orchestras, and audiences. How this is happening is what our work is about.

We are analyzing as the facts are happening. That's the beautiful thing. A good example is that the discussion about how sustainability in China is happening at the moment that China transforms from a rural into an urban society. So this discussion takes place at the same moment, whereas in Europe or in the States, it took place 30 years after, or 50 years after the fact. The highways were already there.

Soon after arriving in China, I understood that I could not compete with the Chinese architects in terms of speed, or production, or skill. Normally, western architects like to do research during their design. Research is an integral part of doing architecture. Not in China! There the research processes are so quick, and the pace is so fast that there's hardly any time for analysis. According to **Rem Koolhaas'** book about the Pearl River Delta, Chinese architects are two and a half thousand times more efficient than western architects. I cannot build faster than a Chinese architect, so I should not compete with that. That's not where my added value is. It's important to make it clear also to clients that if they hire me, they have another type of person at the table than when they hire a Chinese firm. And especially with the book, people see that I have another profile than a Chinese firm, which is mainly aiming at production.

While doing research, it was very nice to come to local design institutes and architecture firms where thousands of architects work, and never receive any journalists, let alone foreigners and foreign journalists. So we had the possibility to talk to their directors for hours and really exchange ideas on how they perceive their position, in this case, the city of Xian. We also had this experience in Guilin and in Guiyang. These are cities of millions of inhabitants that are really exploding, and at the same time, are very much overlooked. And we really spoke to the people that produce all those skyscrapers that you see, but do so anonymously.

The Chinese are very much aware of what's going on in their country, and they are also very much aware of the fact that it's pretty special. People in the West are, in a lot of cases, pretty much ignorant about what's really going on in China. Still, the cities that are now emerging and are growing in central and western China as starting to become players on the worldwide network of cities. People sometimes still overlook the sheer amount of production or people that China represents.

Go West was well received in China. We are now working on the Chinese translation of the book. People are interested, especially since there's not much analysis of the region that we describe, central and western China. The coastal areas are very much explored, also by foreigners, but central and western China not so much. It sounds like a cliché, but the book was not only about the destination, but it's also about the journey. It was a three year trip through China, but also about architecture and about the state of architecture, the current state of affairs, and especially urbanism. And I developed myself, as an architect and a photographer through that whole experience. Did I learn from it, or did I change? Absolutely, a hundred percent.

There's a saying in Chinese that someone who spends a week in China wants to write a book about China, and someone who spends a month wants to write a chapter, and someone who spends a year doesn't want to even write a page. And I think that's very much true because we started working on this research with a sort of grave naïveté. My colleague and I originally decided to explore 20 cities of central and western China. We would try to describe the whole country apart from the coastal region. If I had known more about the undertaking, I would never have dared to take it up, but luckily, I was very, very unprepared.

We are now working on spreading the word. We lecture all around the world, Europe, in the States, and after the Chinese translation, also in China. We've done a couple of things in China already, and with the Chinese book in hand, we can go to the Chinese readers or the readers that read Chinese more easily. One of the main questions that we ask in the book is whether a new type of urbanism is emerging in these cities. Have the Chinese developed a new type of city that we don't know in the States, that we don't know in Europe? The answer is yes. The cities of central and western China are typically different, generally speaking, from other parts of the world. With the emerging power of China in the world, the Chinese should start to export this type of city.

And we are now working on how the Chinese are exporting their models. One of the things that we're working on is a conceptual project in which we propose to export a special economic zone, following the Chinese model, to Europe. So we superimpose the concept of a special economic zone in a certain area in the Netherlands, to see if that could enhance the suffering economy of Europe. Maybe we can use Chinese means to improve the economic situation in the Netherlands.

This also follows a remark of Angela Merkel a couple of months ago, when she said, "Maybe we should introduce the special economic zone in Greece." Actually, we came up with this idea already two and a half years ago, and two months ago, I read this in Der Spiegel. So it turns out that reality is also sort of keeping up with our ideas or, well, maybe they read our website, I don't know. But the thing is it's actually being picked up in Holland pretty well. So we are talking to one of the governors of the province where we proposed this project, and the governor is very interested and wants to organize a committee that starts to do research about feasibility of the concept of a special economic zone within which there are lower taxes, it's easier to set up a company, and it's easier to migrate to work there, et cetera, et cetera.

Especially in Shenzhen, in the early days, this notion of an economic zone was particularly attractive because Hong Kong was across the border. Hong Kong had money and had the know-how and potential investors with the same cultural background as people in Shenzhen. So there was this sort of mutual or polar/bipolar urban model. We propose that same model in Holland, next to Randstad or next to Amsterdam. We propose this as a thinking model, but at the same time, it's pretty much real because, with this idea, the Chinese powers are expanding into other parts of the world.

We also have a more theoretical form of this concept. We're working on an outline for a new book that will be about Chinese cities in Africa as the Chinese influence in Africa increases. The Chinese are very present in Africa, in countries from Angola to South Africa to Egypt. There are one million Chinese living in Africa at this moment. What is the spatial implication of Chinese investors in Angola, of Chinese urban planners planning cities, planning new towns in Luanda? What is the impact of Chinese contractors doing work in Kenya, or special economic zones in Zambia? There's a whole strata of different kinds of urban models that we're exploring already that actually literally come from central China and are just implemented in Africa.

The Chinese urban model strives for harmony and tries to create solutions for the middle class. At the same time, it works with gating off, enclosing and disclosing, which can lead to big problems if groups of people are systematically gated off physically, socially, economically, and culturally. This is one of the biggest threats of Chinese urbanism.

In 20 years, China will have the largest urban society in the world. That means that roughly speaking, one billion people will live in Chinese cities. That is more than any other country in the world. And that means that these people will not only live in cities but also these cities will be drivers for urban culture, right? That is sports, that is academics, that is art, that is museums, that is theaters, et cetera. The way in which China is able to deal with the liberties of these groups or the ability in which the people in China are able to tap into the potential of one billion urban citizens is the biggest potential and the biggest challenge for the Chinese urban model.

If they are able to use it, and if they are able to liberate or to create liberties for their urban citizens, then they will have a powerful urban group of people and the biggest urban class in the world. If not, then the potential for crisis and dissatisfaction will be huge. Because the urban model in China is currently based on an ongoing economic growth, the idea that tomorrow is better than today, and that children will have a better life than their parents in an economic sense, is widespread. Once this model slows down? It is slowing down in Singapore already, which is based on a similar model, and it is slowing down in Shanghai, on the east coast. And then it becomes necessary to replace this economic growth with something else. The question is, what is that?

After releasing 'How the City Moved to Mr. Sun,' Daan founded MORE Architecture and moved back to Amsterdam.

In terms of starting our own firm, Mack Scogin and Merril Elam Architects are basically 15 or so years behind our peer group, doing our own work. We worked in a large firm for almost 20 years, which, when we first started our own, was a bit of an advantage but has been more and more of a challenge for us over the years. I know this sounds like an odd thing to say, but we were running a big firm. We were running a very large firm, 500 people, which is a totally different experience. You're making decisions every day, keeping all those 500 people busy, making it a viable business, etc. At **Heery & Heery International** in Atlanta it was all about a collaborative effort. It was all about getting teams together, and literally controlling the process of the project from start to finish, and privileging time and cost control, design, all of this stuff, trying to make it about end balance and etc. Looking at architecture very seriously, from the standpoint of a fiduciary to the client, all of those things, that was a wonderful experience. I don't regret it really, not a day of it. However, the fact is it has affected our trajectory after that, trying to get in touch with exactly what our sort of personal position and personal way of conducting a practice.

Mack Scogin has no time to do marketing. He's working on projects.

When we left Heery, we had a hard time getting selfish. But the one thing that we have done for the last 25 years is that we are involved in every single project all the way through — both of us in some capacity. And certainly during the design process. We're still collaborators, we have never given up, we love collaborating, we love having young minds, good minds around us all the way through the process. We listen to people, we borrow from people. But we have held on to the sense of control over that whole process, including client relationships. And it's one of the things that has kept us reasonably small compared again to our age peer group who have grown. We've never really experienced significant growth in our firm. And we haven't decided whether we would grow or not grow. We simply chose to stay with our projects. So that's what we've done.

My partner Merrill and I both love the water. Now we slow down to where all we do is get out and cruise around the marshes in South Carolina and Georgia in a little tiny boat. We travel and look at things. If you really get down to it, I think that's so much a part of what our architecture is about. It comes from a lot of just sheer observation. So we make a really big effort to see things, see other architects' work, and go places. We started really late doing all that, opening up this big world to ourselves. Merrill teaches some, and I teach on a regular basis and have for over 25 years. And in a way that opens up and energizes us in all sorts of ways. There are always new insights from young eyes.

There are lots of projects that we've done that are not planar conditions, some of which we have purposefully, consciously tried to make for instance extremely heavy, and I would say failed miserably, but we tried. When you look at the U.S. Courthouse in Austin, Texas, I can understand exactly your reaction to it. But the fact is that's probably the first courthouse that's ever been designed that the word pinwheel has been attached to because both in section and in plan, it is a pinwheel. It literally is in motion in terms of its dispersion of the program. And it for very serious reasons because those serious judges seriously wanted a lot of serious sunlight. And they wanted sunlight in every single room. That's almost an impossibility in a courthouse where there are so many constraints on the separation of service, access from the judges to the public, to the prisoners and all the kind of stuff, the mountain high books of design standards. For a judge to simply say I want sunlight in my courtroom or else, is something that we took seriously. That spun us off that ground line up into the air and created this — you have to look carefully at it because there's not been a courthouse done this way before. There are very few, if any, that have been able to give every courtroom exterior exposure for security reasons. And so it's a transformative project in a very serious way in a serious project. I would say a pinwheel is a little serendipitous in terms of its characterization, but that is what it is. So I don't know about the planar. We've been called everything under the sun from hicks to constructivists to phony colonial to you name it. For whatever reason, we just don't really worry about that too much.

How do we collaborate? Somebody did write one time that it was an ongoing intense creative argument or discussion, maybe argument. How do we collaborate? It's kind of hard to talk about because we've been doing it so long that we don't really think much about it. We had the advantage of going to school together, working together in different arenas all of our professional lives. And so it's been a development process that we haven't worked at. We have not worked at it consciously. We have just done it. In a way, I think that's how you have to do it. You can't sit down and say, "Okay, here are your tasks, and here are my tasks." We've never done that with anything in our lives together. I have no idea what she does with her money. We've never had that kind of definitive role-playing that I would think a lot of people have to establish. It's extremely frustrating for the people around us. They never quite understand how decisions are made or who might make them. But people that value working for us love that. And if they don't, they probably don't stay with us for very long. Although we've never had a lot of people leaving us. That's a terrible answer, but I don't know how else to answer it.

Merrill has a way of seeing things that is truly astonishing to me. One, she sees the foreground, middle ground, background simultaneously in every single thing, all day, every day. In order for me to do that, I have to stop and think about it. It's natural to her. So the point is that I have a great, it's not actually respect, it's a fascination with the way she sees things. I'm always surprised. And then it's always predictable that I'm surprised. That's the only consistent thing. And I think that those are the best collaborations when you're literally not just appreciating somebody else's kind of opinion, that you're challenged by them, the best word I can think of is fascinated by the other person's opinion. There's a give and take, again corny, but there's a kind of give and take way of getting at some decision around things. And on projects, there's no predicting sort of who affects what, when, and how. It's just a kind of organic discussion.

TSh: Competitions were very important for us when we were just starting to learn how to work together. We had worked together on some projects like *Plan Section Sentence*, which was a competition sponsored by Arcade magazine that we entered when we were still working at Miller Hull. We were not a firm; we were barely a couple then. But that was a way of learning how to work together. We participated in something called the *Home House Project*, which was the first thing we ever did together on our own. Home House was important in that regard, and that was our first real taste of success. It gave a little bit of confidence that we really were able to work at the level we wanted to work. Or at least it was in our reach to participate in discussions about contemporary architecture and so forth. So those competitions were really important for us to be able to think about how to work together.

Tricia Stuth and **Ted Shelton** learned how to work together – an important tool for any relationship.

TSt: I'm very proud to say that I've done the ACSA housing competition as a student and was a finalist among maybe 2,500 entries, which I by no means felt that that makes me great, but it certainly gives me the confidence to keep trying. And I think that's what Ted was alluding to. I think that a little bit of recognition gives you confidence.

TSh: For us, the whole point of awards programs is the opportunity to be critical about our own work. And go back and look at it and to think about what was successful, what wasn't, and why. Sometimes we even understand the work in new ways in that there are things embedded in it that we didn't realize at the time. So that's become a pretty interesting thing for us. It is an outgrowth of our positions as academics, where you have to sort of justify everything to a certain extent, have some sort of peer review. So, it's maybe something we wouldn't have done to the extent that we have if we weren't in academic positions as well. But, it's been very beneficial to our work.

TSt: I think the articulation of the competition's brief gives a great toe hold where you can thematically start to address issues that someone has long thought about and framed in ways that help you think about what you've done in the past. The RIBA competition for the *Kilder Observatory* is a great example of that. Kilder Forest is a national forest in Northumbria, England. The competition was very specific about the brief in terms of how the telescopes had to work, why the housing worked this way or that way, but yet it recognized that along with those very prescriptive parts of the program, it was set in a national park that had this really strange landscape. This allowed us to really explore some ideas that we were interested in terms of the relationship between the poetic and the technical, and how the technical should be a poetic act.

TSt: I can't remember exactly who sponsored the *RE:Route* competition right off hand. RE:Route was about transit. And so RE:Route was saying that there are simple, mundane things that just should be more poetic, they should be more beautiful. Knoxville, an area of Ted's research in particular, is like many cities: bisected by an interstate highway system that broke the traditional city fabric and creates real imperceptible boundaries in the city that have affected its growth, development, demographics, all sorts of things. So RE:Route was just trying to say: we now have a lot of underpasses that appear to be boundaries. How might we design, redesign, or develop the underpass so that it would be seen more continuously with the fabric underneath it, and be understood more as a gateway than a boundary? Nobody asked for this particular fix, but it's a problem area and so let's look at it. And I'm not sure exactly, but a city councilman saw it somehow, and called and asked about it. So I brought some of the imagery to look at it with him, and he was very interested at the time. Unfortunately, it didn't happen to go anywhere.

TSh: It was certainly an idea that you and I had talked about quite a bit because, at the time, they were expanding I-40 through Knoxville, and as part of that, they had to rethink the underpasses and so forth. And we saw what they were spending money on as far as lighting and sidewalks and chain-link fence.

TSt: That was window dressing.

TSh: We said: you know, you can take that same money and do something a lot better. And so that was really an idea that we had been talking about.

TSt: And it was maybe a two-week effort. And the competition online was very clear. It was digital only, submitted online, and the winners were discussed online and such.

TSh: The academic world and the practice world inform each other. We're bringing something to the academy through our design work but also the academy is informing what we do as a practice. Right now, all of the students in my studio are registered for the ACSA steel competition. I'm working with Chris Ford from the University of Nebraska, we're collaborating on a studio, and we thought it was important that the final presentation requirements we were going to have for our studio could easily be translated to the final competition requirements that the ACSA was asking for.

TSt: For me, competitions in a classroom have also been related to grant funding for design-build projects. In particular, a project called the *New*

Norris House which was funded by the EPA through its people-planet-prosperity competition, P3. It is about helping students move ideas about sustainable design to the market place. There is a phase one where forty teams are selected from the country, and then a phase two where those forty will exhibit on the National Mall in DC. These are not purely architecture students. This is anybody in the university who believes they have good ideas to promote sustainable design and its implementation. To compete not just against other architects was a really great experience for me and the students to sort of move through and see the forty finalists, see how they were explaining the merits of their ideas and why it was important to study. Ultimately the students that I co-directed won one of the six grants to use as seed-funding for a design-build project that we're doing.

TSh: One thing that was really interesting for the students, in that case, was that they were competing against chemistry students and engineering students, and whoever might think that they had an interesting idea about a sustainable future. It gave the architecture and design students a real glimpse at how adept they are at presenting ideas graphically and verbally. And comparing it to what they were seeing from some of the other competitors, I think it gave them a lot of confidence in their ability to understand how much they had grown in relation to some of their peers in other parts of the university. Whether it's standing up and being interviewed for a podcast that's going out over the web live, or talking to the judges or talking to the general public, or being able to have a graphic component that marries with the spoken component, I think it was really great for them.

TSt: And so we've since done things like the NCARB prize, which are very much about competing for funds only through submitting text and visual boards. Competitions require that you can't seduce merely with words, and you must also explain through what you've designed. And so really trying to help the students see their work: what if you couldn't stand up and verbally present it? What would you be able to convey? And I think that's really valuable and critical and we do that specifically for competitions that they enter but also as a test for internal competitions for the best design work in the college to say: pin it up. People are going to walk around, they may or may not know who did it, but you certainly won't be there to explain it. And how will it be understood?

TSt: We lecture about the unseen sight, which I guess is the thing that permeates our work most profoundly. That allows us to work regardless of site or program or client or theoretical versus something that will be executed to in all those instances, take this idea of the unseen site as ways to find the things that inform the project and find unique ways of framing them, and better understanding them and developing design work that reflects that process.

TSh: The ability and the opportunity to articulate this idea of the unseen site as a way of giving words to something that we've been interested in and not been able to pin down so precisely in the past has been really valuable. When we say unseen sight, what we're saying is the world of histories, and ideas, and cultural practices, all those parts of context that are unseen, and how those inform work. And the interesting thing is that you can take a project that's very on the surface, seemingly pragmatic, small, and unimportant. If you start scratching the surface of something as mundane as the zoning codes or infrastructure or things that we don't usually think of as being very influential and high minded in the built environment, all of a sudden you see that there are a lot of cultural values that say something about the society, that relate to other bigger ideas.

TSt: I guess one of the things that I'm particularly interested in is history. I think history is fascinating, I love to travel and experience historical places and understand their trajectories, their developments, the politics that inform them, how people live in those places. Yet, I really love contemporary architecture and how these two things can coexist in the United States. And the understanding that contemporary architecture is not merely responding to things that inform its form directly or its expression, but that those are an outcome of many more things. And how those ideas of understanding past architectural examples, what the culture they came out of, what the economic condition they came out of, who was involved, how they've been used over time. We can take those topics of conversation and help contemporary architecture gain a greater understanding that helps to see all the things that are informing them such that they are sensitive to history and cognizance of what is informing contemporary architecture.

TSt: That said, the most recent competition that we've entered perhaps is the all coveted Rome Prize. And certainly, our application was about competing to get a chance to use Rome to explore those ideas. So, we look at the ways in which the sewer in Rome might help us understand settlement patterns, and where people live and how they live, and how we might learn from that to translate that to more contemporary conditions of the city's development and the impact that has on lives over time.

TSh: We will continue to cross lines between teaching and practice and building and writing. As we move a little further into our academic careers, the mix of that might change a bit. I think we will continue to do a lot of that and maybe in just slightly different percentages. As far as the larger future of architecture, of course, that's a very big question. One of the things that I'm very interested in these days is how we bring design thinking to problems that have been thought of as traditionally out of bounds for designers, things that have been specifically performative issues like infrastructure, and what can a designer actually bring to questions like that. Interdisciplinary cross-boundary work is something that a lot of people are talking about right now. I think that we don't quite know what that is yet, and a lot of people are trying to feel around for the contours of that issue probably more successfully in landscape architecture right now than in architecture per se. For me, the real question is for the future of cities. We're a rapidly urbanizing planet. We are already an urbanized nation; we're a consumptive nation. So I think that when you start looking at questions of how we're going to live on the planet in the future, it's really a question of how we're going to live in cities. So that's something that I'm very interested in right now.

TSt: That said, we live in the shadow of the Tennessee Valley Authority. The 1930s New Deal, a unique moment where many disciplines together tried to look at the issues confronting the Great Depression. Among the engineers, the planners, the designers, there was an idea about energy, an idea about social responsibilities, and that these things were overlaid with how they expressed a culture's values. The work that Ted's doing with Chris Ford at the University of Nebraska and your students at UT, is engaging students in infrastructural hybrids. The students say, "Yeah, those dams are beautiful and they are very productive today." But how many architects are participating in the major infrastructural questions of the day? And if there aren't many, which it seems at times, then maybe we need to expand our boundaries and our thinking a little bit.

TSh: So then that brings us back sort of full circle to some of the things we were talking about at the beginning, which is when you take those sets of things, and you start to overlap and see where the intersection lies, then that is what led us to this idea of the unseen site, and how we see that as a way of talking about what we do. That it is trying to sort out all these infrastructural forces, regulatory forces, and trying to understand how those might enrich contemporary architecture, and might simultaneously ground contemporary architecture because it understands those forces for its own condition.

I started practice in a larger corporate practice, and left that in order to lead a practice that was project-based and designer-led. In a certain sense, we're architects that have more structure around how we do projects than how we run an office. Along with saying that we're project-driven comes an investment that we make in every one of our projects. Rather than being led by business people, we're led by two designers, Snow and Kreilich, and in that sense, the work that we do is not typical of the studio practice, either. Many studio practices are based on very particular opportunities that have great and clear design investment, and a lot of what we do is based more on conventional project types. Our DNA comes from finding an ability to take something out of a conventional status and move it into something else. The inspiration comes from the projects. At the same time, we're architects who really love construction. We're not theorists who put architecture around the theory; we really look at the project and understand the context of the project, and build from there. And building is not something that's foreign to us or banal in any way; it's always interesting. There isn't a person in our studio who doesn't get huge inspiration from just going to the site, going prior to construction, going during construction. We get inspiration from the world, not from just the spinning of the gears, or reading.

Julie Snow needs to put boundaries on her obsession with the work that she does.

Typically, we are in charge of the building from the initial conception to handing over the key. But more and more now, we're collaborating with other people. For instance, we're doing a ballpark. The contractor and his in house design team are the architects of record. It doesn't mean we don't go to the job site - I was just at the ballpark yesterday – and it doesn't mean that we don't constantly work on the details with our colleagues. We don't like to see the design end at 30 percent design documents. Our clients pay for it. We don't do it for free. Sometimes, I won't be billing for that time, but, for the most part, we structure our agreements so that we can, because our work lives and dies by its details and systems integration. Even when not everything meets the standard that we would hold our projects to, there's something powerful about the project, and maybe with a little squinting, it still looks right.

Most but not all of the project is usually designed when we start construction. There probably isn't enough paper to draw every detail, but I would say that everything is thought through. I know people with Revit think that you're building the whole model, so every detail is thought through. I don't think that's true, but I would say, for instance, on some of the residential projects, we've got a good amount of thought put in by the time we're collaborating with the contractor and subcontractors on site. There are many changes that take place during field operations, and that has nothing necessarily to do with the architect or the contract, but the owner. The project is done when it's built. And sometimes it takes a few more weeks than we might have hoped. I guess the biggest surprise I have ever encountered doing construction was going out to my first job site for a project that I was pretty much the sole author for, and saying, "Oh, my God, it is just like the model, only bigger." It was pretty exciting that what I had in my mind's eye, what you had conceived of, was actually real. Many people build a lot of complexity into their work. And with our work, when it actually arrives, when it actually is built, there is so much complexity with light, and it's just richer than I could ever have imagined. For me, the light and the context just bring it to another level, and it's better than what we conceived. I think it's the opposite with architecture. The idea is never as rich and full as the reality of construction.

What makes me as a woman so interested in construction? Probably the fact that it was expected that I wouldn't understand. But that just wasn't an option for me. I really needed to understand construction. And it isn't understanding it as much as mastering it, really feeling like I've understood how things can be and should be assembled.

We never really know everything we need to know when we design a building, and understanding how much our design consultants and our construction colleagues bring to our process — it's huge. It's important to recognize how much knowledge, experience, and expertise are brought to the table by those groups. They often know what they're doing, but not always.

My education did not prepare me for that. And should it? This is a profession you can learn in five, six years. It's very hard to see students come out of university and really not grasp the basics of how a building is assembled. So one of the first things we try to do in the office is to get people to go through a project end to end. Just to expand that understanding of who needs to know what, when, is certainly one of the huge efforts. It's very rare that you have students come to a job site, or that the universities in the U.S. provide technical education. Co-op, internships are great, but it's a buffet line of six months here and six months there, and by the time you understand how this office does it, you find out this other office does it completely another way. While this is great information to have, I just don't think that technical education in North America is where it is in Europe. When you graduate with a degree in Europe, you are an architect. You can hang up your shingle and go. I remember talking to **Nathalie de Vries** in the Delta Sky Club — she was returning to Amsterdam, and I was going to Minneapolis — and she went to school at Delft or Rotterdam, a technical university, no theory, nothing. And I said, "So if that's the kind of education you had, how did you guys get so interested in theory?" And she said, "We were just dying for it." It was just so interesting to her.

I wouldn't argue for just the technical, but I do think that it's difficult to demand a fully formed conceptual basis of design from students who don't really understand how to assemble. I've taught enough to know that this is the system we have, and I do believe it's working. I think we do need that next three years [for the Masters in Architecture degree] in the studio. I'm still not sure that people, once they're registered architects, are even ready to open a practice in the U.S., and I think it has to do with the way that we work and the idea that the set of documents is so complete. By comparison, more is figured out in the field in the European system. And that's a completely different deal, because Europeans engage with their contractor partner and discuss how things might work.

I think it would be an impossible wish to change the education of an architect. Our students are graded individually, and therefore, collaborative work is anathema to a grading system; it just doesn't seem to work. The whole star system in architecture is based on one person being the author of this work. And so it seems like we're training authors rather than training collaborators. I don't know what the fix is, because we still want to graduate people, we want to give them grades. Pass/fail might be a start.

To be honest, my own decision to become an architect was quite accidental. I was going to college, and I was doing dishes one night with my mom, and she had just spent the weekend with friends of my father, Thelma and **John Dinkeloo**. And John was telling about how he was traveling to London and doing this project, doing that. My father was discouraging me from medicine, and so my mom suggested I try architecture. Little did she know that it would become such a big part of my life. But, yeah, I listened to my mom. What about that? We had a career day, and you could sign up for anything that interested you. So I wrote down architecture, and the counselor brought me in and said, "No, I think you mean interior design." I told her I was pretty sure I meant architecture. She said, "Well, you know, I don't think women do that." And I said, "Well, they might." In fact, it was very funny because it was an Argentinian woman, a friend of my father that was doing the talk on architecture. I made this choice with no information. I was just sure.

I still think architectural education is profoundly applicable to any number of endeavors, whether people practice or not. If someone asked me today, I'd encourage them to pursue it, although my kids would tell me I was not. I think they were looking too closely, they knew too much already. But now I have a son who is a photographer, one daughter in graphic design, and another daughter in psychology, autism research, and I think all three of them have a lot of the visualization skills, a lot of the design thinking, the sort of syncretic thinking, so I think it's a great education.

I went through school and opened a practice, never thinking of myself as a woman architect. I thought of myself as an architect, and I was committed to that. At the same time, I talk to young women, and they think of themselves as women architects, and they see that as a positive. They see that as an important aspect of who they are, and they don't want it to go away, they don't want it to be suppressed. I have to say I'm very impressed by that. I don't know what it means, I don't know where it will take them, but I'll be happy to find out.

I had many mentors, and frankly, many guys who really supported my work. I worked for a rather large corporate firm, and I had a mentor there, an owner of the firm. He had my back and way more than I ever thought. I recognized that much later. He was just a wonderful man. Obviously, this was a smart thing to do to mentor me [laughter], but I was not cut out for the corporate world, and so he had a tough time, and I just appreciate his influences so much. Then there was another designer who taught me an enormous amount. He was one of these brick counter guys he just detailed beautifully, and one just wanted to sit next to him and absorb what he was doing. And just do that, too; it was that kind of mentorship by example. Later, when I started a practice, I had this really interesting mechanical engineer client who told me about his company's philosophy. He thought that that was important for an architect who was designing for him to know, but it was also really important for anybody starting a business to know. He was a huge mentor and had an enormous faith in what I would do, which was great. He also had a way of using architecture to create change in his company, so I was often the prow of the ship that was making change, but I could always say, "Well, Bob says," and everybody would go, "whoa, okay." There are people that I'm learning a ton from, which is good.

My favorite project is whatever's on the drawing board right now or whatever we're working on, or the next project. It's like choosing your favorite child. There's no such thing, they're all wonderful in their own way. There are some projects that have required such an investment that they become miracles in their own right, and so I am constantly grateful that that ever happened because it really looked many times like it wouldn't. We're in the process of delivering a ballpark that's very much like that. The whole process has been arduous with budgets, public opinion, and historic preservation issues. Our project manager from the construction company lived for his mantra, "Opening day." My favorite project is whatever is in the hopper, ready to come out, or it's that one that just is so full of potential and ideas.

When we started, all of our work came out of nothing and was characterized by pragmatism, inventing stuff, and very constrained budgets. I just love those early projects, but as we move forward, we've done more and more complex buildings, programmatically and urbanistically. Some projects have had more robust budgets, which is much easier and, in a certain way, a lot more fun because you can really build well if you have a substantial budget, and you can have a complex program. We've been very interested in the DOS, Department of State, Design Excellence Program. So I think there's something quite interesting happening with embassies, and this could be very interesting to us. This would be a great way to transition into more complex and more generous work. We have great opportunities, and I don't think building well is necessarily constrained by budgets. Building well with more durable materials is.

I think when you start your own practice, you have to have a reason, an obsession. I'm going to make this work! It's a certain sort of stubbornness failure is not an option. I didn't start with a trust fund or go into business with my husband, which is what many women architects do. I always had to make the projects pay. I also didn't follow the model of teaching to support my practice. I did teach when I started, but that was largely because of interest in teaching and the ability to get health insurance for my family. Ultimately I think that the idea of not allowing myself to fail really helped me succeed. It helps to start out with a clear business model that, while the aspirations for our projects are very high, they have to pay for themselves. We have to get enough fees to do that. If the client isn't willing or interested in doing something at that level and isn't willing to create a fee for that, then it's probably not going to be a great fit. Early on, we would be kind of not brutal, but very careful about understanding why our clients were coming to us and making sure that their expectations were our expectations. That was back when people thought, well, I'll just call an architect, and they'll do whatever I tell them, and that wasn't something that we were interested in.

First projects set up an architect's presence in the world. I was not interested in doing a ton of residential projects when we started the practice, because then we would have become that small architectural studio that did houses. And while that's a fantastic place to be, it wasn't where my interests lay.

Other pieces that contribute to a successful practice are being open to collaborations, really understanding that clients come in all forms and sizes, and being entrepreneurial about how we present what we can do and what we can bring. I think the world has changed a lot since I opened a practice, and I am seeing more and more collaborations, more complex collaborations, and I think very fruitful collaborations. Being open to different kinds of practice is important.

I feel convinced that I can convey my standard to a team of people. I mean that's one of the things that the design leader of a project and when I'm talking about the design leader, I'm talking about our whole studio has to be really clear about. We have to know how we articulate the goals of the project.

I had a friend who did a lot of film and music, and he said, "You know, your job is just like mine. You've got to keep the beat." We must keep that beat right through the entire project and make sure that everybody understands those goals. And, if we really want people to play well, we get ideas about the goals of the project from them. They become active participants in creating this idea that's going to move forward. People want a great project. In this collaboration with Ryan Companies on the ballpark, they made a game out of when they would bring us out and ask us what we thought of this or that or, here's a concrete sample for this, here's another concrete sample, here's another one, what do you guys want to do? They would make a game of choosing beforehand, guessing, and they were 99 percent right. They had internalized a lot of our goals and our impressions of the project. And they were great advocates for the project. They're not part of our studio; they're the people we work with, and that means a lot to us that we can actually walk away a little bit. That doesn't mean everything is going to look the way we intended it. Because the construction process was accelerated, there's a lot of squinting, occasionally, on a project like that, but it's going to be great. Again, "Opening day."

I think in the future collaboration is going to be a larger and larger part of how we work. I also see clients understanding architecture in different terms. There used to be the question of function versus aesthetics, and now that has expanded into so many different realms. We talk about our project context, not just the landscape context or the programmatic context but also the cultural, social, economic, and political context. And we know our clients have expectations to change the way they work, change the social dynamic within a working group, or economically revive a district of a town.

I think our whole world is going to expand in terms of what design is expected to do, and that means we're going to have to have many, many more collaborators as part of what we do, which is great. I think that the expansion of practice is a wonderful thing.

My secret history is that I am a sociologist by training by education. When I went to teach at the University of Virginia, I had the opportunity to be in a joint appointment between sociology and urban planning. At UVA, urban planning is in the school of architecture, and, as a result, this whole new design world opened to me. It allowed me to develop some ideas over time that I never would have had I not been surrounded by both designers and architectural historians. I would say that was really the beginning of it.

Daphne Spain explores women's impact on the built environment.

I am interested in women's status and had always studied it from an aspatial perspective before. By beginning to look at the literature in planning and architecture, I realized that there had to be some spatial correlate to women's and men's status. I came from a background of examining racial residential segregation and the effects that had on opportunities and resources for African-Americans, and I thought there might be similarities in terms of limiting or enhancing women's opportunities relative to men's. I looked at three types of places that men and women would live together: the home, the school, and the workplace. I did a type of anthropological study for traditional societies and examined those in which women were separated from men in the home, whether it was a yurt or a ger or a tent. They actually have separate spaces, male and female spaces in the home or in the tent, and I compared women's status in those societies with women's status in societies in which there were no such distinctions between male and female spheres. I found that women's status was higher in those societies where men and women shared space. I did the same thing for educational institutions and for the workplace. The book that came out of that project, Gendered Spaces, was published in 1992, about four years after I started the joint appointment. Part of it was the anthropological look at traditional societies, and part of it was US history. I looked at how homes, schools, and workplaces have become more gender-integrated over time. I made the argument that as women and men have become more integrated in those institutions, women's status has risen as well. That was my claim to fame — I am still coasting. I've been told that the book is used in some architectural classes. It had legs, and that was maybe because I was so engaged with the material. It was all new to me, a new way of thinking about the relationship between status inequalities and space.

I don't know whether women design differently — certainly, there have been very few professional female architects, so it's hard to know. Certainly, **Zaha Hadid** has the reputation, **Jeanne Gang**, who designed the highest residential skyscraper in Chicago. I don't think Hadid does it so much, but Jeanne's building is used as an example of a more naturalistic form. The outside is covered with undulating walls that are responsive to the environment and it looks almost like a cascading waterfall. She certainly has been recognized as someone who has more feminine - or feminist? – approach. But there are certainly plenty of women architects who design in a similar way to men. The one I know that did the type of male work would be **Julia Morgan**, who designed the *Hearst Castle* in San Simeon. I think she also designed YWCA visitor houses, but until I read about her, I didn't really know about that many women architects. There has been a lot more work done in the last 10 years, collections of all the women who were out there just working but who were never heard from. I wouldn't come down one or the other on that, I think if a female architect wants to imbue something more feminine into a building, she might be more likely to think of those details than men would. But they also might just be a product of their education as all of us are. As long as most of the design professors are male, they will work from the canon, but that too is changing. There are more female faculty members; we'll see what happens over time.

Speaking of space, that brings up a counterintuitive example which is **Gaudi**'s. He is certainly all about the waves and the lack of right angles and lack of height other than the *Sagrada Familia*, but who knows what would have inspired him in his attention to the mosaics and that sort of detail. We could say that that showed feminine sensibility. Maybe **Frank Lloyd Wright** had a little bit of that in terms of the horizontal interiors. So maybe there were male architects who were channeling some feminine sensibilities into some of their architecture. If you think about what feels homier, for example, it would be for me more a Frank Lloyd Wright house than a San Simeon type place.

The sociologist in me never discovered the architecture of Venus versus Mars. If I were a psychologist, I might think yes, there is something basic, and certainly, a neuroscientist or a neurobiologist would say there is always some basic biological component. Still, as a sociologist, I place more stock in how one's social circumstances affect the outcome. Many think that if only women were in power, we would have this nicer world. Women in power are pretty much like men in power. They pay attention to some different priorities, but it's the social situation, the status that matters. If there are as many wealthy women as men, what might they commission to be built, would they commission women? Would they commission men? The Mars/Venus thing is too cut and dried for starters. There certainly are so many places along that continuum, and it is the social situation. But speaking of that continuum, our next question will have to be: how do transgender architects design? And since there are more highly visible transgender people — not just architects but I assume maybe more in the arts professions than in the others — what would we expect from them? Would we expect them to design the sex they were born to be, or would they adopt the opposite social characteristics and design more like their adopted or acquired gender? That makes the whole female/male question irrelevant. Or it can maybe answer that question. It would be a great study, but I don't know if there would be a big sample yet, or maybe ever, to be able to look at it.

My book "How Women Saved the City" came out of my exposure to architectural historians and learning so much about late 19th-century architectural history and how it all seemed to be male professionals for architecture and landscape as well. I started asking myself, not why there were no women — it was clear why: they didn't have the education, they didn't have the credentials — but how could women have changed the city when they did not have the professional credentials. There only two avenues open to late 19th century women: the church and women's clubs, voluntary associations. I set about looking for voluntary associations that had some urban building agenda and in chronological order those were the YMCA, the Salvation Army where women played very important leadership roles, the College Settlements Association whose houses were often organized and run by women. **Jane Addams** and *Hull House* were the most famous. And the National Association of Colored Women, which was formed by black Baptist women. Each of those associations rebuilt or repurposed existing buildings. The YWCA is probably the one that built most new buildings, but they also turned other old houses into boarding houses, they had typewriting schools, they had hotels for women. The Settlement Associations certainly re-created row houses, gave them a different life as neighborhood living rooms, which is what they called them. In the case of the Hull House, it expanded from one initial mansion into an entire city block. It was huge. The National Association of Colored Women was creating boarding houses and schools for black women who were being excluded from the YWCA, and the Salvation Army, of course, was building all the working men's and working women's homes. They also built rescue homes for all the women who were having unwed births and had a very progressive approach to women in prostitution. In the 1880s, the commander of the Salvation Army in this country, Evangeline Booth, said something to the effect of, "women need inexpensive places to live in," and, "they would not wind up turning to prostitution if they were paid better wages in the jobs that they do." 'There will always be a need for these rescue homes because of the Niagara of woe brings these women to our doorstep all the time.'

I wanted to see the places that women had created, and it was vernacular architecture, but the title came from the idea that the women in these organizations were helping industrializing cities deal with a huge influx of European immigrants, single girls who were leaving the farm because there was no work for them there, and African American migrants from the South. The settlement houses were mainly in North-Eastern and Mid-Western cities. I called all those spaces redemptive places. They were trying to redeem —

very literally because they were all based on some sort of religion — women who had gone astray in the city, or immigrants who couldn't find work. They were redemptive places for the women who mostly used them - some were for males as well - but they also saved the city from all the chaos and disorder that accompanied the arrivals of so many strangers. I came up with the title because I thought they were saving women and saving cities, but in an unacknowledged way.

That actually came out of a situation where I had completed some work, and someone else had gotten credit for it, or I wasn't getting the credit I thought I deserved, and that was going on at the same time that I was starting this project. So, I thought about all the women who did a great deal for the industrializing city, and yet they got no credit or very little credit for it. I don't think anyone had brought all those organizations together and looked at all these different kinds of places, although there was lots of research that looked at them individually. I loved doing that book, I had great images. It was a great scavenger hunt. I probably worked for five years on it. Every city I went to I would look for old postcards, for YWCA buildings, or I go to the historical society. I focused on Chicago, New York, Boston, and Philadelphia, but these were places that were everywhere, and that was what appealed to me. They certainly had more effects on cities than the City Beautiful Movement. The City Beautiful movement took care of the civic, monumental city, but what about the people?

I really liked that book. I had great hopes for it because I had enjoyed it so much. It came out in 2001, and I was interviewed on the Jim Lehrer NewsHour by Ray Suarez on September 10, 2001, the day before 9/11. When I got the invitation to Jim Lehrer, I thought, "Oh my God, I just won the lottery!" I won the academic lottery. Not to make money from it because academic books just don't pay, but that Ray Suarez liked my book, he's going to interview me on NPR. Too bad, it didn't happen. The interview took place, but it didn't go anywhere. Nothing. It was just erased. According to my publisher, there was a slew of books that came out the year that never made a thing.

Does the city need saving today? Not in the same way, we don't have the same environmental toxins that were present in the industrializing city. We do have the same immigration issues, we certainly have the polarization of wealth that existed in the Gilded Age and the Progressive Era. I've often questioned where are the settlement houses, where are the younger people committed to this. I think Teach for America comes close to that, and nonprofits certainly are expected to do more and more as the government does less and less, and that is another characteristic in common. The settlement houses started the kindergartens in libraries and public baths because municipalities were not doing that. Now we've got basic services missing again: no safety net compared to the '60s / '70s heydays.

I think the private sector is certainly saving the built environment by reinvesting. What you are seeing here in Cincinnati, Over the Rhine, the transformation of the last five years is astonishing. In cities across the country, there's all sorts of building going on, but there is still no one or no program that's interested in the dual city of the haves and have-nots and the vast distance that is developing between the two. We don't seem to have the politicians that want to deal with them.

International relations seem to trump everything that the government is going to do. There is so much demand for that, and so this loss with the move of the development of cities to private industry, there is going to be trouble with the exception apparently of Cincinnati, because Procter & Gamble is behind 3CDC and has designated something like 40% of the housing in Over the Rhine to be affordable. They have bankrolled new businesses and transformed the school system. That's an incredibly unusual corporate citizen, and Cincinnati is probably the size city where it can make a difference, as opposed to a much larger city. One can only hope for more businesses that follow that philanthropic model, but they don't seem to be out there in great abundance. This must be an exciting city to live in and have all this evidence of things that seem to get better. I am sure there are still a lot of underclass that still have a very hard time, but it looks as if there is at least some effort made.

Are women saving the city now? Well, that's the good news/bad news part. A lot of these women in the past were volunteers, or with the settlement house workers. They created their own profession because nursing and teaching were overloaded at the time, so that became social work. None of those other women worked outside the home. Of course, now they do, so there is no more volunteer base. The reserve army of women is gone. They are in the labor force now. Married couples with one or two kids have very little time. People don't have time to do it. Studies show that women who work full time are almost as likely to volunteer as those who work part-time, and women do volunteer more than men do. But women have a lot more opportunities now, paid opportunities, and that, of course, is going to siphon off some of that volunteer work.

The typical woman, if she's marginally well-off, can attend college, can get a job, is still paid a little less than men. Women are still disproportionately represented in the healthcare professions, in nonprofits. It is helping other professions that are all low paid that's where women all are. I would say maybe the combination of a lack of time to volunteer and dependence on lower-wage jobs - maybe they're working for others in their lower-wage jobs – but they are not finding the time to volunteer themselves.

I am probably what you would call an accidental academic; I didn't have a grand scheme as such. I incrementally stepped into the academy after a fraught relationship with studies throughout my earlier years — from TA'ships in school, and research fellowships, it followed by a couple of lecturer positions, and subsequently an assistant professorship. I did my duties, as it were, in all of the ascending tracks, from Northeastern to RISD, then from Harvard to MIT, with some forays into SCI-Arc and Georgia Tech. Currently, I have shifted my focus to Cooper Union, where there are new challenges altogether. I like all of these schools, I have had great experiences in them all, but I also developed a strong set of intellectual biases towards certain issues along the way. I ended up inheriting a position at MIT, which I thought was the place I was least apt to be in, and for which I had the least preparation. It was a great challenge for me: to be surrounded by people who had a vast intellectual capacity in areas that were unfamiliar to me and, therefore, outside of the comfort zones with which I had come to be accustomed.

Nader Tehrani tries to bring the world of practice into teaching.

Some graduate from school and win a major competition in their early 20s, as did **Moshe Safdie** with his ground-breaking design for Habitat. That didn't happen to me. I worked on one project at a time, developing one problem in response. Thematically, I would say that there is a lot of consistency in the work just because of the intellectual focus on materiality, aggregation, the protocols of construction, the evolution of our understanding of construction with digital fabrication, and ways of collaborating differently with the industry. All of this produces a web of connections that build on top of each other. It just turns out that the big commissions that we have acquired, the schools of architecture, are a great audience for the body of knowledge in which I am invested.

But I have also come to realize that the successes of our process have diverged, and what constitutes advancements in the academic context truly matters little to the advancement of commissions, projects, and other audiences. In short, good references produce jobs: people who like me give me jobs, but it is not always linked to the intellectual focus of the work itself. And so, it has also led to the imperative of building a relationship between that which we try to advance in school and that which we focus on in practice, if only to allow them to interrogate each other, inform one another, and test the limits of their own spaces.

We have about 25 people in our office. If you average it out, in 25 years of practice I've gained one person a year. So too, the number of projects has increased, but this has taken a long time. There have been a couple of great and exciting moments in our practice. The first, I would say, was early, when we got the first P/A Award. I'm still committed to the P/A Awards, but I'm saying at that moment when you get your first one, it's one of the most amazing things. The second one was after our second P/A Award, when **Terry Riley** called us and said, "I'd like you to be part of an exhibit called Fabrications at the Museum of Modern Art." I'd hardly turned 30, and being asked to do something major like that, for me, was a huge opportunity, a huge honor, and it was the moment in which the office got into digital fabrication in earnest.

Has my childhood exposure to other cultures influenced me as an architect? I can certainly say that having been born in London, raised in Pakistan, lived in South Africa, Iran, Italy, and the United States, I have been impacted by all these influences. The physical environments of Karachi, Johannesburg, Tehran, Rome, London, and New York could not be more different. If anything, they prepared me for uncertainty because every four years, just when I was planting the seeds of a new foundation, I was projected into a new place. It exposed me to cultural relativism — that the conventions, the norms, and the social codes of one place are not necessarily in alignment with another. And so that prepared me indirectly for understanding that architectural scenarios, languages, and so forth, are different and that things have to be translated at every given point. Learning tolerance, as I moved from this side of the world to the other, and knowing how to communicate in other people's languages, not just literally, but culturally, became important. And certainly, part of my upbringing was really to learn other languages (Farsi, English, Afrikaans, French ... and later Italian and Spanish) but really, it was a stepping-stone for understanding differences in cultures.

Before I came to architecture, I had a fair share of challenges in school, especially in reading and writing, resulting in a less than stellar academic trajectory. I regret that, because to this day, I struggle at writing. That's something that remains a big issue for me. And so, as a person who was weak in literary terms, I came to rely on my visual context as the basis for interpreting the world. Maybe my visuality literacy was a compensatory crutch for me because I couldn't communicate effectively through language.

Later, during my days in architecture school, the shift of our focus was precisely on design. The problem was that, beyond the humanities, we didn't realize how much integrated systems, mechanical engineering, day-lighting, and structural systems impacted our design thinking. As saddle-bagged courses, they each had their own raison d'être, but rarely in conjunction to each other. Though technical in nature, they were obviously critical as program for design alibis, or so I came to discover.

In a practice that requires one to discover one's agency, I think it important to develop a strong sense of self-determination, even if one needs to rely on consultants and experts for those areas of design that require legal and insurance safeguards. The strategic knowledge of these inter-related fields become your ammunition for design, because as we grapple with a world of limited economies, triage in the VE process, speed in an era of 24-hour turn-arounds, and strategic alliances between dispersed fields all become critical to our sensibilities of we are to carve out a space for design –that, in a process that has all but eroded the necessity of slowness. Ironically, it is these necessities that have made me, after all these years, into a good student of technologies.

Today's students come into school quite well-equipped with the digital age because that's the world in which they were born, and somehow, they also come into school with a broad understanding of the global challenges that we face, whether it has to do with energy, global warming or questions of disaster. Many students often confuse their ambitions to solve global problems with their responsibilities of good design, or what design can actually do to participate in addressing phenomena outside the formal, spatial, and material realms. Design cannot do everything. It has its own means and methods, and we need to undertake a closer inspection into its devices, methods, and peculiarities. I would like to relaunch a more robust dialogue about what design can do, and where its political strength lies.

That's one of the challenges students face today. The more access they have to things on the Internet, the easier it is to conceptualize the world in terms of the image: but in turn, I would argue the more responsibility they need to bear to contextualize the very images they sample, borrow, transform and cultivate. Those very images, when isolated from their context, stand to alienate them from their conditions of production, their historical and cultural roots, or their semantic and symbolic richness. Thus, in great part, this is an appeal to address the two urgencies there images may prompt us to rethink: on the one hand to look beyond the image, into the engine that is concealed behind them to see how they work, operate and perform — as it were, the architecture beneath the image, and on the other hand, to internalize the role of the image and its transformative agency in today's culture, and bring to it renewed responsibilities.

From a conceptual point of view, I've always tried to bring the world of practice into teaching so that students are exposed to conditions of certain practices such that they gain the agency to transform them, and not merely to accommodate them. That's very important to the way that we think. At the same time, because of my investments in schools, I've made it a practice to take all of the experimentation we're doing within the halls of the academy to impact the means and methods of how the industry operates. Thus, while I do not see these two worlds as seamless, I do see them as a binary that has to impact each other in aggressive ways.

When I first came to MIT, at the ripe age of 45, I was considered one of the young members of the faculty, however ironic that must sound. Part of my mission there was to reckon with how to build a school, to build a debate, conversation, and a set of polemics. But also, as an older generation of faculty members began to retire, this opened up a host of positions for emerging voices, and in my four years as head, we would be able to bring a dozen new faculty members into that discussion. Thus, hiring people to cultivate that discussion was the first act.

Secondly, the question of a core education had not been raised in a while, so our task was to open up questions of foundational pedagogy and to imagine what we could do to structure the conceptual and technical dialogue of the first two to three years of the program. The discussions were open, but also specific but with a speculative atmosphere; we were ready to test and as much as ready to fail. We did not worry so much about the immediate consequences but rather what we would learn from what we did and how we would build on it as we handed the baton over to the next person. We structured a process, and now about two generations of students have graduated; it's about ten years ago, from this first round of pedagogy. And obviously, things have changed considerably since I was there. Now, my challenges are focused on Cooper Union, its full-tuition agenda, the transition to online learning, and the sustenance of its critical culture.

One of the challenges at MIT was in trying to bring its five discipline groups into conversation; each of them, sophisticated in their own realm, they had all suffered intellectual alienation of the decades. Thus, my project was, in part, to see if there were venues in which they might collaborate: in thesis, inter-disciplinary projects, roundtables, joint lectures, etc. Given their relative autonomy, they were also free to expand on their own independent missions. As a designer, part of my mission was also 'selfish': how to bring their particular brand of intelligence into the studio space, which after many decades of autonomy had suffered its own alienation by being separated from the very world it sought to engage. In having faculty from history/theory, technology, computation, and art into our studio program back in the studio, it cultivated less of the instrumental pedagogies we see in other 'integrated studio' programs, and possibly more of an orchestrated space of productive friction. I'm not sure if we succeeded or if we failed, but let's say it did evoke some collaboration, some dialogue, and that's a work in progress. It was an important way to bring MIT back together while placing it on the map.

The other things I undertook were somehow architectural, as it were. If you've been to MIT, you recognize that the School of Architecture is distributed between three floors and three corridors arranged in a centrifugal fashion such that there is no center. In fact, there is a dome in the center, but a space that cannot be occupied, since the school of architecture is effectively located in the poche space around the vault of the dome. Simply said: it was virtually impossible to find the faculty, students, and cohorts; it was hard to build a community without a space to congregate.

So, I did one very simple thing. We reconfigured a space to become a lecture hall and a crit room, effectively a flexible hall were all activities come together; it could expand and contract. We expanded the café with a lounge area that spread throughout the corridors. But symmetrical about that, we also built an exhibition hall — small and student-run — that might ignite events, conversations, and cultural productions from the bottom up. And, third, we built a fab lab next to the studio spaces to bring together the pedagogies of design, building technology, and computation, while also serving the mission of the overall institution: mens et manus.

Beyond that, of course, I brought in much more aggressive visiting critic studios, and visiting faculty. I reduced the number of students by increasing the number of faculty, so we had a high faculty to student ratio, making the faculty contribute not only to the undergrads, but to the graduate students, the M.Arch research students, and the Ph.D.'s. And I made a plea to my collaborators and enforced a much more aggressive lecture series, symposium series, and things that would light a fire under the school.

We documented these kinds of initiatives through a series of publications of various types. Some of them have to do wit the history of MIT, some of them have to do with studio works and the design work that happens, some of them have to do with the research that happens at MIT, and some have to do with the exhibitions at MIT, but all of these are a way to showcase what happens at MIT. Of them, what stands out is the **Arindam Dutta** book, A Second Modernism: MIT, Architecture, and the Techno-social Moment as well as our own work with **Sarah Hirschman** on Testing to Failure: Design and Research in MIT's Department of Architecture. All of these efforts helped evolve the culture of the school. I'm not sure if the entire shift in culture were pedagogical, but what happened between moments of instruction was also important: socially, discursively, and intellectually.

The demands of this dual life, between practice and the academy, is challenging. The hours are long, the juggling act is imperfect, and the scheduling is dizzying. However, with it comes the pleasure of the two worlds that inform and educate each other, with the idea that the school need not feed practice in any direct way, as much as practice need not abdicate the speculative spirit in its commitment to the social contract. In moments like this, when we are immersed in a pandemic, an economic downturn like never before, and a moment of social reckoning, it is also important to engage these two worlds, as they both offer a platform in which to define the relevance of design within a cultural discourse.

What I like most about the profession of Architecture is that it is so all-encompassing. It is not really about one thing. There is always something new to learn and, depending on the job or the phase of the job, the tasks and the state of the project vary so much. I'm intrigued by the whole process, and that's what I love about it. It's so different from day to day and from project to project. It is always very exciting because, in architecture, we don't always know what's next as far as the work goes. I'm intrigued by all aspects from the beginning of conceptualizing a project all the way to getting that last detail right. They're equally important and, to me, equally intriguing.

The job of a good architect is to take what the client says he wants, to give him that plus more that he really hasn't anticipated. Most architects do that. A client comes with a program and wants x, y, and z, and the architect takes that and puts it into the mix. But the architect also gives them so much more. Some of it the client doesn't even realize or appreciate until the project is over. Architecture works on many different levels. It satisfies the requirement, but more importantly, it pushes boundaries and reaches new limits.

Patrick Tighe supervises construction to get clean and well-executed details.

I don't know if our architecture is process-driven. We are very interested in the way people inhabit space, the way they use space, and the experiential nature of being in a particular space at a particular time. That is very much part of what we do. I'm interested in not just creating a beautiful object but one which has to work on multiple levels — on the urban scale and on the level of the individual. It's important to create a memorable experience so that the individual can remember inhabiting the space, not so much from afar, but from actually from being in it. My work is not about one particular style. That's intentional. I'm not interested in rehashing old ideas. I'm interested in taking those ideas and pushing them further. For me, it's necessary that the work evolve and change and grow and turn into something different. As a result, our work is very different from project to project. And often time, as was the case with the *Tigertail House* in Brentwood [2007] and the *LA Loft* [2006], we were dealing with a certain set of constraints, dealing with very specific site conditions. Part of the work had to be very controlled and concise. And then there were these moments in each of those projects where there's a greater expression, the counterpoint of two entities speaking with each other. When we find two things creating a dialogue, it brings out the importance or difference in each. I like that, I like setting up that contrast so that one can actually feel it and realize it, and it becomes more powerful.

For the *Nodular House* [2008], we won a Progressive Architecture award. Basically, we were asked to do a prefab home by a prefab manufacturer.

We started using their system, their kit of parts to create a house, and the more we did it, we realized that we were just doing what everyone else was doing because, at the time, there were many of these prefab homes on the market. They were all kind of like Dwell Magazine, with the same aesthetic, the same materials, the same box-like form. So we said, "If we're going to do this, let's do something different." And for a long time, we were very into **Le Corbusier**'s idea of the modular, and **Buckminster Fuller**, and at the time I was actually looking at prefabricated pieces from Italy in the 1950s. All of this was in my head, and we designed these utility nodes, which became the Nodular house. These pieces would plug into an existing prefab home system or any home for that matter. And the nodes were pieces of utility: there were kitchens, and bathrooms, and circulation pieces. The idea was that as the family evolved or changed over time, the house would also; so if the family needs another bathroom, it plugs one on, or if the family needs to move it to another location that is possible. With this optimal flexibility came the idea of fabricating these pieces. We were looking at new methods of fabrication using technology and prefabrication. The form of the pieces ended up being a result of the program within. It wasn't so much a kind of formal expression; we weren't trying to start with an aesthetic. It came from this process of figuring out what these things needed to be, and that's what they became.

Most of my projects are relatively low budgets. I have to work really hard to get clean and well-executed details, and then make sure that those details get into a job. Often they are the first thing to go. But I feel that they are really worth fighting for. To me, the project needs to be successful on all levels. The overall big picture needs to work, but also the details are really important because they complete the project, and are what one really notices and remembers. But we also do affordable housing projects where we don't have the luxury of getting that detail, and we have to let go and focus on more basic areas. And I understand that. As an architect, I have to choose my battles or strategically know when to fight for a certain element. Strategizing is half the game to get it right. In the end, it's not about me; it's about getting a good project for the client and the people that use it.

That is why we are involved in construction supervision. We do it for our projects, and we are there a lot. It is one thing to draw on a piece of paper, but there is another thing to actually make sure from a general contractor, down to a sub, down to a sub's worker, that a piece is executed. And oftentimes, something is missed, and the architect has to sometimes step in and make sure that those things get done right. It's important that, if not me, some of my office has an eye on what's going on and really watches out for the client. The architect's job is to make sure that the project is built as per the plans, as per the way the client signed off on it. It's really an obligation that the architect has to the client.

I am from the east, I love the east coast, and I go back often. But I live on the west coast and I love it there, too. Architecturally it's a very exciting place to be. I teach at Sci-Arc, so I'm part of that whole group. Even with the recession, there's still an energy and a sense of optimism in the air. Even in these times, there's a sense that in LA, we can do things that others can't do in other parts of the country, and we try to push that even further. So for me, it's a good fit, I love the place, I love the energy. The architecture community there is great. There's a lot of opportunity in LA, and I want to be part of that.

The work in my office and my teaching at Sci-Arc are interconnected. Teaching is a great source of inspiration, and I learn from the students by being there, seeing the work. It often sparks ideas that get transferred into my own work. I'm so glad that I can do both right now and that I'm not just in my office all the time. I'm also out and talking about architecture and being part of the dialogue. That's really important to be involved and be part of the discussion. The profession changes so much, and I don't think academia is really keeping up the pace in which the profession is evolving. It's trying to but is always a couple steps behind. And with this whole reevaluation of the way architecture is practiced in the last few years, I don't think even architects know yet what the new reality is. It's not necessarily the schools' fault, because the schools can't keep up with what they don't know, and architects don't know yet really what the new reality is. We have a lot to reevaluate once the dust settles on where the profession is going in the next few years.

Architects have revamped their offices and taken a new look at the way they run their practices. The office of the future is going to be much more diverse and nimble and ready to change and evolve. That is super important, and it's exciting, too, because it means that we have to be on our toes, and be able to respond to the new climate. It's all about adaptation, really.

The person who is driven and who puts in the time is going to make it no matter what. Most architects I know, the ones that are successful, are so successful because they worked their asses off. Yeah, they get a few breaks here and there, but they work their asses off. And I think that's the key right there, putting in the work and doing good work.

I think of myself as an urbanist. I'm interested in cities, in describing cities, and intervening in them, and so I think the disciplines are often trying to catch up to where cities are. I first noticed it in graduate school, that, if you were looking at American cities, the future was landscape. All the European authors on American cities we read were suggesting that you had to learn something about landscape. And I knew nothing. I hadn't had a course, I hadn't attended a lecture, I hadn't read a book, nothing. What I began to see was a generation of urbanists who were using landscape as a medium and yet not in a way that traditional landscape architecture had been using it. This was a group of people from Western Europe, parts of North America, and parts of Australia and New Zealand, who began searching for a way to describe this kind of work in which what was being done was a kind of urban design. But it was a kind of urban design in which building fabric or street grid or let's call them neo-traditional techniques of town planning were not the primary order. The primary order was given by the ecological or environmental driver. And from that, a new kind of urbanism emerged, what we call today landscape urbanism. This kind of urbanism describes a body of practices in which designers across disciplines and professions engage in city-making. But instead of beginning first with the building as the primary building block in a way that much of traditional urbanism has been framed, or even the street grid or fabric per se, they tend to begin with environmental or ecological drivers.

Charles Waldheim can't think of a more interesting object of study than cities.

When I came out of graduate school a long time ago in the last century, the logic that was given, the conventional wisdom, was to "learn how to build." And so the center of much of what I was given over a set of values had to do with the craft of making things, and the career trajectory that was imagined for leading graduates of leading design schools had to do with "learning how to put a building together."

This produced a situation where architecture, at least in North America, wasn't always addressing the social, environmental, urban conditions that, of course, architecture has always had purchase on. But it appears that the obsession with craft, materiality, and tectonics is really vulnerable. That, of course, was also a moment when the other disciplines in and around the built environment were equally radicalized about their own autonomy. I mean, in landscape architecture, there was a generation who were post '68 radicalized around environmentalism, and for all the right reasons, similarly, planning was radicalized around social agency and political and juridical models, and again, for all the right reasons. But that trajectory tended to leave architecture unmarred from these other social or environmental or urban agencies.

This produced a condition for my generation, where we were essentially invited to make a kind of false choice. We could either do quote "architecture with a capital A," as in its own autonomous forms and as a cultural venue, cultural destination. And the trade-off was that if we were to pursue that, we were giving over the social and environmental and external reference to our field to other disciplines both practically and on the level of conscience. And this left the field open for a kind of neo-traditionalism within urbanism, and for many, many years, leading progressive architects, not even to say avant-gardist architects, and even those in the discipline of architecture were essentially arguing for that autonomy at the expense of saying "well, if you want to be engaged in social, environmental, or urban questions, we're more than happy to allow that to essentially be given over to neo-traditional models." I've described that as a Faustian bargain," I never understood why it was made at a certain point in time because for architecture to have its own autonomy was quite a valuable moment. The irony is that when the urban arts pursued their own extremities or their own autonomy, it was only through design culture that ecology, for example, has really come to the fore, or that potentially social questions could come to the fore.

Today we have these enormous challenges, and yet we can see teams which are growing in complexity and scale — in response to the complexity of the problems. And it's an open question on a project basis: will the leader of that team come from landscape architecture, will it be an urbanist, will it be an architect or a graphic designer? This fluidity about which professional will lead the team is actually reflective of a kind of tension that we have about the professions of education, keeping pace with where cities are going.

The phase zero is the formation of the team: who's on the team, and advising who should join the team, local partners, international talent, a mix of disciplines. What's really interesting these days is the mechanism whereby the talent sorts itself out. It produces conditions where, you know, a major urban park is designed by a graphic designer.

The formation of the team is 51 percent of the exercise. In that regard, the design industry is looking a lot more like advertising these days in the sense that you have increasingly a very small number of fairly well capitalized multi-national firms of which there's a franchise in many major markets. Increasingly in global culture, we find ourselves in processes where talent is being selected, extra-nationally, continentally, or even globally.

Those tendencies are with us to stay, but one position that's available is to retreat from that and to work hyper locally. And many people have done that to very good effect, and I would say that that's an interesting way of practicing. The other way of practicing, which is to acknowledge that increasingly we live in a very complex global world, means we will probably be called on to intervene as professionals in a wide variety of places where we have little context or experience, and so we must think about training professionals for either of those — for the hyper-local or the global. We spend time talking about and thinking about the value of working on sites that you cannot visit and what it means to access a site digitally, and how that changes the work that we do and the way that we educate people.

I teach at the Harvard Graduate School of Design, and just now, we're having a lot of conversations about the relationship between deep immersion in disciplinary knowledge and professional knowledge, and then the relationship between those fields and their margins or externalities. And at the same time, I use design culture as a general characterization to help expand or unpack architecture, because it's autobiographical of my own experience but also in part because when architecture is tempted by a kind of fundamentalist strain or streak, as any discipline, any profession can be, there is a kind of tension between going back to fundamentals and then expanding with new problems.

This is something that I advise my students on: the first thing is that there are quite a lot of roles to play. There's a lot of interesting work to be done and to be absolutely fearless if not arrogant but confident about pursuing one's own interest. What's really important is that maybe we spend less time talking about competitions as one vehicle and talk more what the importance of having professionals and peers advising on selection processes. And so in that regard, the obvious, and I think good advice is to choose your partners wisely. A lot of energy and attention obviously goes into the formation of those relationships, and they tend to be, on the one hand, loose yet enduring. And if you look at other industries like film or advertising or other creative activities, they have these kinds of decentralized networks and undercapitalized types that come together on a project basis. In that regard, cultivate a set of disciplinary consultants and colleagues that you can work with effectively on short notice. That, for me, is really quite important.

Originally I wanted to be a journalist. Or perhaps, more precisely, as time went on, I wanted to be a publisher. So I went into journalism at Berkeley. And journalism was all writing, as you might expect, and I found out relatively quickly that I was not a writer. But I was interested in the artistic part of it. I liked layout, I liked books, the way they felt. All I could do in the Journalism Department, if I wanted to be in production, was sell ads. So I sold ads. I had a year of that, and I decided that wasn't going anywhere. I either had to change schools or my major.

I went through the catalog, and I found this thing called Landscape Architecture. It was one-third landscape, courses of all sorts, one-third architecture, courses of all sorts, and one-third other things, courses of all sorts. I thought that's probably as good a background for a publisher as anything. I went with a fraternity brother of mine, at the end of my sophomore year, and we took a sophomore studio. We were making models, and we used toothbrushes and, you know, speckled things. I loved it. My fraternity brother friend hated it, and he went screaming from the room. I stayed.

To **Peter Walker** Landscape Urbanism is a Presbyterian confirmation. Its promotors know what God wants, and they tell you.

I learned relatively quickly that school is not just about learning a craft or a profession. To spend too much time on those aspects is a waste of curriculum time. However, students must have some sense of craft, and it doesn't matter whether they're working on old fashioned craft like grading and drainage, and plants, they need to know that it exists. When I first graduated from Harvard, a lot of us felt that we really knew something nobody else knew. Some felt they were too weak to get a job, which is one of the feelings I had had, and some were so arrogant, they thought they could rule the world without any more knowledge. Balancing those two extremes is vital, and accepting that some of the things we learn in school have no direct application, but some other things are important perspectives for any student.

I must have taken 10 history courses, art history, architectural history, landscape history, American history. I did pay a lot of attention, and I wish I had paid even more attention because I found it the most useful thing, useful because there is nothing new under the sun, and knowledge needs to pop up when we need it. We can't take every project from zero, and we have to rely on some underpinning. Evaluating things that are happening now by putting them into a historical perspective is a wonderful approach. Knowing history, knowing where things "fit" has been the most important tool, other than talent, and ambition, that I got in school. And I always tell students that that's the thing they should focus on.

Toward the end of my schooling, I got a little nervous about where I was going to work and how I was going to get a job, and how I was going to make a living. I went to the chairman and asked him what he thought about my going to work for the National Park Service. My parents were Depression babies, teachers, and were always saying, "Be very secure." The chairman started laughing, because I was one of the better people in the school at that time, and he said, "Look, Pete, you can go to work for an office, and any time you don't like that, you can go to National Park Service, and they will take you with open arms. You go to work in the National Park Service, and if it doesn't work out, the offices will think what the hell was he doing in the National Park Service." The following week he got me an interview at **Larry Halprin**'s, and I went and showed him all my work from school. Larry, a bit of a prickly pear, said that he really hated the design I was doing, but he gave me a job anyway. He didn't like the **Garrett Eckbo** and **Burle Marx** kind of forms I did; he was more **Thomas Church**, more about plants, but he wasn't as jazzy as they were. I started to really learn when I went to work for Halprin. And through him, I knew Church, and so I got into that kind of design.

At that time, everybody was doing residences, which I figured I would do. But when I got to Harvard, **Hideo Sasaki** had a completely different view of what was coming. This was early in the '50s. He saw that with the GI Bill, schools were going to be huge, universities were exploding, and urban renewal had just started. They were going to rebuild cities, and the transportation, the highway program, that all had to be thought through. He just gave me this huge view, like taking me up in the ivory tower. It was such a huge prospect, actually, much larger than I could imagine myself doing. And I never went back to the garden thing. I got interested in housing in new towns, which was a subset of this fantastic thing Sasaki was explaining to me. That's really how I became a landscape architect.

I was working for Sasaki, and we were working for **Saarinen**, for **Skidmore**, for **Anderson Beckwith**, all good firms. We had gotten this job called Foothill College in California, and one of the provisos was that we open a little office during construction out there. Because I was the only one who had worked in California and knew anything about it, it was logical that I would go out and do that. I figured we would do Foothill College, and in three years, I'd be back in Boston. But just as Sasaki had said, this place was just exploding with urban renewal, expansion of suburbs, shopping centers, schools, everything. I didn't get back for almost 20 years. The office got to be huge, got to be 200 people, and it was only in '72 and '73 during a downturn that our office shrunk to only100. There had never been an office like that on the West Coast before, where the norm was typically five or six people.

It's very hard to work in retreat — they always say that the most difficult move in military life is retreat — and I was just exhausted. So when the economy turned back up again, I turned the office over to one of my partners, a guy named Kal Platt, and took a job teaching at Harvard, just one class. I had left in order to do a job, and then I went back because I was just tired of doing all that. By then, I was collecting modern paintings, and I was also doing some painting. Boston was wonderful because I could work the week there, and Friday afternoons, I'd go to New York and spend the weekend. I got a little loft down there. **Donald Judd**, **Frank Stella**, and **Andy Warhol** had been at it about 10 years by the time I kind of arrived. I'd go out every Saturday, and there would be two or three shows that just blew my mind. It was an incredible time for art.

Art influenced what I did from the very beginning. I was teaching first a seminar on contemporary heroes basically, Halprin, Church, Eckbo, all of the people who were still alive. Then I was teaching a studio that was art-based. We would go and look at art, we would analyze it, we would do projects which were engaged in art, and we would end up at the end of it doing a memorial, ironically, and using those same ideas as devices for engaging a public and pulling them into the memorial spirit. We did several Kennedy memorials, we did Roosevelt one year, we did the Holocaust. We would change the subjects, but it was still trying to take art and then make a piece that had to speak, not just of itself but also of somebody else in response to a narrative.

Then Jerry McCue became Dean at the GSD. First, Jerry asked me to take over Urban Design and find him a new chair. I ran the search, and we got **Moshe Safdie**. And then Jerry said that we need a new chairman at Landscape. I wasn't that happy about that. I was willing to do it for a bit, but I was no Sasaki, and I wanted to practice. So I did that for three years. It was fascinating; I got to reorganize the program. I didn't know anything about academics, I just taught I mean, I just worked. So it was good for me, and it was time to think. Out of that came a little experimental office, a typical academic office. I had a little space in the square. I basically hired students, and we did experimental projects and competitions. We even won a few. That became the office I have now.

When I had worked in California, I never was fired, ever. In my new little office, I was fired fairly regularly, particularly because I was going to my old clients, but I wasn't the same person; I had changed. When they said, "No, no, this isn't what we want," I'd say, "No, it is what you want." And then they'd fire me. Good friends would fire me. It was a different stance, and that was happening in the '70s.

The big thing that's going on now is a thing called Landscape Urbanism, which is a combination of McHargian notions of larger systems applied to mechanical systems. **Ian McHarg** used to think that form would come out of plumbing and water distribution and transportation systems, not just on the surface, but also underground. It's interesting that no form has come out of that. This is not to say that it had no influence and not to say that it wasn't useful, but it isn't the basis of form; rather, it's the basis of a different kind of analysis. And we all use it. Landscape Urbanism is an attempt to revive that larger sort of landscape base idea of planning. It has all the strengths of the McHargian stuff and all the weaknesses because McHarg never did become the basis of design. He brought architects in, and some of them have been really good designers, and he went into practice with Wallace, who was a really good planner, economic-based, demographic-based, and having a good sense of physicality, but the theory never really worked.

I don't think Landscape Urbanism is going to work, either, because I think it has the same kind of large vision, without a client base. You can't do it at the site level, you can't do it at the city level. Like McHarg's approach, it really needs to be done at the regional level, and it needs to involve watersheds and things like that. That's what you would have to have to make Landscape Urbanism work, even if it did find a formal way of developing, I just don't see who in America would do it. We should probably spend more time on global warming and get right at the real problem. I don't think our real problem is building.

Sasaki thought that we could solve larger units, cities, parts of cities, universities, and so forth, with the Bauhausian idea of getting landscape architects, engineers, architects, planners together to design this ideal city. That didn't work. So I'm not much for theories, because they were hypotheses that were never proven anywhere in any degree. I think the fallacy in them is that the information, the area, is so vast, no one could learn it. One of the troubles that Ian McHarg had with his students was that they'd spend so much time learning these various forms of natural science, learning the vocabulary, and so forth, that there wasn't any time in the curriculum for them to actually apply it. If he hadn't been getting all the English architects, there would have been no design at all. But a lot of people were already designers before they went into that course, so the fact that he didn't teach design did not matter much. I knew two or three young people who didn't have an undergraduate degree in design and went in, and they were just bewildered, and some of them are bewildered to this day.

I have often thought about what if I hadn't gone back to California, what if I'd stayed with Sasaki, whom I respected, would the firm have sagged? Stu Dawson and I were the firm's landscape designers, and there were a number of other people who were really important to the firm - planners, architects, and so forth. Sasaki was very interested in the Bauhausian idea of collaboration, which is to put everybody in a room. It works in academia where we could have a wonderful class with an engineer, and a planner, and so forth, and we did them at Harvard. Those were great classes, but Sasaki tried to do that with the firm. And if there are brilliant people carrying out each of those roles, and designers that were strong enough to stand up and play the role, it might work. But in the nature of things, landscape architect budgets are largely a tenth of the total. You can't wield an awful lot of power from that position. Even in the office, they were about a tenth of the fees, so they didn't have equal power.

Sasaki's notion of equality and that the best idea would win didn't work, of course; it bureaucratized like all organizations do and consolidated power in one place or another. They weren't wonderful architects. For a moment in time, they were wonderful landscape architects, but it didn't sustain. I thought if I had gone back after Foothills, that perhaps Stu and I would have been strong enough to hold the end up because Sasaki wasn't going to, he was too interested in the whole. On the other hand, the firm we did make was quite interesting and made its contribution, and this firm, the one I'm in now, is quite interesting and has been making contributions. So it doesn't have to be done just one way.

Ultimately, I find that I've worked with so many good architects, and they were all so different in their approaches. Interestingly, we tend to make heroes out of people who have been unable to sell anything while we look askance at people who are too able to sell something. But that is an essential part of getting design done. And finding patrons, I remember **Martha Schwartz** and I, when we were practicing together — we spent a long time thinking about the patrons. Martha decided that the art mavens were the patrons. And that, in a sense, made her do smaller things because that's the sort of thing they could commission. I decided that institutions were the patrons, which was **Mies van der Rohe**'s notion. And he would get his hooks into an institution, and he would do four or five things. Saarinen was more like that, too, where he was very, very good at handling and getting people to try things. When we look back at some of his buildings, you wonder how the hell he ever got permission. I've done two airports, and airport people are the least imaginative of audiences. On the one hand, they're all about money, and on the other hand, they're all about expediency, sometimes both at once. To get TWA to build that building, I can't imagine it. Saarinen was very good. I watched him in action. He was very good. And I learned something from every architect I worked with.

I'm always finding students, architectural students, too, who don't go and see things. They've had so many slide lectures that they don't think they have to go and see anything. At Harvard, we got in a car, went to New Harmony, went to Columbus, went to Chicago. We saw all the stuff that we had been told about, and were able to replace those slide images with images in our heads of walking around these spaces and seeing it. That was so powerful to me, that firsthand impression. I virtually can't do a project without going to the site and kind of wandering around and thinking about it. That's what field trips are about.

I've been catching up all my life trying to go to enough places, with enough time to think about them. I love to go to places with students because I then have to explain what it is, and in doing that, I lock into it in a way that couldn't be done otherwise. We do teach people how to read, and we do teach students how to read purposefully, how to get information, and how to organize it. But it's a lot harder to learn to see. How do you learn to systematize that, and how do you learn to draw out of that?

I think that is very important now because computers have replaced reality, in a sense. Computers are wonderful, we make money with them, but they come between us and reality. They're like the slideshow, in that they're a substitute for reality, and they're also becoming a substitute for drawing. They're a substitute for using our hands. I know I'm old fashioned, but I still think that the "hands-on" is tremendously important. And that's what I would tell students who are in school now. Actually seeing and actually drawing – these will stand them in good stead. I've come to believe in it, maybe absolutely.

My roots are an amalgam of things and places. I did a semester abroad at the Architectural Association (AA) while I was at the University of Virginia, and traveled for a year at the SOM fellowship between my first and second year at Princeton. At Virginia, we had the legacy of Cornell and Syracuse, the period of **Five Architects**, early postmodern, and an emphasis on diagraming, drawing, using a very narrow bandwidth of visual means to present. **Richard Meier** was one of our gods in terms of his diagraming and clarity. Architecture was perceived as a language; it could be taught; it could be communicated in a set of shared formal strategies that are understood.

We were very sheltered at Virginia. And we thought everyone did the same thing we did. What was great about going to the AA was that I vividly remember seeing **Nigel Coates**' work and asking myself, "Where is this guy from? This is insane." I didn't understand his work at the time. However, **Gordon Benson** and **Alan Forsyth**, the professors I had, were among the more Corbusian, were more the ilk, and there was a bit of self-selection that went on in choosing to be in their studio. But even they were quite a bit far out, farther out than what I had been used to. And there was this level of passion and commitment that was great. Some of our faculty at Virginia had that, too, but there was an intensity about how they went about things at the AA that I hadn't been exposed to before.

Adam Yarinsky wanted to be an architect since first grade.

I went to Princeton, which was similar to Virginia but had a more expansive view in terms of a theoretical, philosophical standpoint. Professors like **Alan Colquhoun** or **Tony Vidler**, provided us with a deeper grounding in some of the things we were doing in cultural terms; how buildings were historically conceived in terms of their culture, as well as the physical parameters of the specific project. Alan Colquhoun was my thesis advisor, and I graduated from Princeton in 1987. It was at the beginning of the end of the era of postmodernism. I felt fortunate to understand the limitations but also the strengths of the movement. I took architectural history every semester for six years of my education. From the more general courses at Virginia to Vidler's course called Ledoux, Soan, Schinkel, or Colquhoun's history of architectural theory, I have always felt really engaged about it. I've just always loved history.

I am a huge fan of **Adolf Loos** if one can be a fan of an architect who's been dead for 75, 80 years. I am very much attracted to Alvaro Siza's work. And I also admire **Gigon & Guyer, Herzog & de Meuron, Zumthor**, those architects that have an intensity about material, spatial qualities of their work, an integrity to the work from a constructional and material standpoint.

Almost twenty years ago, I founded Architecture Research Office with **Stephen Cassell**. I felt that through a different approach to architecture, we could perhaps achieve a balance: make great architecture, have a well-managed firm, have fun. Ultimately, we thought of the practice as a form of inquiry and wanted to continue to learn through our work. I wanted to be an architect since I was in first grade, so I'm one of these strange people who think of it as their life. I don't really think about it as a career or profession. The idea of having that kind of level of control over my own practice just seemed very natural. And of course, starting out, I didn't think of any of the risks. But of course, we've been through three economic downturns now, and all of that so ... but it's good.

My partners and I are all generalists, I would say, and we are all interested in design and also the management aspects that we don't generally distinguish from design. So we don't have a firm where there's a rainmaker or a businessperson. We have a business manager who's not an architect, and we have a business development person who's not an architect. But, from a practical standpoint on a day-to-day level, we collaborate about design.

From an administrative standpoint, one principal is usually the principal in charge of a project. (S)he has either more direct contact with the client or is ultimately responsible for running the project team, which might have a project manager, a project architect depending upon the size. So we do divide things up like that. The process of who gets what project has always been relatively organic and has always seemed to fall out to where there's been a balance. We certainly think about who should be listed if we're going after a project, because of someone's workload or things like that. But it has generally speaking not been an issue. At this point in our careers, we're more than happy not to be the administrative lead on a project, because we know that we can still have a connection with the design. We usually find that the person who is the collaborating principal is an outside voice who can be an advocate for aspects of the design. We try to use that productively to critique each other. The office is set up like a studio. We sit out in the room with other people. We have about 25 people altogether, and we try to be as non-hierarchical in that respect as possible.

Typically when we start a new project, we gather information. That information can be everything from factual information about the site, dimensions, surrounding buildings, or program. We're often defining the program with a client, so we're engaged in interviewing, measuring, helping the client transform broader goals into specific, tangible program needs, and associated costs. We've done a lot of programming and predesign work, especially in the last decade. We like to think that information gathering builds an informed intuition about the project design. So we don't necessarily come into a project with an a priori final result. We do have inclinations of what might be a way we should study the project, or areas we don't necessarily want to explore because we think they might not be as productive.

Following the information gathering stage, which is not necessarily a strictly defined phase, we begin to test ideas with as many visual means as possible: physical models, computer models, obviously two-dimensional drawings. We cycle through alternatives not just to sort of grind through options but also to build a sense of what we think is the appropriate fit of the architecture to the project's goals. A subset of this phase is working with clients to figure out the intangible aspect of their mission. How to give form to those, or how to facilitate those through the architecture. It's not just, "We need x number of classrooms." In the case of our renovation of the Princeton School of Architecture, the question was how to take an opaque building and literally open it up to the surrounding liberal arts campus. We explored how to make a visual connection to what was going on inside.

When we initially present to a client, we don't necessarily present multiple alternatives if we can explain very clearly why it is we've decided to do what we're doing. We like to think of our clients as collaborators, and we don't mind involving them in our process by explaining certain options that we've studied. So we try not to just say, "here's what you have to do." These days, some of our clients have objectives that are at odds with what we feel is the most appropriate way to study the project, not the design, but the process of how to get the best result in terms of architecture. So we spend a lot of time just figuring out how to keep our process on track so the outcome will be more successful. We do a fair number of mockups, especially for key elements. We like to identify parts of projects to be areas for specific exploration. We did a fitness facility for a large corporate client, the new *Goldman Sachs Headquarter*, where we created a custom backlit resin ceiling panel that was used to cover 20,000 square feet of open workout space.

Architecture should be experienced with directness toward material qualities; construction integrity enters in very early in the process. One example is the *US Armed Forces Recruiting Station* we did in Times Square. Here the reflectivity and transparency of glass were a fundamental carrier of the intentions of the project. It's something that we thought about from the initial rendering, which is a façade, but at night, with the reflection of the buildings surrounding Times Square, the façade is the image of the American flag that merges with the surrounding commercial signage. In that sense, it was very direct. We thought about that within the first few weeks of the project. And we think about material and constructional quality early on, because we try to calibrate the architecture to what we feel the budget can handle. So rather than saying at the end of the project that we really thought this should be a stone building but it turned out to be concrete block or brick, we like to think at the beginning that this is a brick building, so we're going to make it a really great brick building. That doesn't mean we don't explore alternatives, but we're conscious of the economic reality. We want it to be successful on those terms.

Doing work for higher education or for public clients, the construction quality can be an issue. That can be particularly challenging, especially when we put a tremendous amount of care into the construction documents, knowing that it's not going to have the best contractor. If there isn't somebody on the contractor's side who cares, we can't compensate for it beyond a certain point. That I find is the most challenging. Other challenging things are when I feel that our process has a risk of being hijacked by the particular way a client needs to have the work or the design process occur. But that doesn't mean that we can't work with large groups of people or complicated processes. The more I do it, these twenty years on, the more opinionated about our process I get; we shouldn't squeeze things too tight into certain time periods or anything like that. Every project goes through challenges. It's a little like having kids. Hopefully, parents are satisfied with how their children exist in the world. So the education and public projects I'm working on now are the most challenging. I think most architects would agree with that.

There's a bunch of projects I would love to do. Any kind of major cultural institution like a museum or a performing arts center is a great project, not only because of the program but because they potentially will exist in perpetuity and be an integral part of the culture that's created them. So those are maybe at the pinnacle of what any architect would want to do. In direct proportion to that permanence, they have that public scrutiny and complexity and difficulty in achieving it. So they are very challenging to do well, but if you can pull it off, they're really amazing.

I would love to do a public housing project. We just don't have that program really in the United States anymore. We have affordable housing done by developers, and New York City does it, but it's a type of project usually done by firms that specialize in it. And it's not often that a client will open that up to others who haven't done one before. So it's very hard to do that, but the **Michael Maltzan** projects are really commendable in terms of the discipline. Even if the budget is super tight, we can bring a lot to the project, just by being creative and caring about things. So that type of project definitely excites me.

My partner Stephen Cassell and I decided early on that the practice would be our main focus but that we wanted to teach and do it intermittently. I think that there's a demand in different institutions for people like us who have one foot in the academy and one foot in the practice. We can bring a different perspective to the students. And that demand has led to very consistent offers to teach.

The idea of having studios that are integrated design studios is very helpful because students are exposed to how structure and mechanical systems can be woven into an architectural strategy. But beyond that? Some architects criticize the academy because they say students are not prepared. But I don't think they have to be prepared in the same way. Knowing how to make a building, that's something that we, as practitioners, contribute to the development of students up to a point. I mean, that's why students apprentice. Students need to develop a greater consciousness of the historical and social context in which buildings have been made in the past. Not because that's the way they'll be made in the future, but so they can begin to think critically about the work they're doing in the present. That's probably the biggest thing that I would advocate for. And it takes particularly enlightened teachers like Vidler or Colquhoun or **Beatriz Colomina**, a great teacher I had at Princeton, **Mark Wigley**, and others, who can make history and theory relevant to the practice of architecture today. That's important. Otherwise, it's just people looking at magazines and books and copying stuff. It's got to be more than that.

Having been to all those schools, we've also done three architecture school planning projects. We did a master plan for Cornell, we did the five-year plan for the Harvard Graduate School of Design, and we are doing work for them, and we're doing the programming, planning study for the University of Michigan. There are something like 100 architecture schools in the United States, and each one has a unique culture and legacy, and it's fascinating to me that they have this specificity growing out of various circumstances. So it's pretty interesting. I wouldn't have thought when I was a student, about the diversity that's out there.

We did a year and a half study on design quality in the federal government for the GSA and the NEA. We interviewed about forty people across different disciplines, not just architects but graphic designers, industrial designers, mechanical and structural engineers. And one of the concerns I have is that there is a misconception that everything is design. That's what has already happened with business schools teaching design. There's a way architects think about problems which is great and benefits other disciplines, but we also do still make buildings. People will need buildings to live in, to occupy, to create interior space so that we can survive in different climates, support programs, etc. As broad as design can become, there's still going to be building. I'm talking about expanding architecture beyond making buildings to thinking about how we design processes and how we create public space and understand infrastructure systems. Being nimble about our work and how we create it is important. Sometimes it's designing a process, and it's not a building; sometimes, it's very intensely designing a building.

Concerns about sustainability are going to be increasingly enmeshed in what we do, so there won't be any dividing line between design quality and sustainability. It will be the same thing. I've always thought about daylight being important and intelligent, efficient use of material is important, building orientation on the site being vital. So those are things that get inculcated into the profession through a rubric of sustainability. I think that's a good thing. It isn't just a fad. It is necessary given the scarcity of resources in the world that we live in; we need to be more intelligent about what we do. What's great about the way people are being taught these days is the recognition that the things an architect does are diverse. You don't have to be the star designer of a building to be successful. You could go work somewhere else and be a client of architects, and you could be just a concerned citizen and get a graduate degree in something else and not be an architect. But that the ability to think critically, the ability to care about your environment, those are invaluable skills. Today, architecture is understood to be a field where graduates can assume a variety of positions in our society. I think that's very important.

Interior design was never a career that I thought I was going to end up being in, although I have always admired it from a distance. So I am thrilled to be working in it now because I find that there is so much overlap between the two disciplines of architecture and interior design. I think that having both perspectives, the architectural perspective and the interior perspective, is valuable for architects and for interior designers to have. It just makes us better at what we do when we have an understanding of how space is utilized in a cohesive manner.

In fact, it is not just my architectural education that prepared me well for being an interior designer but also all the education that I have had prior to that. My undergraduate studies were not in architecture or interior design. I studied chemistry and economics because I was a premed student at the University of Virginia. Although I sometimes jokingly say that it was kind of waste, the truth is that it really prepared me very well to think critically and in a different way from a lot of interior designers or even a lot of architects. My advice to design students is not to be so narrowly focused on just studying design, but to make sure they expose themselves to a wide breadth of subject matters. It is important to be well versed in science, to have an understanding of math, to understand history, to understand literature. We never know how the brain is going to take that information, process it, and how it is going to end manifesting in your work. But certainly, it is going to be a competitive advantage.

Vern Yip hosts home makeover shows and appeared on TLC's Trading Spaces.

I don't think that my getting an MBA changed the way that I design. But I certainly think that it made me more sensitive to everything that goes into making a project real. Not many of us go into architecture or interior design to just spend all of our time creating projects that are just on paper and are never going to be realized. My hope is that the spaces I design actually get built. And as a result of getting built, and as a result of being well designed, they impact people's lives in a positive way. To get a project built necessitates some understanding of what it takes to get it to that point. No matter what, today, everyone benefits from having some understanding of how to run a business, how to be entrepreneurial, how to actually make a living. At the end of the day, we want to be able to clothe and feed ourselves and to be able to support doing what we love. In order to get there, we benefit from having some understanding of the business world.

What person seeks to be an architect or interior designer and then goes and studies chemistry and economics in his undergraduate degree? Someone could sort of look at that and say, "You are kind of messed up. Maybe those four years were a waste of time." I was pretty old when I went to get my first professional degree, my Master of Architecture at Georgia Tech. A lot of people going into that situation have studied architecture for four years, and then they are going for an additional two, or they have a five-year degree, and they are going for an additional one. But here I was, starting graduate school with an economics and chemistry degree. Many people would look at that and say: wow, big mistake. But I just choose to look at it differently. I have to say that as soon as I made this change, this dramatic shift from being a premed student and studying chemistry and economics, to studying architecture and being in the world of design, I immediately felt like I had changed from being a fish swimming upstream to a fish swimming downstream. I immediately felt like the DNA in my body was responding and was telling me that I was finally on the path that I was supposed to be on. As soon as I shifted onto this design path, it did feel like the doors were suddenly opening for me, and the stars were aligning, and I was on the path that I am supposed to be on. And then it just became about really hard work and perseverance. I always kept my eyes open for opportunities.

My first job was being responsible for laying out the toilet stalls and the urinals, but even though that was not that much fun, I threw myself into it and took this attitude that I was going to be the absolute best—nobody was going to be able to lay out toilet stalls and urinals better than I. By taking that attitude, eventually an opportunity is going to open up. Many people would say, "Oh, you got two undergraduate degrees, you got two graduate degrees, and you started off working 80 hours a week for twenty thousand dollars a year. That has got to be a huge blunder. That has got to be a huge failure." But I don't look at it that way. First, we should really be doing things only if we are passionate about it. If we are not passionate about it, it is just way too hard. Second, if we really, really apply ourselves and are the first person at work and the last to leave, we will make it. We will get to where we want to be.

When I first started in television, I went from working at a really large firm, the largest firm in the southeast, to going out on my own, and then having access to some very, very high-end clients, and then launching into this show that really was new to the US. No show had ever been on the air before like Trading Spaces. It was sort of like the wild, wild west. Everybody was trying to figure out how to do these kinds of shows. It was like boot camp because we were expected to do everything. Not only to design the space and pick the colors and the materials and all those kinds of things, but we were also expected to paint the walls, install the flooring, hang the lighting, hang the pictures, and move the furniture in. I don't think most interior designers do that, right? Interior design is about coming up with the design and turning in the documents and ordering the things, and then there are people there who execute it. But even though it was incredibly difficult, it was helpful, and it made me a better designer. I now understand with my own two hands how to install different materials and what needs to go into it and what conditions need to be in place. And honestly, I command a lot of respect when I am talking to a contractor or a subcontractor and can speak their language. They know that I am not somebody who, on a whim, just happened to pick a material but that I actually know how it should be installed and what the challenges are and how to circumvent those challenges. I am not saying it is mandatory that everybody do that. But I found it to be incredibly helpful and difficult.

I love being part of television because making a television show is a very, very creative process. It is a confluence of practical skills with creative skills. The process of making a show is a tremendous effort that requires many people. There are producers on-site, and they are making sure that the right shots are being taken, and the right bits are being photographed or shot for the show, at any given point. There are multiple camera people, audio people, grips, production assistants, and people who are on set to provide food and drink. The whole crew is able to work; there are people who are there lending a hand and making sure that furniture gets moved into the right place, that the room gets painting. Anybody in the field experiences that process of a project going from a to b, from conception to completion, but we compress it, and we also shoot it. So we have compressed the time, work on tighter budgets, and shoot it for a show. Making a television show like Trading Spaces requires all of these people on location. And this doesn't even take into account all the others who are editing and programming. It is very much a collaborative effort to make a television show.

By the point that I actually get involved, the homeowner or the client that we are going to be focusing on for a show has already been selected, if there is such a person. Sometimes I work on designs that do not really have homeowner involvement. For example, we give away an urban home every year as part of a show called HGTV Urban Oasis. My goal in those instances is to have that space embody what that city is about. So at that point, my client becomes the city. But when there is a homeowner involved, that person has already been selected, and I am not part of that process. Someone has already interviewed them, found out the things that are critical to them — their likes and their dislikes, things that are working for them in the space, things that are not and what they are hoping to see — often times there will be a taped interview that I will get to watch. Typically I receive a packet about two, maybe two and a half weeks, ahead of time. And it is up to me at that point to analyze that information. I will view it multiple times. To me, that file is like gold, that is where everything is. It is even helpful when they are interviewing them in spaces that we are not focusing on because I get a sense of who they are. Unlike a traditional client interview, there is not that opportunity to talk to them in person at length and then touch base with them throughout the design process. I am working in a bit of a vacuum, but I have all this information, so it is up to me to really pay attention, to read between the lines, and to be very sensitive to what is unfolding in front of me.

After I get that information and the dimensions of the room — overall width, overall length, height, where existing junction boxes are, where existing outlets are — I will draw the physical room as is in a CAD program and then I begin the process of space planning. For me, a successful room is the confluence of function and aesthetics. I would much rather have a room that functions well but maybe isn't aesthetically pleasing than a room that is aesthetically pleasing but doesn't function as well. So I always start with the function, and I always make sure that the space plan works for what the clients are expressing they need to have happen in that room. This usually happens within five or six hours, and then it becomes a process of finding those things that are reflective of their taste and their requirements, and making sure that everything fits within the overall budget. I usually know that I have certain givens that immediately come out of my budget. I have paint unless we are doing a wall covering of some sort or something like that. And I have x number of dollars set aside for supplies that we are always going to have to have on hand, for hardware and other basic necessities. But then it becomes more difficult: am I doing something to the flooring, what kind of light fixtures are going to go into this room, what kind of furniture? And then I must make sure that those things can be made available very quickly. I would say it usually takes me about two days in total to nail down everything that is going to go into that space. After that, it is a logistical exercise. It is about making sure those elements can get from point a to point b. We usually have some sort of off-site storage facility where we hold everything until it is time for the day of transformation. Everything gets loaded into a truck by a team, and that team makes sure that everything gets to the location in time.

In the remaining days before the actual transformation, I am making sure that I flush out the design completely, that all elevations are there, all dimension strings are accounted for. If I am doing any kind of custom furniture, I check that I have dimensioned it completely and that all of this information is coordinated ahead of time with the producer, any handy person who is on set, and the camera person, so they know their angles, they know if I am using a mirror, how they are going to be able to shoot that, and what colors the room is going to be. All of that information is important for them to know way ahead of time so that they can make sure that shooting the show is as seamless as possible. We usually do two to three rooms in two and a half days, and that includes the onset of demolition. So it is the demolition and then putting it back together and getting it finished out, and all the furniture and everything gets hung and installed, and then we reveal the work.

There is no give on the back end. Often designers and architects with private client projects have a reputation for taking more time than they are really allocated. But in our business and our industry, there is no additional time. The deadline is the deadline. The room must be a hundred percent complete by the time the homeowners are shown in the room. Not only do we want to be respectful of their time and make sure that we are showing them the room when we told them we were going to, but it is also very, very costly to have all of these people on set. If we go into what we call overtime, it is ridiculously expensive. It becomes not feasible.

The first time I see the clients is when they leave. I see them at the very, very beginning, but there is no time to pull them aside and have us talk about this in more detail. No, it is basically an introduction and saying that I will see them in a few days. The next time I see them is when they come back, and we show them the work. I don't know if they are being polite or grateful, but I have been very lucky. I have never had anybody complain. I am very proud of that, but it could in large part due to the fact that they are just being nice. Who knows? But I think that the best compliment I can get in that scenario is always "I feel like you have known me my whole life," or "I feel like you have been inside my head," or "this feels so much like me but better than I could have imagined." That is always the goal. The goal for me is to really give them the best version of who they are in their space, to have that manifested.

I think that it is sometimes contrary to the idea of what being a successful designer really is about that I develop a brand and a style, and if you walk into my space, you immediately know that this is my work. I think that that is a popular notion, and it is a very egocentric notion. But this is architecture and interior design, two professions that are not free of people who are egocentric. But what we do with the TV show is totally different. I put my ego aside, and I am honestly invested in you, taking all of your information, processing it, and then manifesting it in the best possible way. I love that. I am very, very proud of that. A lot of times, clients have styles that I don't like at all, but it is okay. It is not my house. It is not my space. I don't have to live there. You want a home that looks like a motorcycle? I can make it look like a motorcycle. You want a home that is a log cabin? We can do that. But it is about trying to figure out what the essence of that it. When somebody says that he really wants a home that looks like the inside of a NASCAR, I have to figure out what is it about having that kind of space, about being inside of NASCAR that really motivates him and really makes him happy — is it the color? Is it the texture? Is it the light? Is it the finishes? Is it the fact that it feels dynamic — versus just taking it on a really literal level? I could just give everybody everything on a literal level but it is only going to satisfy them for a small amount of time. At some point, they are going to want more. It is always my goal to dig a little bit deeper and figure out what it is about x, y, or z that the client really loves. I know you really love it, which I think it is great that you have identified that, but what is the essence of that? And how can I capture that essence and manifest it in an interesting way that he will love for a while?

Often I have the chance to rethink or redo the function of a space. In one of the first projects, we had a living room dining room combination, and there was no need for that in that particular house. The homeowner wanted it to be converted into office space slash music practice space. Or a breakfast room converted into an office. That particular show, Deserving Design, was very much focused on people who were giving back to the community and were making their communities a better place by starting a nonprofit or dedicating their time or efforts. They needed to carve out workspace or office space out of space that wasn't working for them in that capacity. We converted many dining rooms, living rooms, breakfast rooms, guest rooms into workable office spaces, or multi-function spaces, or guest rooms that could also accommodate a home office. I would say at least 50 percent of the time, we are completely changing the function in that space to better work for them.

I definitely think there are also some constants. Function is a huge constant, and so is space planning. For me, everybody starts with a space plan. But how it is manifested aesthetically has to be responsive to who those people are. In many instances, we work with people who reach for the same kinds of language, meaning, "I love Pottery Barn, I love Crate and Barrel." And I think in many of those instances what they are saying is, "I think what makes me happy is warm, traditional furniture. I don't want it fussy, but I want it to be comfortable." I am okay with that. I am totally fine with that because, at the end of the day, I love the fact that somebody actually has the ability to vocalize what they love and what is important to them.

I have never gone back to see how clients inhabited their world. I will tell you why: I just feel like I have done my job. I really have become invested in them. I really have become invested in the process of giving them the space that hopefully they are really happy with. I know it is never going to look like when I left it. Every picture frame in place, every book lined up perfectly; it is not supposed to. At the end of the day, it is supposed to be a growing, living organism that adapts to the clients as they live their lives and reflects the changes in the experiences that they have been through. So I am happy for that to actually happen. All of us worked very, very hard to give them this space, and we hope they are happy with it. They should do with it as they please.

The work we are doing for HGTV has nothing to do with stage design. In fact, there is very little that intersects with what we do on television and creating a stage set. The spaces that we are creating are meant to be spaces that are fully inhabited and are meant to function on a day to day level. So it actually is much, much harder because it has to look great in person, and it has to function completely, 100 percent, none of the design can be sacrificed. And on top of that, it has to look great on camera. So there is this additional layer that interior designers don't normally have to be responsible for. Normally every interior designer wants his space to function well and to look great in person. The additional layer has to be able to translate into a photograph, to camera. That is something else we are responsible for. But the design always takes precedent. If I am proposing what is right for the space but is going to be difficult to shoot, I let everybody know ahead of time, and we can make sure that we have the right equipment on board, the right lighting, the right everything to make sure that when we actually shoot it on camera or get it photographed, that it is a true translation of what it looks like in person. So there is a lot of additional coordination ahead of time.

I am on another show called Design Star, a competition show, and the winner of that show gets his own show on our network, so it is a huge prize. You cannot sacrifice the design in order for it to look great on camera, but it still has to look great on camera. For many contestants who come from the interior design world and private practice, this is one of the hardest lessons to learn. But most of them pick up on it. It is a lot of work, but it is worth it.

I think that what we are doing for TV could be a model for future practice. After Trading Spaces started airing — it was revolutionary for television at that time — it started impacting what was being made available in the marketplace. Big box and mass merchandise retailers all of a sudden became much more sensitized to offering items that were affordable and had good design inculcated. Now we take well-designed items that are affordable, have quality, and are widely available for granted. That really wasn't the case before Trading Spaces became widely popular and spawned all these shelter publications and knock-off shows and successors. It immediately caused the expectations of the public to shift. And that impacted how we practice, especially in the residential sector. In the commercial sector, it is what it is. It is always going to be a certain way. It is necessary for sustaining this profession that we adapt accordingly to this idea that design has been democratized. I am not saying that we are going to become a profession where we not only design but have to do the installation and the painting. I am saying that is not harmful to have that knowledge base to give you a better understanding of how materials work, and now you can manipulate those materials. Maybe I use them in different ways because I have a different understanding of them than I previously did. It definitely makes the designer much more solution-oriented. I think that that is really good and I already see it happening. Interior designers are practicing in different ways. I don't want to have interior design or architecture be antiquated professions that eventually die out because they are not needed anymore. We just have to adapt as things change.

This collection would not have seen the light of day without Dean Robert Probst, who, ten years ago, had me develop content for an architectural monthly to be published by my college. Lee Aviv assisted with procuring the interviews for a first volume and did the first transcriptions. The magazine never materialized, but the interview project continued, helped by Sarah Kusuma, who also prepared the web template still awaiting content. Thanks to Colleen Wimmel, who transcribed hours and hours for a "collegiate" rate, and my academic directors William Williams, Michael McInturf, and Ed Mitchell, who supported the endeavor by allowing me to interview our guest speakers. Special thanks go to Peter Zellner, who put me in touch with ORO Publishing. I was fortunate to have so many colleagues who willingly recounted their architectural background and shared their dreams for the profession. Without their stories, there would be no book.

Acknowledgments and Apologies

Finally, thousand thanks to my editor, Ellen Layne, who took me under her linguistic wings. She helped me keep the narratives flowing and guided me across the treacherous world of architectural jargon.

In order to keep the narrative flow intact, I have edited the interviews rather heavily and removed my questions. I hope to have done justice to each individual. All the mistakes are mine.

Index